Essential Meeting Blueprints for Managers

Effective meetings made easy

Sharlyn Lauby

Impackt Publishing
We Mean Business

Essential Meeting Blueprints for Managers

First published: March 2015

Production reference: 1030315

Published by Impackt Publishing Ltd.
Livery Place
35 Livery Street
Birmingham B3 2PB, UK.

ISBN 978-1-78300-082-1

www.impacktpub.com

Credits

Author

Sharlyn Lauby

Reviewers

Yaagneshwaran Ganesh

Almitra Karnik

Acquisition Editor

Nick Falkowski

Content Development Editor

Sweny Sukumaran

Copy Editors

Sharvari H. Baet

Madhunikita Sunil
Chindarkar

Utkarsha S. Kadam

Project Coordinators

Priyanka Goel

Rashi Khivansara

Proofreaders

Simran Bhogal

Maria Gould

Ameesha Green

Paul Hindle

Graphics

Sheetal Aute

Abhinash Sahu

Production Coordinator

Melwyn D'sa

Cover Work

Simon Cardew

About the Author

Sharlyn Lauby is the president of ITM Group Inc. (http://www.itmgroupinc.com), a consulting firm that focuses on developing training solutions that engage and retain talent in the workplace. A 22-year business professional, Sharlyn was vice president of human resources for one of the world's largest organizational consulting firms prior to starting ITM Group. She has designed and implemented highly successful programs for employee retention, internal and external customer satisfaction, and leadership development. She is a recipient of the Human Resources Professional of the Year Award presented by the Human Resource Association of Broward County (HRABC) and the Sam Walton Emerging Entrepreneur award, which recognizes women business owners for their community contributions.

She is also the author of the blog *HR Bartender* (http://www.hrbartender.com), a friendly place to talk about workplace issues. The blog has been recognized as one of the *Top 10 Business Blogs Worth Reading* by the Society for Human Resource Management (SHRM). Publications such as *Reuters, The New York Times, ABC News*, and *The Wall Street Journal* have sought out her expertise on topics related to human resources and the workplace.

Her personal goal in life is to find the best cheeseburger on the planet.

Acknowledgments

The acknowledgments section has always been one of my favorite parts in any book. It's an opportunity to look behind the curtain and understand the many people who are involved in this project.

First, my thanks to Nick Falkowski at Packt Publishing for giving me this opportunity, and to Sweny Sukumaran, Priyanka Goel, and Rashi Khivansara for answering all my questions, offering valuable critiques, and being a wonderful source of support.

This book would never have existed if it wasn't for all the meetings I've organized, managed, lead, and participated in. My thanks to all of the companies, organizations, and people I've ever sat in a meeting with. I've learned a lot from you. Productive and fun meetings do exist.

Thank you to the wonderful business professionals who shared their expertise in this book. You certainly didn't have to, but I'm so glad you did.

To my fabulous clients who allow me to be a part of their organization. Thanks to you, I work on great projects with great people. And to the terrific people who read and share my writing on HR Bartender, you are treasured.

Lastly, my love and admiration to my husband Keith, who still listens to my crazy ideas. I'm one very lucky girl.

Thank you all. Cheers!

Sharlyn Lauby

About the Reviewers

Yaagneshwaran Ganesh (YG) is a marketing enthusiast with years of experience who believes in aligning marketing operations to the organization strategy. He heads the global marketing operations at Corporater Inc. and is responsible for marketing strategy development and execution across 10 countries.

YG is known for his influential marketing articles on LinkedIn, ManagementNext.com, EPMChannel, and many more. He has an uncanny knack for inbound marketing, strategy execution, event management, market research analysis, and brand management. He is also proficient at strategy frameworks and metrics and strategic business planning, and is known for his ability to point out the source of problems.

He is a published fiction/nonfiction author and his books have received great reviews from *UK Daily* and *Morning Star* and appreciation from Adam Grant, the Wharton Professor and New York Times bestselling author of *Give and Take*. YG is currently working on a strategic marketing title.

Almitra Karnik is currently a senior product and solutions marketing manager at Twilio Inc., where she leads the marketing efforts around the entire Twilio technology platform. She develops targeted benefit-selling strategies for customers, including messaging, positioning, competitive analysis, and measurable Go-To-Market campaigns along with thought leadership and AR/PR engagements. She was formerly a product and solutions marketing manager at Cisco Systems, as well as product marketing manager at EMC Corporation. She began her career as a software developer at EMC Corporation.

Almitra has a master's degree in computer science from the University of Massachusetts and an MBA in marketing management from Santa Clara University.

I would like to thank my husband, Amit Sharma, for being my inspiration and guide not only during the course of this book, but throughout my professional career.

Contents

Preface   1

Chapter 1: Meeting Roles, Responsibilities, and Activities   9

Task and process roles within meetings   10
   Task functions   10
   Process functions   10
Task responsibilities within meetings   11
Process responsibilities within meetings   12
Meeting activities   13
   Problem-solving activities   13
     The Situation-Target-Proposal (STP) model   14
   Decision-making activities   20
     Minority decision-making techniques   20
     Majority decision-making techniques   22
   Smartly tracking your progress   28
     Definition of SMART   28
     Benefits of using SMART   29
Summary   31

Chapter 2: Regularly Scheduled Status Updates   33

Goal of the meeting   33
   Daily meetings   34
   Weekly meetings   35
   Monthly meetings   36
   Quarterly meetings   36
   Annual meetings   37
   Regular meetings must have value   38
Common challenges and how to overcome them   38
Before the meeting   40
During the meeting   42
   Welcome activity for groups   42
   Balancing old and new agenda items   43
     The parking lot   44

Wrapping up the meeting   44
    The power play   44
Using today's technology   45
After the meeting   46
5 tips for a better meeting   47
Summary   49

Chapter 3: Brainstorming   51

The goal of brainstorming   51
Common challenges when brainstorming   52
Before a brainstorming session   53
During the brainstorming session   54
    Selecting the facilitator   55
    Keys to effective facilitation   56
    Case study – brainstorm in a box   57
Using improv techniques to improve idea generation   58
Using power to control the brainstorming environment   59
Using technology in your brainstorming session   62
After the brainstorming session   62
5 tips for better brainstorming   64
Summary   65

Chapter 4: Networking Meetings   67

Networking goals   67
    Building relationships   67
    Leveraging the relationship   68
        Your business card is a networking tool   69
        Job search   70
        Requests for information   71
        Business connections and partnerships   72
Types of networking meetings   75
Common networking challenges and how to overcome them   76
    One-sided conversations   76
    All take and no give   77
Before you go to a networking meeting   78
During the meeting   80
    Saying no   81
Connection power–how to get more of it   82
Technology and networking   83
After the networking meeting   84
    Following-up   84
    When and how to ask for a favor   84
5 tips for better networking   85
Summary   88

Chapter 5: Training Meetings   89

What is a training meeting?   89
The goal of a training meeting   91
  Communication versus training   91
  Presentations are not training   92
  Is a training meeting the best approach?   94
Training meeting challenges   95
  Training, facilitating, and presenting   98
  "Flipping" training   99
Before training occurs   100
  Setting up the meeting room   101
During training   102
  Introduction   102
    Discovering participant expectations   103
  Discussion/demonstration   104
  Testing/practice   104
  Feedback/debrief   105
  Wrap up   106
Modern perceptions about power and training   107
  Training as a reward   108
  Individuals owning their professional development   108
Technology in training   109
After training occurs   110
  Evaluation   111
5 tips for better training   112
Summary   115

Chapter 6: Employee Performance Conversations   117

The goal of performance conversations   117
  Setting relevant goals   118
  Comparing performance to the company standard   119
Common challenges when discussing performance   120
  Tacit approval   120
Before meeting with the employee   122
  When to hold the meeting   122
  Where to hold the meeting   123
  Who to invite to the meeting   124
  Plan the conversation   124
During the employee meeting   124
  How to start the meeting   125
  Conducting the performance conversation   126
    Example – positive employee performance meeting   127
    Example – improvement-needed performance meeting   127
Using workplace power during the meeting   128
  What if the employee comes up with a bad idea?   129

Performance discussions and appraisals   129
   Redefining the performance review   130
Technology versus a face-to-face meeting   131
After the meeting is over   131
5 tips for better performance conversations   133
Summary   135

Chapter 7: Focus Groups   137

What is a focus group?   137
   Focus group goals   138
   Benefits of focus groups   139
   Pitfalls of focus groups   139
Best use of focus groups   139
   Focus groups versus surveys   140
   Focus groups versus individual interviews   140
Common focus group challenges   140
   Selecting the right participants   140
   Developing engaging questions   141
Before the focus group   142
   Using an outside facilitator   142
   Meeting logistics   143
   Creating a meeting agenda   143
During the focus group   144
   Tell participants the purpose   144
   Setting ground rules   145
   Taking meeting minutes or notes   145
   Exercising active listening skills   145
     Nonverbal skills   146
     Following skills   146
     Reflecting skills   147
     Soliciting questions   148
   Staying on time   149
   How workplace power can impact a focus group   150
   Ending the focus group meeting   150
After the focus group   151
Using today's technology in focus groups   151
5 tips for better focus groups   152
Summary   156

Chapter 8: Pitch Meetings   157

How to develop a pitch   158
What's a pitch meeting?   158
   The goal of a pitch meeting   159
The biggest challenge when pitching an idea   159
How to create support for your idea   160
Before the pitch meeting   163

During a pitch meeting   165
Take legitimate power seriously   168
Bringing technology into the meeting   169
After the pitch   171
    Having a pitch turned down isn't about you   171
5 tips for better pitch meetings   172
Summary   175

Chapter 9: Strategic Planning   177

Creating a strategy and being strategic aren't the same thing   178
The business case for strategic planning   179
Strategic planning meeting benefits   179
Frequency of strategic planning meetings   180
Common strategic planning challenges   180
Before the strategic planning meeting   181
    Meeting location   181
    Session facilitator   182
    Meeting participants   182
Step 1 – Formulation   182
    Mission   183
      Developing a mission statement   183
    Vision   185
    Values   186
Communicating company mission, vision, and values   188
Step 2 – Development   188
    Conducting a SWOT analysis   189
    Documenting the conversation   191
      Mind map   191
      Fishbone diagram   192
      5 whys   192
Step 3 – Implementation   193
Power and its impact on strategic planning   194
Bringing technology to strategic planning   195
Step 4 – Evaluation   196
5 tips for better strategic planning   197
Summary   201

Chapter 10: Project Meetings   203

What is a project team?   203
Roles within a project   204
    Project manager   204
    Project sponsor   205
    Cheerleaders   206
The goal of a project meeting   206
Common project meeting challenges   207
Before a project meeting   210

During a project meeting   212
  The cost of a meeting   212
  The cost of finishing the project on time   213
    SMART milestones   214
    Gantt chart   214
  Using expert power on your project team   215
  Seating arrangements   216
After a project meeting   216
Today's project management technology   218
5 tips for better project meetings   218
Summary   221

Chapter 11: The Work Doesn't End When the Meeting is Over   223

The meeting after the meeting   223
Gossip after the meeting   226
Recovering from a bad meeting   226
  The meeting leader is unprepared   226
  Meeting participants are unprepared   227
  The wrong people attending the meeting   228
  Participants take over the meeting   229
  Meetings that go off track   230
  Meetings that run too long (or too short)   231
Monitoring progress after the meeting   232
Summary   233

Appendix: References and Resources   235

Preface

"Kill stupid meetings."

That was the response to the question "Which company rule would you get rid of?"

According to the management-consulting firm Bain & Company, employees spend between 21 and 28 hours a week in meetings and this number continues to rise in double-digit percentages. No wonder we hate meetings! They consume a major amount of our time. Nothing is more dreaded in our professional lives than the business meeting.

My guess is we've all been in a worthless meeting, so I don't need to waste time telling you about the impact of bad meetings. We're here to talk about conducting valuable meetings. But for a second, think about the impact of a poorly run meeting on the organization. Here's an example:

> *A department holds a weekly meeting. For the purposes of simple math, let's say 10 people attend the meeting and they each make $50,000/annually ($24/hour). Their department meeting costs $240 each week or $12,000 a year. If the meeting is run well and produces good outcomes, the $12,000 could be money well spent. If not, think about what the company is wasting.*

But as much as we would all like to abolish the business meeting, that's just not practical. This book will help you manage the meeting process, whether you're leading the meeting or attending it. If we commit ourselves to having better meetings, then they shouldn't be a nuisance in our day. They should be viewed as necessary and serve a valuable business purpose.

In this book, I will examine the three most common types of business meetings: informational, decision-making, and feedback. Within each section, we'll explore the different formats based upon the goals you're trying to accomplish. **Productive meetings** do one of these things:

➤ Provide information

➤ Create a mechanism for decision-making

➤ Allow opportunities for feedback and discussions

Informational meetings allow participants to hear the same message in the same way. Consistency is an important consideration for informational meetings. A perfect example of an informational meeting is the weekly or monthly department meeting.

Now, you could argue that e-mail provides the same opportunity but it really doesn't. As popular as e-mail is for business communications, there have never been any generally accepted guidelines when it comes to e-mail business communications. Except of course that using all caps is considered shouting and even then, people ignore that rule all the time.

How many times have we heard "Didn't you get the memo?" or "I didn't get the e-mail."? Informational meetings put the people who need to know the information in the same place at the same time. Everyone is there to learn and understand the information.

Another advantage to informational meetings is not only that participants hear the same message but that the sender of the message gets confirmation that each person heard it. Sending a memo or e-mail only guarantees the message was sent. It doesn't guarantee the message was read or understood.

Please note I didn't say to agree with the information. It's possible with informational meetings that participants might wholeheartedly disagree. But the meeting accomplished its goal—to convey information.

Decision-making meetings provide participants with an opportunity to agree on a course of action. The focus is to reach a decision. This means everyone who is invited to the meeting is expected to contribute toward the decision. It's important to note that all decision-making meetings are not and should not be consensus-building activities.

Consensus building and decision-making are two different things. There are several ways for groups to reach a decision. Consensus building is one of them and is considered a very valuable business tool. However, not every decision should be made using consensus building. For example, consensus building would take too long during times of crisis.

Typically, the individuals being asked to make the decision are also responsible for carrying out whatever has been decided. Participants might not necessarily be in love with the decision that was reached but all participants are expected to support the decision. Each participant is held accountable for backing the decision.

Decision-making meetings are similar to informational meetings in that at some point during the meeting, they convey information. But in contrast to informational meetings, decision-making meetings have an element of agreement in them. Participants must agree that any information being presented is valid and relevant. Otherwise, they will never reach a decision.

Feedback meetings combine the messaging of the informational meeting with the action of the decision-making meeting. Where feedback meetings deviate is in the relationship between when the feedback was given, when decisions are made, and who makes the decisions.

For example, in the decision-making meeting, all participants must agree with and support the outcome. During the feedback meeting, there can be varying degrees of agreement and support depending upon who is making the decision. An example would be a marketing focus group with customers. The customers are providing valuable feedback but ultimately they don't make the decision.

It's also possible there's a gap between the feedback meeting and any decision, because participants might not see their feedback translating into action(s). Participants attending feedback meetings must have a lot of trust in the process and feel secure that their feedback is being given proper consideration, whether they can see the results or not.

Another purpose of feedback meetings is to create a mechanism for future feedback. This is what makes the feedback meetings so tricky. Anyone attending a feedback meeting must understand how and when their feedback is being used so they are comfortable with participating in future feedback meetings.

Sometimes organizations, in an effort to be super-efficient, try to combine meeting types. This usually ends up with disastrous results. For instance, a department will have their regularly monthly status meeting (which is an information meeting). Right before the meeting, the department manager sees their vice president and invites them to the meeting, which is fine; vice presidents can attend meetings. However, the department manager also decides this is a good time to solicit feedback from the employees on a new procedure. Here's what happens:

> ➤ The manager isn't prepared to effectively explain the new procedure. The employees end up asking a whole bunch of questions the manager can't answer. The manager looks unprepared in front of their boss.

> ➤ The employees think that the vice president wanted to hear their feedback, even though the vice president knew nothing about it. If the employee feedback isn't taken seriously, the employees get frustrated.

Business meetings have specific goals. If we, as business professionals, plan and conduct meetings to their intended goals, they wouldn't be the nuisance everyone makes them out to be.

And if a meeting doesn't meet one of those goals—providing information, making decisions, or creating feedback—then we probably shouldn't have the meeting. Simple as that.

This book outlines the most common types of business meetings by category: informational meetings, decision-making meetings, and feedback meetings. It's written to take the pain out of planning meetings. It will offer suggestions to put some fun into routine meetings. And it shows you how to shake off a terrible meeting because, no matter how hard we try, we'll never be able to eradicate the world of bad meetings. We can, however, make them a bit more tolerable, and a whole lot more effective and efficient.

What this book covers

Chapter 1, Meeting Roles, Responsibilities, and Activities, gets you started with the fundamentals of running and participating in a good meeting. We'll cover the different roles individuals play in meetings and how to help those individuals be successful during the meeting. We will also talk about the different ways that groups make decisions during the meeting and how to determine the best decision-making method for your group. Lastly, I'll share my secret weapon for keeping track of the outcomes discussed during the meeting—SMART plans.

Chapter 2, Regularly Scheduled Status Updates, deals with one of the most common types of meetings (and often one of the most complained about meetings!): regularly scheduled status updates. In this chapter, we'll discuss different types of status meetings and how to choose the best one for your agenda. I'll also share some resources to keep this regular meeting from getting stale and boring.

Chapter 3, Brainstorming, discusses how brainstorming meetings can be tough to manage because the outcomes aren't always immediately apparent. But brainstorming performs a valuable function and is necessary for organizational innovation and creativity. In this chapter, I'll outline the common challenges to brainstorming (such as negativity) and some techniques to overcome them. I'll also share some new methods being shared that you might want to experiment with the next time you decide to call a brainstorming session.

Chapter 4, Networking Meetings, covers networking meetings (or synergy meetings), which are essential to our own professional development. We need to build contacts and business relationships. These opportunities help us find jobs, get customers, and grow our business. However, there's nothing worse than a networking meeting that comes across as "gimme, gimme, gimme". Networking is about exchange and dialog. This chapter will show you a few approaches to make that happen.

Chapter 5, Training Meetings, discusses how training meetings are for those times when something needs to be learned. We're not talking about formal classroom training here. Most organizational learning takes place one-on-one, informally and just in time. The key to a successful training meeting is structuring the conversation properly. During this chapter, I'll show you how to create an effective training meeting.

Chapter 6, Employee Performance Conversations, discusses how employee performance conversations aren't the ones mandated by the Human Resources department. Every day, managers and employees have conversations about performance—both good and not-so-great. Performance conversations are not punishment. They are essential to accomplishing goals. In this chapter, I'll provide a script for having conversations that will engage employees.

Chapter 7, Focus Groups, explains how focus groups happen both inside and outside organizations as a way to solicit input. They also happen on social media channels in the form of crowdsourcing. Getting different and fresh perspectives can make or break an idea, and as so much is riding on focus group findings, proper preparation is a must. I'll offer some suggestions for creating focus group sessions that give you useable results.

Chapter 8, Pitch Meetings, discusses pitch meetings that are called for the purpose of selling an idea, project, vendor, and so on. The meeting can be internal, for example, selling the idea for a different marketing campaign, or external, selling a company on the purchase of a new leadership training program. We might have a tendency to think pitch meetings are only for sales professionals. In today's business world, pitches are made at every level in the organization.

Chapter 9, Strategic Planning, explains how strategic planning is the foundation for which many of these other meetings are formed. Strategy sessions often get canceled or delayed because they are viewed as a luxury—not as a necessity —or because strategic planning outcomes are voluminous binders that are propped up on a shelf and never referenced again. During this chapter, I'll share my four-step progression for strategic planning that keeps the process from getting out of hand.

Chapter 10, Project Meetings, discusses how project meetings are specifically designed for groups or teams that meet in order to accomplish a task. It might be an implementation team for a technology solution or a group of employees planning the company picnic. What makes this type of meeting distinctive is that, at some point, the project will be over and the group disbanded. We'll talk about the unique challenges these groups face when they meet and today's dynamic of project meetings with virtual teams.

Chapter 11, The Work Doesn't End When the Meeting is Over, reminds us that once we leave the meeting, the work really begins. Keeping participants engaged and making sure office politics doesn't overturn the decisions agreed upon by the group can be a full-time job. In this chapter, we'll talk about how to maintain momentum in between meetings and some tips for how to recover when the meeting doesn't go as planned.

Appendix, References and Resources, contains all the references and resources that have been used in various chapters of this book.

For each type of meeting, you can expect to see some common elements, which are as follows:

> **Goals of the meeting**: Establishing a clear and concise meeting goal will keep the meeting, the leader of the meeting, and the participants on track and focused. I'll give you tips and resources to help you develop sound meeting goals.

> **Common challenges and how to overcome them**: We'll talk about the top challenges that can occur during each type of meeting and outline some suggestions to deal with them.

> **Before meeting activities**: Preparation is everything. I'll give you a list of things to do prior to the meeting including discussions about who to invite, agendas, pre-work, and logistics.

> **During the meeting**: This is the most important part so it needs to go right. I'll share a practical meeting outline and advice to help you manage difficult participants.

- ➤ **The "Power" play**: As much as we don't want to admit it, office politics and workplace power can impact business meetings. In this section, we'll discuss some common scenarios and how using your workplace power in a responsible way can bring positive results. Everyone has power. It's understanding what kind and when to use it.

- ➤ **Bringing today's technology into the meeting**: Business professionals today must know how to leverage technology to achieve results. I'll share examples so you can incorporate technology into your meetings or use technology for virtual teams.

- ➤ **After the meeting**: It's hard keeping participants and projects on track outside of the formal meeting, and the answer isn't to just call another meeting. I'll share recommendations you can use to follow-up after the meeting.

- ➤ **5 Tips for a Better Meeting**: For each meeting, I'll present ideas, suggestions, and best practices from business people that you can use to master successful meetings.

Who this book is for

Business meetings do not have to be necessary evils. This book is for anyone who has to plan a business meeting. From the first-time manager to a seasoned professional, this book will help you turn those stale, boring meetings into something that brings value and possibly even a bit of fun.

Human resources blogger William Tincup writes on the *Human Capitalist* blog that the key to a successful meeting is the time allotted. "60 minute meetings are lazy, ineffective and the bane of our existence. Prepare more before the meeting; speak in cogent terms— whatever it takes. No scheduled meetings for more than 30 minutes." While I agree with Tincup that timing is important, it's not the driver for effective meetings; preparation and content are.

Meetings, like many other things in our business lives, are about properly managing resources. Well-run meetings can provide valuable information, help companies solve problems, and allow employees to make better decisions. In fact, when we gain the skills to run terrific meetings, it can even help advance your career.

Whether it lasts for 10 minutes or 2 hours, being able to plan and run a business meeting is an essential skill for any professional. One of the greatest compliments I've ever received as a business professional was "You lead a great meeting." That's what you want to be known for.

Conventions

In this book, you will find a number of styles of text that distinguish between different kinds of information. Here are some examples of these styles, and an explanation of their meaning.

New terms and important words are shown in bold.

	For Reference
	For Reference appear like this

	Lists
	Lists appear like this

	Action Point
	Action points appear like this

	Make a note
	Warnings or important notes appear in a box like this.

	Tip
	Tips and tricks appear like this.

Reader feedback

Feedback from our readers is always welcome. Let us know what you think about this book—what you liked or may have disliked. Reader feedback is important for us to develop titles that you really get the most out of.

To send us general feedback, simply send an e-mail to feedback@impacktpub.com, and mention the book title via the subject of your message.

If there is a topic that you have expertise in and you are interested in either writing or contributing to a book, see our author guide on www.impacktpub.com/authors.

Customer support

Now that you are the proud owner of a Packt book, we have a number of things to help you to get the most from your purchase.

Errata

Although we have taken every care to ensure the accuracy of our content, mistakes do happen. If you find a mistake in one of our books—maybe a mistake in the text or the code—we would be grateful if you would report this to us. By doing so, you can save other readers from frustration and help us improve subsequent versions of this book. If you find any errata, please report them by visiting `http://www.impacktpub.com/support`, selecting your book, clicking on the errata submission form link, and entering the details of your errata. Once your errata are verified, your submission will be accepted and the errata will be uploaded on our website, or added to any list of existing errata, under the Errata section of that title. Any existing errata can be viewed by selecting your title from `http://www.impacktpub.com/support`.

Piracy

Piracy of copyright material on the Internet is an ongoing problem across all media. At Packt, we take the protection of our copyright and licenses very seriously. If you come across any illegal copies of our works, in any form, on the Internet, please provide us with the location address or website name immediately so that we can pursue a remedy.

Please contact us at `copyright@impacktpub.com` with a link to the suspected pirated material.

We appreciate your help in protecting our authors, and our ability to bring you valuable content.

Questions

You can contact us at `questions@impacktpub.com` if you are having a problem with any aspect of the book, and we will do our best to address it.

>1

Meeting Roles, Responsibilities, and Activities

An efficient meeting gets things done. A bad meeting is a time waster.

The top four complaints that I hear about meetings are:

1. "We have too many."
2. "They're too long."
3. "Our meetings go off track."
4. "We don't get anything accomplished."

To keep the meeting focused so you can get things done, it's essential to establish a few fundamentals about meetings. People need to know the reason they're being asked to attend the meeting. They need to understand the purpose of the meeting.

Bringing structure to meetings isn't a constraint. On the contrary, it's a strategic way to engage and empower meeting participants. When individuals are aware of the role they have in a meeting, they come prepared to fulfill that role. When companies call meetings with a specific agenda and purpose, the participants know beforehand that the meeting isn't a waste of time. There is a specific objective that needs to be achieved.

In the *Preface*, I shared the three reasons that meetings are held—to provide information, create a mechanism for decision-making, and allow feedback and discussion. Now, we'll talk about the different roles and responsibilities individuals can assume during a meeting. I'll add to that discussion by sharing some decision-making and problem-solving techniques you can use in your meetings. We'll wrap up with one of my favorite methods for taking meeting minutes.

Task and process roles within meetings

A number of roles must be played in any group if it is going to get its work done, while at the same time keeping its members involved and committed. These roles generally serve one of two functions: **Task** and **Process**.

Although attention is almost always focused on the task functions, the presence or absence of process functions will often make the difference between a successful and an unsuccessful meeting. Knowledge of both task and process functions can help individuals become more valuable and useful meeting participants.

Task functions

Simply put, task functions have to do with the content of the work itself.

When the purpose of the meeting is to convey information, then the data and information is the task. An example would be the weekly staff meeting, where the task might revolve around the sales department sharing the clients who will be visiting headquarters during the upcoming week.

In a meeting where the goal is to reach a decision, the task is related to the facts and figures being used to make that decision. For example, if the meeting is to decide where the company will hold its annual shareholder meeting, the participants should be prepared to come with information about possible locations, the number of attendees, and schedule availability of key stakeholders.

During a feedback meeting, the task is the actual feedback itself. For instance, a manager is meeting with one of her employees to share compliments from a customer. The task is the nice story that the manager is going to tell her employee.

Process functions

The process function deals with the nature of working relationships in the group and the flow of communication between group members.

One of the first process dynamics that meeting participants need to conquer is the issue of trust. Regardless of the purpose of the meeting, participants will not open up and engage with the group if they do not feel they can trust the other participants. This has a direct impact on the effectiveness of the meeting.

Back in the 1940s, Kenneth Benne and Paul Sheats defined several different roles a person can play during a team meeting. Over the years, their work has been refined but here are a few of the most common meeting responsibilities related to task and process functions.

Task responsibilities within meetings

Task responsibilities relate to getting the work done. They involve the people who are going to take a project from start to finish. When we're involved in meetings where people will have to do something after the meeting, we want these people to participate. They know the work or they have a strong opinion about the job. Their insight is critical to the success of the project. There are four different task responsibilities:

> **Information giving responsibilities** involve providing facts and information. They provide personal experience relevant to the task.
>
> *"I have some books about problem solving we can use."*
>
> *"Bob told me about a blog that offers writing tips and resources."*
>
> The person in this role could be considered a **subject matter expert** (**SME**).

> **Opinion giving responsibilities** include offering views or opinions concerning information, suggestions, or alternatives.
>
> *"This is good work but I think we can do better."*
>
> *"Mary brings up an excellent point about shipping schedules."*

> **Information seeking responsibilities** consist of asking for information and details pertinent to the task as well as seeking clarification of suggestions in terms of their factual accuracy.
>
> *"Lisa, can you share with us what happened the last time the system encountered this glitch?"*
>
> *"You've been with the company a long time. Have you ever seen this situation before?"*

> **Opinion seeking responsibilities** consist of asking for views or opinions concerning the task.
>
> *"Tom, what do you think about our idea?"*
>
> *"I'd like to hear what the group thinks about this data."*

Task responsibilities do not necessarily have to be assigned to individuals. Sometimes a person's job title might be an indicator of their responsibility. For example, if the vice president of operations comes to a department meeting, they might have an opinion-giving role. It wouldn't be unusual to hear, "This is good work but I think we can do better." Or the chief information officer attending a meeting in an information seeking role asking, "Lisa, can you share what happened the last time the system encountered this glitch?". When the person's job title isn't an immediate indicator, the individual's abilities could be. For instance, the person with an effective questioning ability might be a natural opinion seeker. And of course, it's always possible to assign responsibilities. For instance, the employee with a great questioning technique might be very quiet during meetings. The meeting chair can have a private conversation with the employee, convey how impressive the employee's questioning skills are, and ask them to take a lead role during meetings. This provides feedback to the employee about something they do well and shares how that skill can benefit the entire group.

Process responsibilities within meetings

Process responsibilities can also be known as maintenance roles. These roles contribute to the overall group itself. They help to build healthy communication, enable collaboration and consensus building, and create a positive working experience.

> ➤ **Gatekeeping responsibilities** involve encouraging or facilitating communication from or between group members.
>
> *"I think we need to hear what Mark has to say on this subject."*
>
> *"Let's give Nancy the opportunity to weigh in."*

> ➤ **Focusing responsibilities** define the position of the group in relationship to its task by pointing to departures or raising questions about the direction the group is taking; keeping the group on time and on track.
>
> *"Our goal is to select a software vendor."*
>
> *"How does this relate to the group's assignment?"*

> ➤ **Paraphrasing** is defined as restating in different words what someone else has said to ensure accurate communication.
>
> *"Just to confirm, we're going to recommend that the implementation date is changed to accommodate holiday vacation schedules."*
>
> *"Basically, the IT department is saying that we need a larger server to adequately accommodate the extra users."*

Tip

About paraphrasing

We defined paraphrasing above as the restating of different words to ensure accuracy. It's very different from what is known as "parroting." That's when someone repeats back the exact same words. When someone "parrots" a reply, it could be a sign that they are struggling to understand. Not always, but it will be important to confirm their understanding another way.

It's not necessary to call them out during the meeting with "Are you sure you comprehend?". A person might feel embarrassed and just say yes to end the questioning.

One way to reconfirm understanding is to do the restating yourself at a moment when you're recapping the meeting. For example, "Just to confirm, Justin is going to restate the deliverable here." If Justin has questions or needs additional clarification, the opportunity has been raised to address those issues.

> ➤ **Summarizing** is reviewing the progress of the group from time to time by identifying what the major topics of discussion have been or by describing the major positions that have emerged to that point.

> *"So, we've decided to hold our strategic planning meeting on the first week of October."*

> *"Thanks for the report. Our key takeaway is that sales are projected to be down for the second quarter."*

Often we place the responsibility for filling all these functions on a single individual—the leader of the group. In most groups, though, so many things are going on at one time that one person cannot possibly perform all of these functions. Group leaders should consider sharing these roles and responsibilities within the group. When the work can be distributed more evenly, the likelihood of achieving the group's objectives in both the task and process functions will be significantly enhanced.

In addition, when you give everyone in the meeting a responsibility, it makes them accountable. Tina Samuels writes on Liz Strauss' *Successful (and Outstanding) Blog* that meetings are often unproductive because people don't respect time.

> *"Start the meeting on time so latecomers will find ways to catch up on their own. People will soon shape up and arrive on time because latecomers are embarrassed walking in when others are embroiled in deep discussions. This will save time for the whole group and the meeting will achieve its purpose."*

Meeting activities

Certain activities can make or break a meeting. Participants must know how to problem solve. Not just as an individual but in a group setting. They also need to be able to make decisions.

In both cases, if the group's problem-solving or decision-making capabilities are inadequate, a meeting could go on for what seems like forever. Whether you're a for-profit business with employees or a non-profit business with a volunteer board, you must provide people with the tools to effectively make decisions and solve problems.

Problem-solving activities

In my work with a wide variety of individuals, groups, and organizations over the last twenty years, I've come to the conclusion that many people are not very good problem solvers. They often muddle through, do nothing, adapt, or produce solutions that actually make things worse.

Effective problem solving requires the courage to confront an issue, the commitment to do something, and above all, the willingness to assume responsibility for correcting the matter. When a group meets for the purpose of solving a problem, they need a set of problem-solving tools and strategies to guide them through the process.

This problem-solving model is one I've used for years. It takes into account three basic assumptions about problems in general:

➤ **Problem solving should be holistic**: Typically, we think of problem solving as either a rational, logical, left-brain process, or a creative, imaginative, and right-brain one. The truth is we require the use of both sides of the brain. People must be rational at times and creative at others. Using a holistic approach creates a comprehensive design and can be used to address any problem.

➤ **Most problems are complex**: If we look at the world in simple terms, then we will see problems as nothing more than puzzles that can be solved with some sense of finality. However, if we view the world in terms of complexity, then we realize problems are complex, interrelated, and incapable at times of a simple solution. Sometimes the answer is to find ways of managing the problem rather than outright solving them. The problems that people encounter aren't always simple and don't offer the illusion of a quick fix.

➤ **There is no substitute for effective interpersonal skills**: I firmly believe that if a group is unable or unwilling to communicate openly and honestly with each other, then there's no problem-solving strategy that will help them. Problem solving requires both an effective method for solving problems, as well as an effective process of interpersonal communication.

The Situation-Target-Proposal (STP) model

Problem solving using the **Situation-Target-Proposal** (**STP**) model allows for information to be organized into three interrelated phases:

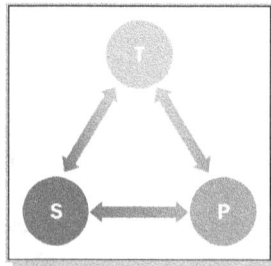

S: Identifying the situation

The situation phase involves identifying relevant information about the current status of an issue. It represents the starting point of the problem that needs to be solved. The situation includes both facts and opinions about the current state of affairs, as well as predictions about the possibility of change.

A word of caution here. Conducting assessments or analysis should be an important part of the process. It helps clearly identify the situation, so we can make good decisions about where we want to go and how to solve the problem. That being said, sometimes we will not be able to collect all the information we might want. External factors such as time or budgeted resources might impact the amount of information we're able to gather.

We have to be realistic about the relevance of information during this phase. One way to do that is by concentrating on information that helps understand the current situation. It's equally important to make certain that the information gathered is objective in nature. Here are six questions you can ask to ensure that all of the relevant information has been collected:

> ➤ Who is involved?
> ➤ What is specifically wrong?
> ➤ Where is the problem taking place?
> ➤ When did the problem begin?
> ➤ When was the problem first observed?
> ➤ What is the extent or pattern of the problem?

Additionally, we have to confirm that our sources of information are valid. The credibility of the data source helps the group determine whether the information is valid. For certain problems, citing only one data source might be sufficient. Complex problems might demand that time, money, and company resources are used to collect a variety of information.

Here's an example we can use to discuss gathering information about a situation. Larry, the department manager, is scheduled to have a conversation with his boss Nancy, about a member of his team Frank. To prepare for his meeting with Nancy, Larry drafts some talking points about Frank's performance.

To: Nancy

From: Larry

Re: Frank's Performance

Thank you for meeting with me today to discuss Frank's performance. Frank has been a valuable employee, and I would like to review his case very carefully before taking any further action.

Last November, Frank began working in my department as a part time salesperson. I was so impressed with his eagerness and ability to work under pressure that I offered him a full time position, which he accepted in January. He worked out well in that position, and in May, I promoted him to assistant manager.

> *Even though Frank seemed to be doing well at his new role, we are both aware of the amount of sick time he has taken since late August and the increasing number of customer complaints we've received about his work. I talked with him a couple of times within the last month and he assured me that he only needs a little more time to adjust to the new position. I realize he is under some pressure. Although, we've had no complaints for the past week, we agree something needs to be done.*
>
> *I am sure that part of the difficulty stems from Frank's rapid move from salesperson to assistant manager. The average time in the position of salesperson before promotion is about eighteen months to two years. But with the resignation of my former assistant manager, I needed someone right away and thought that Frank could handle the job.*
>
> *Because of the pressure then and the introduction of the new fall products, I have not been able to find time to send Frank to the two-week corporate training course that is offered for new managers. This lack of training may have contributed to the problem.*
>
> *In addition, we've spent a considerable amount of time working together since your arrival in June. As a result, I might not have spent enough time with Frank.*
>
> *Finally, if I were to lose Frank, that is, from his resignation or involuntary termination, I have no one to replace him.*

In this memo, Larry does several things right:

> ➤ Larry articulates his concerns. The fact that Larry is taking action is a positive. It can be tempting to ignore the situation or hope that everything works out on its own. Those approaches are not fair to anyone, especially the employee.

> ➤ He provides some history of the situation. This has been going on for months. In fairness to Nancy, she probably doesn't have the situation memorized. In writing this type of memo, Larry has the opportunity to refresh himself with the details at the same time. This allows Nancy and Larry to have the best information when they meet.

> ➤ Larry takes responsibility. This situation is not totally Frank's fault and Larry admits that. A good manager knows how to take responsibility and uses it as an opportunity to make the situation better.

Larry could have improved the memo by adding more details, possibly including attachments of key conversations that had transpired. He could have also given Nancy a heads-up on possible solutions to the situation. This would better prepare Nancy in terms of approving a solution or offering one of her own.

T: Targeting the answer

The target phase involves determining the desired outcome. The target represents what one wants to accomplish and what they want to avoid. It's the end point, the termination of the problems solving process, and the desired result. Terms commonly used to talk about the target include goals, aims, ends, purposes, and objectives.

Tip

Goals versus objectives

This is a good time to discuss the definitions of goals and objectives. We often use the terms interchangeably. I know I've been guilty of it myself. Goals are broad and abstract in nature. They tend to focus on the long-term and are usually difficult to measure. An example of a goal is:

Managers need to be successful coaching employees.

Objectives are narrow and precise. They usually are focused on the short-term and can be measured. A sample objective is:

Larry needs to have a coaching plan in place for Frank by the end of the week.

When you're attempting to solve a problem that involves an organization, you must be certain that the answer you've established is consistent with the company's values. Here are ten questions you can ask to clarify the target or desired state:

➤ What are we trying to accomplish?

➤ If the problem were solved, what exactly would be happening?

> What would look different?

> What would feel different?

> What would be different?

> When is this happening?

> Where is it happening?

➤ How would I know that the desired outcome has occurred?

➤ What would be the benchmarks of success?

➤ How could I provide to someone proof that the problem has been solved?

Let's revisit our example with Larry and the meeting with his boss about Frank's performance. Some of the questions Larry might expect should include:

➤ How would you know if Frank was doing his job well? Larry should expect to outline in very specific terms what satisfactory performance looks like. "Doing well" is not an adequate descriptor. The same with "no more problems." It might be helpful to refer to Frank's job description to understand the specifics.

➤ What about Larry's relationship with his boss Nancy? Is it where you'd like for it to be? Larry needs to feel comfortable with his boss for several reasons. First, he should be comfortable sharing this employee challenge and admitting that on some level he, in part, created it. By moving Frank up in the organization quickly, Larry must accept responsibility for this situation. Lastly, he must feel comfortable asking his boss for support in solving the situation.

> ➤ What options are available (besides replacing Frank)? There are many different ways to approach this situation that don't involve disciplinary action or termination. Sometimes, we are too quick to consider these options. Frank can still attend the corporate training program for new managers. He can also work closer with Larry, and possibly Nancy, to get additional guidance.

P: Proposing the solution

The proposal phase involves developing specific action proposals aimed at changing the current situation into the desired target. The proposal outlines the plan or strategy to be used to change the way things are into the way one would like them to be.

This is often where problem solving activities can fail. The urge can be strong to "do something" — anything to fix the problem. It's important to resist this urge and evaluate the situation as well as determining the target.

Developing solutions doesn't have to be a difficult activity. Most of us can generate ideas using comparisons. There are three ways to generate proposals.

> ➤ Compare the current situation to a previous similar situation. Ask the question, "Have we been in this situation before?". Find out what happened and how the matter was resolved. Example: "Has the company ever promoted an employee too early? How did the employee perform? What did the company do to ensure their success?"
>
> Depending upon the answer, Larry might be able to identify other options to help Frank's performance; options that have worked in the past.

> ➤ Compare the current target to a previous one. Again, trying to use the past to help solve the current problem only this time the focus is a bit different. For instance, "How does the company correct poor performance?" might generate a very different set of options than the previous questions.
>
> Maybe the company has never promoted an employee too early before. But they have run into situations where employees have missed corporate training and started to struggle with their performance. Larry can use those instances to develop alternatives for Frank.

> ➤ Lastly, compare the current situation to the current target. Figure out how to get from where you currently are to where you want to be. This could involve multiple steps. We have to explore this option when dealing with new problems or situations where new solutions have emerged. An example would be if our poor performing employee Frank can attend a new training class that maybe others haven't because the program wasn't offered.
>
> The company has never had an employee performance issue before. They do have a standard operating procedure that outlines the steps managers should take if they are faced with a performance matter. Larry can use the procedure to create an action plan with Frank.

The key to creating good solutions is to avoid the tendency to reject any idea that's new. Phrases such as "We don't have the time," "It's not in the budget," and "We tried that years ago and it didn't work" can kill momentum and stop progress. Another key to creating good solutions is to resist the urge to be right. The goal of problem solving isn't to be the person who came up with the solution. It's to fix the problem.

When considering solutions, the group can use four criteria to determine the best outcome:

> ➤ **Is the solution appropriate?** The proposal should respond to the cause of the problem. One way to decide whether that's the case is to provide a detailed scenario that shows how the proposal will move the present situation to the target state.
>
> When Larry and Frank finally meet regarding his performance, the solutions they come up with should address Frank's performance issues. Larry indicated that one of Frank's issues is customer complaints. Part of the solution might be customer service training. That directly relates to the problem they're trying to solve.

> ➤ **Is the solution attainable?** Identify the current resources available and the resources needed to implement the proposal. The proposal should be successfully implemented using the resources available.
>
> The solutions proposed must be attainable by either Frank or the company. So, if the solution includes training, then those training programs must be available and affordable. Frank must be willing to attend and participate.

> ➤ **Is the solution attractive?** The people responsible for implementing the proposal should understand why this proposal was selected and how it works. Everyone doesn't have to love the solution, but they should support it to some degree.
>
> Frank should be able to explain his current behavior as well as what is expected of him. He should know why the training solution was proposed and he should be willing to participate in the training.

> ➤ Is the solution adaptable? Change is inevitable. The solution should have the ability to be modified if circumstances change or new information becomes available.
>
> At some point during Frank's training program, the corporate office announces a training schedule change. Instead of attending a two-week program, participants will attend a one-week program then complete one-week of self-study online.

Once the best solution is selected, the group can focus their efforts on identifying alternatives, creating a pilot test when applicable, and developing an implementation plan. In thinking about the implementation plan, the group might want to consider breaking down the solution into smaller components or milestones. It becomes easier to monitor and evaluate results.

A major strength of the Situation-Target-Proposal model is its flexibility. It's often possible to start anywhere in the model and move in any direction. It's even possible to work all three phases at the same time. However, when a group is new to problem solving or working together for the first time, it makes sense to use the model in logical order starting with the situational assessment.

Becoming a more effective problem solver can be achieved by learning to assess a problem as it currently exists (situation), establish the desired solution (target), and determine the action to be taken (proposal).

Decision-making activities

A frustration during many meetings stems from confusion about the real purpose of the meeting. Consequently, the first step toward more effective meetings is to clarify the purpose for which people have been brought together.

Decision-making is perhaps the most difficult of three kinds of meetings to master. Yet decision-making is often central to an effective work group. If decision-making processes remain misunderstood or unchanged, little improvement can be expected in the quality or implementation of the decisions being made.

Decisions can be made and identified in a number of ways. Perhaps the simplest way of describing decisions is to see if they are made by the minority or the majority. The following are brief descriptions of different kinds of minority and majority decisions.

Minority decision-making techniques

Minority decision-making techniques are the ones used by a small groups, that is, the minority, to influence the decision of the larger group. There are five different techniques:

> ➤ **Plop** results when a group member makes a suggestion that meets with no response from the group as a whole. It falls, "plop." Not only is there no recognition or evaluation of the suggestion by the group, but the individual who offered the suggestion feels ignored and possibly rejected. They feel that no one will listen.
>
> *Barry: "I think we should have a paintball team building activity."*
>
> *Group: (silence)*
>
> *Tina: "Let's have a bowling team."*
>
> *Group: "Yes! Sounds like a fun idea."*
>
> While the plop technique might appear harsh, it can be very useful when a person just refuses to believe the idea doesn't have any merit. In my experience, I've seen people get together prior to a meeting and someone presents an idea. The group says it will not be well received and the originator of the idea replies, "I'm going to let the group decide." At the meeting, the originator offers the idea and no one responds. It sends the same message without calling the idea stupid.

➤ **Kill** happens when a suggestion offered by one member of the group is rejected at once, either by one or more of the powerful members of the group or by the group as a whole.

Patty: "I think we should be given access to Facebook on our work computers."

Mary: "That's the stupidest idea I've ever heard."

Calling an idea stupid is definitely harsh and can lead to strained work relationships. However, immediately rejecting an idea isn't always a terrible idea. When an idea doesn't mesh with company culture or the company doesn't have the funds to pursue the idea, then it's best to give a swift, direct "no" than lead the person to believe otherwise.

➤ **Self-authorized decisions** occur when a group member suggests a course of action and immediately proceeds upon that course on the assumption that no one disagreed. They assume since no one said "no" the group has given its approval. Such action can lead a group down blind alleys. Even if others agree with the decision, they may still resent the way it was made. No one knows how much support the decision will receive.

Tom: "I've signed the department up for Spanish lessons."

Mel: "Why?"

Tom: "I mentioned it at the last meeting. No one had any objections."

Leading people to believe their ideas are still alive can add to self-authorized decision making. Years ago, I had a client whose CEO wanted to empower the team to make decisions. The team suggested the implementation of a software program. The CEO didn't say no but also didn't say yes. So the team purchased the system to the tune of $75,000. The CEO was furious when she found out. But as the team told her, "You wanted us to make decisions and you didn't say no."

➤ **Handclasp** takes place when a suggestion made by one member elicits a reaction of support and permission to proceed from another. The group may move into action without sufficient testing as to whether the proposal is acceptable to the group as a whole.

Nancy: "Every manager should write an article for the company newsletter."

Paul: "Great idea! Do you think everyone will want to do it?"

Nancy: "Sure, why wouldn't they? You and I think it's a great idea."

Handclasp decisions often occur when individuals do not know the proper channel for approvals. It's great when employees can get together, problem-solve issues, and develop solutions. But before those solutions are implemented, they must be approved.

➤ **Minority support** comes about when a minority of the group makes a decision with which the majority may not agree. This can lead to little future support by the group as a whole for the action taken.

George: "I just left a meeting with the company's vice president.
We think all employees should start parking on the south side of the
building."

Every decision cannot be made with the entire organization. Some decisions will be made by a small minority of people. Common examples include the company benefits program or the annual budget. People might offer feedback during the process but typically a small group finalizes the decision.

The key to minority decision making is knowing when to utilize these. Every business decision cannot be made with everyone in the room. Even decisions like handclasp, which might appear to be ineffective, can end up being very valuable if the proposed decision is presented in the right way.

Majority decision-making techniques

Majority decision-making techniques are used by large groups to make decisions. Because the group is larger, these techniques can be used in an open forum or anonymously. Sometimes conducting an anonymous "vote" or gathering anonymous feedback can encourage greater participation.

➤ **Simple majority** is often determined by voting. Many groups make the mistake of assuming that simply because the majority supports the decision, the minority will come along willingly. They may or they may not resent the action and when called on, give no more than token support at best or actively sabotage the decision at worst.

Charlie: "How many people want to hold the holiday party on Saturday
night?"

Group: Majority says yes

Controller: "But if we hold it on a Thursday, we can have a nicer party."

➤ **Consensus** is successful when all members have contributed to the decision and feel that they have had a fair chance to influence the discussion. Those few members who would not prefer the majority decision nevertheless understand it and are fully prepared to support it.

Tip

Consensus building activity

A colleague of mine shared a consensus building activity that she really likes. It was developed by Kristin Arnold and is simple to use. During a meeting, take a survey of the group using a 5L scale:

Loathe—Lament—Live—Like—Love

Give each participant a chance to rate their feelings about the decision:

- They loathe (or hate) it.
- They lament or will gripe about it afterward.
- They can live with it.
- They like it.
- They really, really love it.

The goal with consensus building is to get everyone to live with the decision. Where consensus building efforts fail is when people try to convince everyone to like or love the decision. It's possible that will never happen. The goal of consensus building is to have everyone live with the decision. If a group pushes too much for someone to like or love a decision, they run the risk of having people secretly lament it.

Lamenting is worrisome because this is an area where decisions can be undermined. A person doesn't say they can live with the decision. They want the option of praising the decision if it goes well and distancing themselves if it goes poorly. Surveying the group to make sure everyone can live with the decision allows the group to hold people accountable for supporting the decision.

I was once a part of a committee that, when it became time to make a decision, the people opposed to the decision would conveniently go to the restroom or have to take an urgent phone call. It was obvious. That way, if they didn't like the decision, they could say they didn't vote to support it. And if it was a good decision, they could say they supported it the whole time.

> **Unanimity**, in most cases, is impossible to obtain, inefficient, and unneeded. Here, everyone completely agrees with the decision that is being made and intends to support it.

Once the group understands how decisions are made, there becomes a second challenge that has to do with the decision itself. Groups have to balance two issues when making decisions: decision adequacy and commitment.

> **Decision adequacy** refers to the quality of the decision

> **Commitment** is the concern for the degree of support the group will have once the decision is made

The level of emphasis that an individual or a group gives these two issues (that is, decision adequacy and commitment) can effectively describe their orientation toward decision-making and the kind of decisions they are likely to reach. Needless to say, the concern for the adequacy of the decision and the concern for the commitment of the group to the decision are independent of each other. A high degree of concern for one does not necessarily indicate a high degree of concern for the other. Case in point:

➤ Groups can make great decisions that no one likes and will support

➤ Groups can make bad decisions that everyone likes and will support

Consequently, we can provide a framework for dealing with decision-making by placing these concerns on the horizontal (adequacy) and vertical (commitment) axis of a decision-making grid. Each axis is scaled from one to nine to show the level of emphasis placed on that particular concern. Thus, nine on the horizontal axis would indicate a maximum degree of concern for the adequacy of the decision, while one on the vertical axis would indicate a minimum concern for the commitment of the group to that decision. Within this decision-making grid, it is possible to identify five major approaches to decision-making:

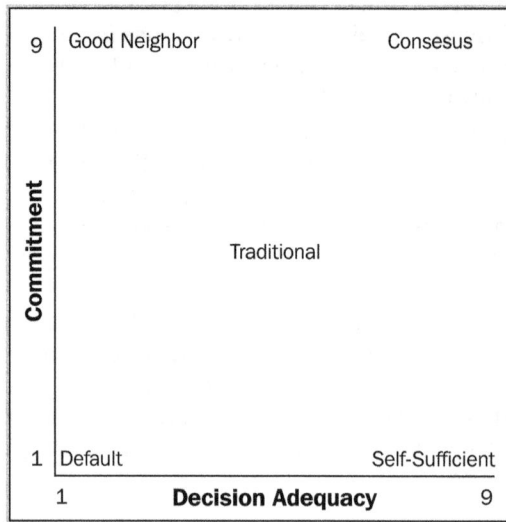

9	Good Neighbor	Consesus
Commitment	Traditional	
1	Default	Self-Sufficient
	1	**Decision Adequacy** 9

Self-Sufficient decision-making (9/1)

Self-sufficient or 9/1 decision-making expresses a maximum concern for adequacy and a minimum concern for commitment. The individual is confident in their own ability as a decision maker. The facts (as they see them) dictate the nature of the decision. For this person, a group is simply not a good place to make a decision. If the decision is an excellent one, the group will probably go along with it but, in any event, it is the quality of the decision that is most important.

A 9/1 decision maker functions as if they hold the final responsibility for the decision. In some instances, this attitude may be quite appropriate. In a crisis or when a particular individual actually does know more than the other group members (and they are willing to acknowledge that expertise), self-sufficient decision-making may be necessary and even effective. Here are two examples where this has happened to me:

➤ Our director of sales and marketing pitched a new campaign to the senior leadership team. We didn't hate the idea but were a bit unsure. Ultimately, the director of sales and marketing is responsible and accountable for the decision. He also has the expertise to make this decision on his own.

➤ During a hurricane, the director of facilities makes the decision to send certain employees home. He does this based upon his experience during the last hurricane. The other members of the emergency team support his decision based upon his experience and expertise.

However, in most instances, 9/1 decision-making is based not on expertise but manipulation. To the extent that the 9/1 decision-maker has formal or informal power, their ideas will be reflected in the final decision. If the 9/1 decision-maker is without power, they may soon become frustrated and withdraw from the group.

Good Neighbor decision-making (1/9)

At the opposite pole from the 9/1 position is the 1/9 or good neighbor decision-maker. This person expresses a minimum concern for the adequacy of the decision and a maximum concern for the commitment of the group to the decision. The primary value for a good neighbor is harmony. Goodwill within the group and avoidance of conflict are the most important objectives.

When the issue under discussion is relatively trivial or when the continued existence of the group is more important than anything else, a 1/9 approach to decision-making will be most productive.

On the other hand, because underneath the good neighbor's emphasis on openness and trust often lies an actual mistrust of power and fear of conflict, the 1/9 decision-maker may emphasize a superficial sort of togetherness that avoids the confrontation and conflict needed for adequate decision-making. If this conflict does break out, the good neighbor, like the frustrated 9/1, may withdraw from the decision-making process because they view conflict in a negative way.

Default decision-making (1/1)

Essentially, default or 1/1 decision-makers avoid making decisions. Often this position is a reaction to the stress of group decision-making. At times, they are operating out of conformity, self-protection, or both.

The 1/1 decision maker is not interested in either adequacy or commitment. It's possible the 1/1 decision-maker may be working in a highly regulated or bureaucratic organization where the guidelines are clearly defined by policies and procedures. In these cases, the 1/1 decision-maker rightly argues, it only makes more sense to follow the book than to invest very much energy in decision-making.

Traditional decision-making (5/5)

The traditional or 5/5 decision-maker expresses an equal concern for adequacy and commitment. However, they usually see these concerns not as complimentary, but as standing in opposition to each other. They do not believe that the group can make an excellent decision that will also produce a high level of commitment. Essentially the traditional decision-maker is more concerned with the adequacy of the decision than with the group's commitment to it but also realizes they may need to trade off and compromise to get enough support within the group. Usually that support takes the form of a numerical majority and the decision is usually made by a vote.

While it might not sound like it on the surface, in many cases, this approach to decision-making is quite appropriate. If the group making the decision is particularly large or if the minority can be expected to at least "go along" with the decision of the majority, 5/5 decision-making will probably be the best way to proceed.

Furthermore, if the group faces any conflict surrounding basic value issues or the allocation of limited resources, the compromise and give and take activities that characterize 5/5 decision-making will be required. Unfortunately, 5/5 decision-making can mean people spend the bulk of their time building majority support, which reduces the amount of time available to spend on the adequacy of the decision-making process itself. Finally, traditional decision-making may get stalled during implementation. If the minority is not willing to support the decision of the majority, the resources needed for the effective implementation of the decision may not be present.

Consensus decision-making (9/9)

Each of the four approaches to decision-making we've discussed so far assumes that adequacy and commitment are irreconcilable and that a group cannot produce a decision that is at the same time a good one with a high level of group support. The consensus or 9/9 decision-maker, on the other hand, expresses a maximum concern for both adequacy and commitment. They believe that the best decisions can be reached if all the resources of the group can be used. Consequently, the consensus decision-maker strives for a high level of involvement from all the members of the group as a good place to make decisions. Differences in opinion are seen as a source of new ideas and not to be avoided. If everyone can be involved in the decision, the 9/9 decision-maker believes not only will the decision be the best one possible, but it will also have the greatest degree of support. Genuine consensus will produce the best possible decisions.

Consensus decision-making has a number of advantages over other methods.

The time needed to reach a decision by consensus will be greater than the time a self-sufficient decision-maker will take. However, over the long run, the consensus approach may actually save time. The 9/1 decision-maker has a tendency to make the same decisions over and over because decisions reached on a 9/1 basis have no group commitment behind them. A decision made by consensus will tend to stand up over time since, once a decision is made by consensus, its implementation is usually assured.

Even decisions reached by a majority vote may be difficult to implement. Traditional 5/5 decision-makers are involved in developing majority support. Each new decision involves a new struggle and a new vote, leaving little time for the group to learn ways to improve the process of decision-making itself. A group using a consensus approach to decision-making is one that is aware of its own process and can learn from experience.

Because consensus decision-making does take time, it is usually not an appropriate method for routine or relatively trivial decisions. Consensus should instead be reserved for major decisions that require both a high level of decision adequacy and a significant commitment of the group to the decision. When the decision is important and when everyone needs to be involved in both making and implementing the decision, the time and effort demanded by consensus decision making will be well spent.

Tip

Effective consensus building

In his article *Decisions, Decisions, Decisions*, author Jay Hall shares several strategies for building consensus:

- Avoid arguing for your own position. Present your ideas as succinctly and logically as possible, but listen to the other team members' reactions and consider them carefully before pressing your point of view further.

- Do not assume that someone must win and someone must lose when discussion reaches a stalemate. Instead, look for the next most acceptable alternative for all parties.

- Do not change your mind just to avoid conflict and to reach agreement and harmony. Be suspicious when agreement seems to come too quickly and easily. Explore the reasons and be sure everyone accepts the solution for basically similar reasons. Change your mind when questions and discussion have produced objective and logically sound foundations.

- Avoid conflict-reducing techniques such as majority votes, averages, coin-flips, rock-paper-scissors, and bargaining. When a dissenting member finally agrees, don't think that they must be rewarded by having their own way on some later point.

- Expect differences of opinion. Seek them out and try to involve everyone in the decision process. Disagreements can help the group's decision because, with a wide range of information and opinions, there is a greater chance that the group will hit upon more adequate solutions.

When conducting a meeting for the purpose of reaching a decision, the procedures used to reach a final decision are critical. Employing the proper technique keeps the meeting focused, the participants engaged, and ensures implementation success.

Smartly tracking your progress

Whether we're having a meeting to give feedback, convey information or make a decision, documenting what occurs during the meeting is essential. The way meetings are recorded can have an impact on the outcome of the meeting.

Everyone takes notes during meetings. We all do it differently. Where years ago the only thing you saw at meetings were legal pads and pens, today people come with laptops and tablets. We can write with pens, pencils, our fingers, or styluses.

Many participants want agendas, handouts, and minutes in electronic format. This allows participants to move information into the programs that are most productive for them. It saves the environment by using less paper. The connected generation, defined as individuals willing and open to digital content and communications, might also argue that they are more accustomed to using a keyboard. It's faster than writing. Electronic meeting files can also be put into folders and shared with participants.

Meeting participants should be allowed to take notes any way that works for them. It's their notes. They will be held accountable for delivering whatever they agreed to. That's what I want to talk about—documenting what everyone agreed to during the meeting.

Definition of SMART

Years ago, I worked for a company where, every time something went wrong, our President wanted a meeting to discuss how we were going to fix the problem. Afterward, we had to create something called "a SMART plan" explaining the steps we were going to take. Sad to say, we developed a lot of SMART plans. I thought it was some sort of punishment.

It wasn't until I started studying for my human resources certification that I learned SMART plans have been around for many years and weren't some dreamt up form of torture from senior leadership. The project management term was first used in 1981 by George T. Doran. SMART is an acronym:

> ➤ **Specific** represents exactly what you would like to accomplish. Think of it as the who, what, where, when, which, and why of the goal.

> ➤ **Measurable answers** the question of how success is measured.

> ➤ **Actionable (also seen as Achievable, Attainable)** outlines the steps it will take to complete the goal.

> ➤ **Responsible (some versions use Realistic or Relevant)** identifies the people needed to reach this goal.

> ➤ **Time-bound (or Trackable)** establishes the time frame to achieve the goal.

Over the years, I've found the SMART acronym easy to remember, so I mold it for creating meeting minutes. I can't think of a better way to outline what happens at a meeting:

> ➤ What are we going to do? (Specific)
>
> ➤ How will we measure our success? (Measurable)
>
> ➤ What are the steps that will help us attain our goal? (Attainable)
>
> ➤ Who will be responsible for each step? (Responsible)
>
> ➤ When will the task be completed? (Timely)

Tip

About SMART plans

On a personal note, one thing that frustrates me to no end when someone presents a topic at a conference or meeting and in the last couple of minutes of their explanation, they say something to the effect of "... and I challenge each of you to leave this meeting and create your own personal action plan to...".

Frankly, they should tell us how to create an action plan. So to minimize my frustrations, I've learned that every time someone challenges me to develop an action plan, I try to work it into a SMART plan format. Works every time.

Benefits of using SMART

In my experience, I've found the biggest benefit of SMART plans is they allow me to steer conversations in the right direction. For each item, we have to address all of the steps: specific, measureable, actionable, responsible, and timely. It's often easy to get someone to say "We need to do this or that." Others may chime into the conversation and add, "Well, in order to accomplish the goal, we must do these ten things."

So, you get a lot of ideas. Then the conversation gets quiet.

SMART allows you to guide the conversation along. Here's an example: We're in a meeting and someone says, "I'm tired of the copiers not working right. Let's upgrade our copier machines." On the surface, this seems like a fine idea. Everyone agrees.

After the meeting, the facilities director comes to you and says, "I don't have a problem upgrading the copiers, but it's going to cost us thousands of dollars because we have a contract." Later, the technology director comes to you and says, "I don't have a problem upgrading the copiers, but we should consider wireless printing options. It will allow printing from anywhere in the building, but we need to do some rewiring (and there's a cost)."

You're thinking—why didn't this come up at the meeting?!

SMART keeps the discussion on track. Now when the copier gets brought up, someone can say to the facilities director, "It sounds like a good idea. What would be involved from your perspective?". They get the chance to answer.

The same goes for the technology director. You can ask them, "Are there any new technologies we need to consider?".

Now the whole group is informed and can make a good decision. It also saved a lot of time after the meeting with conversations that should have happened during the meeting.

SMART goals are particularly valuable in the areas of measurement, responsibility, and timeliness.

I used to work with someone whose entire goal during a meeting was not to be assigned anything. It was so obvious that his co-workers would joke about it—during the meeting!

Using a SMART format to keep track of the meeting gives you the ability to make sure every action step has a person responsible. It ensures that the person who will be held accountable for completing the step is committed to getting it done. It also helps the group understand the allocation of resources.

As you're putting together the SMART plan, you can see if one person is ending up with too many responsibilities and shift the workload. You can also see if someone who should have a role in the plan does.

Next, a great way to create commitment to the plan is by giving the people responsible for each actionable step the opportunity to choose their deadline. An individual can't say that some other person imposed an unrealistic deadline because they agreed to it. Participants also get to see how their action step impacts the other parts of the plan.

A participant knows up front their role and the impact of not meeting the goal. If you're leading or managing a group, this is the essence of holding people accountable for performance. Set the level of expectation. Have that discussion in the meeting.

Lastly, SMART formats provide participants with the ability to see and celebrate their success. When goals or action steps are created, everyone should understand what success looks like. This is the measurement component. Participants will use this information as motivation and validation that the plan was good.

If we use the copier example, upgrading the copiers will cost money and the inconvenience of rewiring the office. The measurement is that the copier will break 50 percent less and employees can print from anywhere in the building. Employees are willing to complete the action steps asked of them because the measurement (aka sign of success) is attractive. Who wouldn't like to cut the amount of time dealing with paper jams in half?

Using the SMART plan for meeting minutes also helps direct conversations toward key discussions like "We have a great idea here... now who's going to take ownership for getting it done?" and "Thanks Joe for leading this task, when can we expect it to be completed?"

Summary

The first rule of meetings is to understand why the meeting is being held and what role each person plays towards the meetings success. People will attend meetings when they understand the reason for them. They will participate and engage if they feel they are a part of the agenda.

During the meeting, groups can use problem-solving models such as the Situation-Target-Proposal (STP) and decision-making techniques like consensus building to create relevant and constructive discussions. The concept behind SMART plans can guide conversations and bring a consistent documentation process.

In the next chapter, we'll talk about the most common type of meeting: daily, weekly, and monthly status meetings. This meeting is probably criticized the most and often contains a lot of what we just discussed: problem solving and decision-making. How can we take the dreaded status meeting and turn it into something productive? Let's discuss in *Chapter 2, Regularly Scheduled Status Updates.*

>2
Regularly Scheduled Status Updates

The first meeting I want to talk about is probably the one we attend the most. It's the regularly scheduled meeting to exchange information. This meeting might be held daily, weekly, monthly, quarterly, or annually. It could be conducted via phone call or in-person.

Regularly scheduled status meetings are the ones that show up on our calendar before the agenda has even been decided. For that reason, they often become the ones we dread the most. It doesn't have to be that way!

When used properly, status meetings have an important role in organizations. This chapter will outline how to turn that "every Tuesday at 2 o'clock" meeting into something valuable and worthwhile.

Goal of the meeting

The goal of the status meeting is based upon two factors:

➤ Meeting frequency
➤ Attendees

Meeting frequency refers to how often the meeting is conducted. A daily meeting will have a different goal than a weekly meeting. Weekly meetings should be different from monthly meetings, and so on.

The frequency of a meeting is usually driven by the organizational culture. Alexa Von Tobel is the founder and CEO of LearnVest.com, a financial-management and lifestyle website. In an article, she wrote for Inc.com, Von Tobel shares how often LearnVest. com conducts status meetings. "We hold an all-hands meeting every two weeks and I do a 'State of the Union' address to everyone, every three months. That may not work for your start-up, but it's certainly worked for us." In the same article, she points out that it's okay to change how often meetings are held. "Over the years, I found that having meetings once a week was too much—we didn't have enough updates worth stopping the whole team for—but having the meetings once a month wasn't frequent enough to cover all the changes. Every month to three months is ideal for going over larger plans." But it obviously wasn't frequent enough for their ongoing operation.

The second factor, attendees, ties the goal of the meeting to whoever is in attendance. For example, a department meeting is only going to talk about issues relevant to that department. A "State of the Union" or town hall meeting usually has the entire organization present, so it will focus on issues that pertain to the entire company.

While we're on the subject of attendees, let's take a moment to emphasize the importance of having the right people at the meeting. In future chapters, we'll address this further but when it comes to accomplishing goals during a status meeting, it goes without saying that the right people need to be present. Status meetings can sometimes get off track or become unproductive because the attendee list is unclear.

> ➤ Everyone attends because "it's only a status meeting". The meeting becomes too large and it's difficult to manage.

> ➤ Key players don't attend because "it's only a status meeting". They don't realize the importance of being there.

This isn't to say that new faces can't show up in status meetings. If a regular attendee goes on vacation, someone should be present to handle their responsibilities, that is, taking notes. It's also a good way to train people for future responsibilities.

I recall years ago being asked to fill in for the board secretary at a volunteer meeting. I attended and took notes. A couple of months later, I was asked again and I obliged. The third time, I was asked whether I wanted to assume the role of board secretary. At the time, I didn't realize it but the current secretary was having challenges and needed to resign. She didn't want to leave the board in a lurch, so she quietly trained me and then felt comfortable leaving the board.

Over the years, I've found that regularly scheduled status meetings have the following goals.

Daily meetings

Typically, a daily meeting is totally focused on what's happening over the next 24 hours. I've worked for hotel companies that would hold a daily operational meeting to discuss the groups that were in the hotel each day, any special guests or VIPs that were visiting, and events the staff needed to know about. The meeting was held twice a day—once for the morning shift and again for the evening shift. One person from the morning shift was required to attend the evening meeting to do a quick debrief of the day's activities.

Another instance when I've seen daily meetings was during times of crisis or emergency. These meetings start when the potential crisis becomes evident and ends when the emergency is over. Two examples come to mind; first, in times of a weather disaster, daily meetings were established to keep everyone informed of the situation. It's essential that everyone have the same information about the projected impact of the storm. I live in a place that is subject to hurricanes. When the weather service announced that our location was in the path of a hurricane, a daily update meeting was automatically established. Depending upon the course of the storm, the frequency of the update meeting could be increased. I've seen the updates occur as frequently as three or four times a day, in conjunction with announcements from the National Weather Service.

The second example of a temporary daily meeting is when the business is faced with a crisis. Many years ago, I was a member of an emergency response team for an airline crash. When the response team was deployed, a daily status meeting was established to keep everyone involved. In these instances, the company needs to make sure that everyone in the team has the same information, is aware of updates to the situation, and handles any challenges in a consistent manner. If your business is in the public eye because of an emergency, a daily meeting can allow you to react to issues faster.

The goal of a daily meeting is the short-term focus on a specific set of tasks or activities. It should be a quick meeting that takes minutes, not hours. The most successful daily meetings I've been involved in are stand-up meetings. They're held in places where there's no table and chairs—there's no opportunity for people to get comfy and they're held at non-traditional times.

Many meetings are held on the hour or half-hour. The most effective daily meetings I've seen have been held at times such as ten minutes past the hour or fifty minutes past the hour. It forces people to show up on time and focus. The person in charge of this meeting faithfully started the meeting on time.

Weekly meetings

Where the daily meeting is driven by a specific time frame (what's happening today?) or an incident (where is the storm heading?), the weekly meeting is about the participants. It's more of a true status meeting, with each participant sharing their current projects.

The goal for this type of meeting is for participants to talk about what they have accomplished and what assistance or resources they need to finish. The meeting becomes a way to keep projects moving forward. Employees that share what they've accomplished are not only letting others know about their success, but giving others a resource if they are faced with a similar situation.

> Mary: "I'm creating a post template for contributors to the company blog. Hopefully, it will make the process easier when writing and help with search engine optimization."

> Tom: "Terrific idea. Sue mentioned at last week's staff meeting that we've contracted with a SEO consultant for our website update. She might have some ideas or be able to ask our consultant for recommendations."

Unfortunately, this meeting can also morph from a spirit of collaboration into showmanship. People can use the meeting as a stage to showcase their talents. The point of the weekly meeting isn't to justify your next merit increase or promotion. It's to let others know what's taking place within the group. So efforts aren't duplicated; time isn't wasted, and resources are optimized.

The ideal length for this meeting is less than one hour. The reason I say this is because, at the point this meeting is longer than an hour, then it's possible the agenda is too aggressive and the meeting is becoming more than the sharing of information.

Monthly meetings

This type of meeting allows more time to discuss issues versus reporting what's taking place (as in the weekly meeting). As a general rule, the people who attend this meeting usually have the authority to put out fires on a daily basis. The agenda isn't focused on daily problems. Those are being handled on a daily or weekly basis.

The monthly meeting has more of a strategic tone. It's not about setting business strategy. We're going to cover that in a later chapter, but we all know there are situations that seem to evolve over time and they take more than five minutes to resolve. Many times the issues being discussed during the monthly meeting are trends that have surfaced as a result of the daily or weekly meetings.

Let me give you an example. As a human resources professional, one of the activities that fell under my responsibility was training. When the company was implementing a new training program, it would take months to design the program, pilot the content to a focus group, and then roll out the program to the entire organization. It wasn't necessary for me to report daily or even weekly about what was happening with the program. I did share the status of the program implementation monthly as well as share any upcoming items for consideration.

Another example is monthly finance meetings. On a personal level, many families have a monthly budget conversation so they can keep track of their spending. Businesses have monthly finance meetings to discuss projections for revenue and expenses. They use those meetings to possibly reforecast annual budgets. Only if matters are dire, would this be a weekly or daily meeting.

Monthly meetings can take longer than an hour because of the increased amount of discussion. The thing to remember is that the people attending the monthly meeting usually have their fair share of daily and weekly meetings to attend so being respectful of their time is important.

Quarterly meetings

If your organization is conducting quarterly meetings, it's usually for two reasons. First, there's some obligation to have a regular meeting but the content of the meeting doesn't justify meeting more than once a quarter. I've worked for companies where the safety committee met once a quarter. It's not a reflection that safety isn't important—that's precisely why regular meetings were scheduled. But the company had a solid safety program that was well managed and didn't have a lot of accidents to discuss. It's balancing the need to keep the topic at the top of your mind (in this case, safety) with participant time.

Another example is volunteer boards or advisory boards that meet quarterly. There's staff that is managing the daily operation and the board gets together quarterly to discuss issues or offer feedback. This leads to the second reason that organizations conduct quarterly meetings—to present information. Certain publicly traded organizations also meet quarterly to "look back" on past performance, that is, revenue, expenses, and so on and share information with investors for the next quarter.

I currently participate as a member of the Society for Human Resource Management's (SHRM) special expertise panel on Ethics and Corporate Social Responsibility / Sustainability. We meet via phone once a quarter. The meeting lasts one hour. The meetings are a combination of SHRM updates and presentations about our area of interest.

Quarterly meetings are great for groups that need to know results from another group. It could be a nonprofit board president sharing fundraising results with the board, or the sales director sharing financial results with stockholders, or even a group of employees presenting their suggestions for the company's annual summer picnic to senior management.

Depending upon the agenda, quarterly meetings can take as little as an hour or go up to half or full days. I used to participate in a state-wide human resources association that met quarterly. The meetings lasted a full-day. Since the participants met in person and were traveling from all over the state, it was important to create a full agenda and make the most of the time we spent together.

An important consideration when groups meet quarterly is keeping the group connected. You've probably noticed as the span of time between meetings gets longer, the content of the meeting is changing. That's because the longer the time in between meetings, the greater challenge in keeping participants focused.

Annual meetings

This type of meeting provides an opportunity to reach large groups of people. They are very important for that reason. Everyone is able to hear the same message, said the same way. Remember that old game "telephone"? One person whispers a message into another person's ear. The receiver of the message then repeats it to someone else. The message is relayed through several people. At the end, the first person and last person compare whether the message remained the same. Many times, the message at the end is nothing remotely close to the original message. That's why annual meetings exist.

This doesn't mean that annual meetings have to become lectures. I've learned a format for conducting large group meetings that works very well and provides an element of discussion. Here's how it works: for your meeting, set the room in small tables where table-talk can take place. After presenting the information, give participants an opportunity to ask questions. Often participants are hesitant to stand up in front of the group, especially if they have a sensitive question or comment to make.

Allow participants at each table to work in groups to develop questions and/or comments. They can also designate a spokesperson to ask the question. The spokesperson is merely that, a spokesperson. They don't have to be the person who wanted the question asked.

This approach encourages participation and discussion without apprehension. A variation on this style of meeting is to give participants index cards to write their comments and give them to a moderator to read for response. Any questions not answered in the allotted time can be answered and posted via a company intranet.

This format for an annual meeting works well when presenting company information such as a new change to benefits or results from an employee satisfaction survey. It keeps the meeting structured. I know many CEOs who were reluctant to hold an all-employee meeting as they feared it would become a free-for-all.

Regular meetings must have value

The most important consideration for regularly scheduled meetings is their value. In short, is the meeting worth the time spent? Scott Berkun, author of the book The Year Without Pants, wrote a piece suggesting that recurring meetings at some point live out their usefulness. "The frequency and nature of meetings is an artifact of culture. An organization with long, or frequent, status meetings expresses the micromanagement in the culture. I once worked on a team that had 2 hour status meetings every Friday. You could hear souls dying, or killing themselves, every fifteen minutes."

While I agree with Berkun that long status meetings with no sense of purpose can destroy morale and productivity, I do believe there are ways to breathe life into the regular status meeting. It starts with the goal. As I've outlined here, ask the question "What's the purpose of this meeting?" The answer should tell you whether the meeting is needed. It should also tell you how often to hold the meeting and who should attend the meeting. Maybe the answer isn't to kill status meetings. It's to have them on the right schedule with the right people.

Common challenges and how to overcome them

Dustin Moskovitz and Jason Womack, writing for TheBuildNetwork, cited a *Psychology Today* study that said 70 percent of employees say status update meetings don't help them get any work done. They suggest that the way to cure ineffective meetings is to manage meeting time rigorously, including setting days of the week when meetings are not allowed. One company calls it "No Meeting Wednesday."

I agree that status meetings often get a bad reputation for being time wasters. It's a common challenge. The meeting becomes a time waster in two ways:

➤ Holding the meeting when it's not needed
➤ The meeting lasts too long

However, declaring a day of the week when meetings cannot be held seems like you're trading off one problem for another. For example, what if the company has a huge presentation to a client on Thursday and needs a last minute meeting on Wednesday to review details? Does the company risk losing a piece of business because of "No Meeting Wednesday"? Of course not.

But take that situation one step further. If the company does hold a meeting on Wednesday because it's essential for the sales department, the floodgates open and other meetings get held on Wednesday because whoever scheduled the meeting will say their meeting is just as important.

So those kinds of edicts aren't long-term solutions. Yes, the date, time, and location of the meeting are important. The meeting should be set based upon operational needs. In my corporate life, we didn't expect anyone from the accounting department to show up to meetings during month-end closing of the financials; only in situations where it was an urgent matter. That's the proper way to manage the meeting—think of your participants and hold the meeting at a time and place that will encourage their participation.

Status meetings should be focused on conveying information. When there is no information to share, the meeting should be cancelled. This truly demonstrates respect for participants and eliminates ineffective meetings.

The second big time waster is when the meeting rambles on much longer than it should. There are three reasons this can happen:

> ➤ Participants are not prepared and they are unable to communicate in a succinct manner.

> ➤ Boredom sets in, participants stop listening, and they ask questions about material that has already been discussed

> ➤ An individual participant goes over their allotted time on the agenda

One way to keep meetings brief is to hold "stand-up meetings". These are exactly as described—a meeting where everyone stands for the entire duration of the meeting. Not to imply that anyone is lazy but stand-up meetings keep the flow of information moving. Standing sends the message that the meeting will not be long. The minute people start sitting, it says "get comfortable, we're going to be here for a while".

Status meetings should only last as long as valuable information is being shared. If the meeting needs to last longer than it's practical for standing, then the next best way to keep the meeting from becoming a big snooze fest is by controlling the agenda.

Somewhat related to time wasting is the challenge of a participant "hijacking" the meeting. This is when someone asks a question or makes a comment that completely changes the agenda of the meeting. Here are a few things to keep in mind when you have a hijacked meeting:

> ➤ **Who hijacked the meeting?** If this person is your boss or your boss' boss, then it might be in your best interest to grin and bear it. Everyone in the room understands what happened and is smart enough to realize that you're going to have to schedule another meeting to accomplish the planned agenda.
>
> If the person trying to hijack the meeting isn't your boss, then either the meeting chair or the person handling focusing responsibilities mentioned in *Chapter 1, Meeting Roles, Responsibilities, and Activities*, can recommend the discussion be held for another time—either at the end of the meeting once the agenda is completed or for the next meeting when everyone would have time to prepare.

➤ **How did the hijacking take place?** What I mean here, is think about how the change took place. There's a fine line between a 5-minute off-topic discussion and a 30-minute conversation that derails the meeting. Is it the result of the meeting chair not keeping the group focused and on track? Maybe a participant bullied their way to controlling the conversation? Take a moment to understand how the situation happened.

➤ **What was the new conversation?** I've seen situations where meetings have been hijacked and the topic that the conversation was changed to was more valuable than the original agenda. A good example is when the CEO hijacks your meeting to share information about a new customer or answer questions about those acquisition rumors going around. Conversely, I've seen times when the new agenda was a long-winded, self-absorbed effort to impress a member of senior leadership. Obviously, a change in discussion for the benefit of the business is okay; using the meeting as a platform to brag isn't.

Depending upon the situation, it is possible to get the meeting back on track. The longer the agenda is side-tracked, the more difficult it can be to get the group focused again. The key to keeping status meetings relevant and engaging is balancing the desire for group discussion with respect for the participants' time.

Before the meeting

Meetings that are held on a regular basis need agendas. They don't have to be printed agendas; they can be e-mailed, although printed agendas can be helpful. In my experience, participants can forget to bring agendas, even when you tell them to print and bring the agenda to the meeting. This causes a delay at the beginning of the meeting, because someone will have to go print a handful of agendas.

For some meetings, a printed agenda isn't practical. The stand-up meeting I mentioned earlier didn't have a printed agenda, but the format was exactly the same every day:

➤ The Operations Manager opened the meeting and shared any noteworthy items.

➤ The Sales Director discussed special visitors and VIPs.

➤ The Human Resources Director shared important employee announcements.

➤ There was an open floor for any other matters.

The meeting was simple and straightforward. If the Sales Director wasn't present, he sent the assistant director to report in his place. Everyone knew the agenda and it was followed.

Make a note

Can't attend? Send a replacement!

Individuals need to get comfortable with the idea that meetings will occur without them when they're out sick or on vacation. Sending someone in your place allows participants to get the information they need in a timely manner. Remember—that's what the status meeting is all about.

It also allows the person replacing you at the meeting to learn new skills. Someday, they will be running their own meetings and need to be comfortable with delegating to someone else.

Now a slight variation was our weekly executive committee meeting. The meeting had the same format each week:

➤ The General Manager discussed overall operations.

➤ The Chief Financial Officer discussed overall finances.

➤ The Sales Director shared revenue projections and potential clients.

➤ The Human Resources Director shared relevant employee announcements.

➤ The Operations Directors shared status on current and upcoming projects.

Occasionally, something would surface during the meeting where the group agreed they wanted a presentation on an issue (for example, an overview of the new expense reimbursement procedure or review of performance management process) or to engage in a longer discussion (for example, summer dress code guidelines or the status on the sale of a division). In those cases, the agenda might be modified slightly to accommodate the conversation. The modifications to the meeting agenda could be to eliminate the status reporting for the week or to extend the meeting.

Even when meetings have a regular format, a written agenda can be incredibly valuable. I've served on a couple boards where a printed agenda was prepared prior to the meeting. The actual flow of the meeting really didn't change. What changed were the topics of discussion.

Meeting leaders can send out feedback forms prior to a meeting and ask whether anyone would like time on the agenda. If you do ask participants what topics they would like to discuss during the meeting, be prepared to manage the feedback.

➤ **Topic and time**: Not only do you need to know the topic for discussion but how long the discussion will take. This is part of proper time management.

➤ **Inappropriate topics:** Be prepared to address suggestions that could be inappropriate for the meeting. For example, a budget conversation that hasn't been approved.

➤ **Private conversations:** Some topics are best handled privately versus in a meeting. Again, be prepared to respond to requests adding agenda items that are best dealt with in a one-on-one conversation.

> ➤ **Limited time:** If there are lots of requests, priorities will have to be established. Maybe a topic can be scheduled for a later meeting, or another meeting scheduled to deal with a specific issue.

As a chair of the meeting, I included on the agenda not only the items that participants wanted to discuss but also the items I wanted to hear about. So when meeting participants notoriously would avoid discussing certain issues, I put them on the agenda. That way they knew in advance their discussion was expected, and I wasn't accused of surprising anyone.

The printed agenda was helpful for participants, especially when a vote or final decision needed to be made. A notation on the agenda told everyone in advance that an action would be requested. Participants could make sure they were prepared to discuss their views.

Lastly, a printed agenda can help with the preparation of minutes for the meeting. Taking minutes is a tough job and the agenda can serve as a reminder of what discussions took place and decisions that were made.

During the meeting

A regularly scheduled status meeting should have four parts:

> ➤ Welcome
> ➤ Outstanding agenda items
> ➤ New agenda items
> ➤ Action steps and wrap-up

During the welcome, the meeting chair should convey any meeting logistics, introduce new participants, and provide some introductory points. If the group meets in the same place, then everyone probably knows the logistics, for example where the bathrooms are located. But for groups that rotate their location, this is important. In addition, for groups that meet infrequently, including a planned activity during the introduction to connect the participants is important.

Welcome activity for groups

Groups that meet quarterly or annually need a moment to reconnect before getting down to the business of the meeting. Think of reconnecting as being similar to a training icebreaker. The goal is the same: participants get to learn about each other and become comfortable with their surroundings.

The reconnect activity can be a traditional introduction by each person. It doesn't have to be elaborate. One of my favorite icebreakers is to have participants interview a partner then introduce their partner to the group. One of the questions in the interview is related to the meeting agenda, so I have some background information about the group. Examples include:

➤ Do you prefer to work alone or in groups?

➤ Name one quality in the best team you've ever been a part of.

Another question during the interview can be totally fun. This is a wonderful way to create some laughter and give the participants something to chat about outside the meeting. Examples include:

➤ Name one person (living or not) that you'd like to have dinner with.

➤ Where did you go on your last vacation?

Balancing old and new agenda items

Next on the agenda are outstanding items. These are the issues from the last meeting that may have been updated and need to be reported on. This is where, sometimes, I think the meeting can go off track. It's important to bring up issues and to let the group know when action items have been finalized. But this does not have to consume the entire meeting. Participants are not there to tell you the ten steps they took to accomplish a task. If they are, there's another problem—trust. The purpose of covering outstanding items is for participants to inform the group where they are in the process and to ask for assistance if necessary.

It can become confusing when old and new agenda items are discussed at the same time. This is a challenge when the meeting agenda follows a department and not a topic. For instance, when the meeting agenda is: operations goes first, sales second, and finance third, typically the meeting will blend new and old agenda items at the same time. It's based upon the department.

On the other hand, an agenda that follows topics can separate the old and new agenda items. An example would be under old agenda items to discuss the current status of the website revision. At which time, all impacted departments would participate. Then under new agenda items someone might bring up the 4th quarter forecast.

Both formats are fine. If you structure the agenda by department, realize the meeting might need more control to keep the conversations focused. A resource that could help keep discussions on track is the parking lot.

The parking lot

For those times when you are discussing old agenda items and someone brings up a new topic, the parking lot can be a lifesaver. The parking lot is a list of items that the group needs to discuss, but not necessarily in the current meeting (after all, it's not on the agenda). When the new topic is brought up, someone can make note of this new topic. Typically, this is done by the person responsible for focusing, which we discussed in *Chapter 1, Meeting Roles, Responsibilities, and Activities.* You can use a flip chart, piece of paper, or a note taking computer program to keep track of parking lot items.

If there's time after the agenda has been accomplished, the group can start to discuss parking lot items. If not, the group can decide to include parking lot items on the next meeting agenda or deal with them outside the meeting format completely.

Wrapping up the meeting

Once the group has discussed the agenda, it's time to wrap up the meeting. Before adjourning, the person responsible for summarizing (discussed in *Chapter 1, Meeting Roles, Responsibilities, and Activities*) should recap the decisions made, action steps agreed upon, and the follow-up that will occur after the meeting. Remember the goal of meetings and consensus building; it's not to have everyone to fall in love with the plan. Consensus building is about each person being able to live with the plan.

Status meetings are about sharing information. Participants should be able to live with any decisions or action steps.

The power play

Workplace power is active during meetings. In the case of status meetings, informational power is prevalent. This type of power is defined as influencing the behavior of others with information. We often hear it in terms of the old cliché "Knowledge is power." Therefore, individuals with a lot of information can use that to influence a decision or action during the meeting.

An example of using information power badly comes from Andy Porter, Vice President of Human Resources with Merrimack Pharmaceuticals. He writes on the blog *Fistful of Talent* about power manifesting itself into meetings via office drama similar to a reality television program. "There's some ridiculous, cringeworthy argument going on that you don't quite understand and makes you feel a little uncomfortable and embarrassed. But like any good reality show, you take some guilty pleasure in showing up for this meeting. You know it's a waste of time, but you keep showing up for the sheer entertainment value of the whole debacle."

This is what happens when individuals don't share information the right way. It appears to be manipulative. Behind the scenes, employees are plotting to embarrass the manipulator for their behavior. Office drama ensues. If you're part of the drama, you just want it to go away as quickly and painlessly as possible. If you're watching, as painful as it may be, it can also turn into a guilty pleasure to watch.

The reality is that if this kind of drama can happen to someone else, it can possibly happen to ourselves. So it needs to be stopped. Informational power is important, and we must use it responsibly. During the meeting, if you have information that the group should consider, it should be shared.

There could be times when we're unsure about sharing information. Maybe we don't know whether the information is appropriate for the entire group because it's confidential. Or we don't want to share the story with all of the participants because it's embarrassing to someone in the room. In these cases, it's appropriate to contact the meeting leader after the meeting, share the information, and explain why the information was not disclosed during the meeting.

The meeting leader has an obligation at that point to do two things. First, they should offer some guidance about how to handle similar situations in the future. Next time, you'll know whether you should share the information in the meeting or bring it to the leader afterward. Secondly, the leader needs to decide how to proceed with the new information.

The incorrect way to respond is by not sharing the information with anyone. If the meeting participants discover that you had information and didn't share it, not only does it impact the team's performance, but it can have a negative impact on your personal credibility.

Using today's technology

Because status meetings can be easily held over the phone, technology is an important consideration. Employees who work virtually have the benefit of using computers, laptops, tablets, and even their smartphones to participate in meetings. The challenge becomes making sure that when the meeting is being held using technology that participants are paying attention.

Program Manager Nicole Steinbok presented a concept at the event Seattle Ignite 9 called the *22 Minute Meeting*. She explains that 30 and 60 minutes don't leave any time to get things done between meetings, so 22 minutes allows us to hold a meeting and still sort things out in between. Since the meeting is short, Steinbok recommends banning the use of technology. For 22 minutes you ought to be able to completely focus.

Theoretically, this is totally true. For a short meeting, like a stand-up meeting, people should be able to focus on the content and not check their devices. The longer the meeting, the more you have to manage technology.

Making sure that technology doesn't disrupt your meeting is all about setting expectations. Not just for the meeting but within the organization. Here are three pieces of technology etiquette that must be addressed:

> ➤ **Response time**: Having a smartphone doesn't mean that every request must be answered immediately. I remember conducting a focus group as part of a customer service training program I was designing. We asked participants what was an acceptable amount of time to reply to an e-mail+. Their answer? 24-hours. In your organization, it might be different but having some sense of appropriate response times keeps individuals from checking their devices during meetings.

➤ **Interruptions**: Even when the company has clearly defined appropriate response times, there will be instances when a participant is expecting an urgent message. It could be personal or professional—everything from a text message saying a parent's surgery went well to the last piece of information for a critical proposal. People who are waiting for a message need to have a way to both participate in the meeting and keep an eye out for the response.

➤ **Notifications**: This is especially true for long or unexpected meetings. We might do a great job of managing our technology, but that doesn't mean everyone else does. We might be at a meeting and get an urgent request. Participants need to be in a position where they can let others know what they are currently doing and when they can respond. True, some requests might dictate that a person leave the meeting but those are rare.

After the meeting

I mentioned earlier that taking meeting minutes is a tough job. It's also a very essential role. Minutes are the record of the meeting. They are necessary for so many reasons:

➤ **Distribution beyond the meeting:** Often, meeting minutes are distributed to absent participants and to interested parties that were not in attendance. I would share executive team meeting minutes with my department. And I would share department meeting minutes with my boss.

➤ **Record of discussion**: If there is ever a question about a decision made during the meeting, the minutes can serve as a resource. For instance, the decision to change the date of the employee holiday party; various dates were discussed but which one was finally agreed upon?

➤ **Planning tool for in-between meetings**: This is why I love SMART plans. The person responsible for the action steps agreed upon during the meeting can use the minutes as a planning tool.

➤ **Defense of a decision**: While none of us want to focus on this aspect, in today's litigious society, we do have to think of meeting minutes as a formal record that could be submitted in court.

Meeting minutes can be one or all of these things. It can be tempting to not prepare meeting minutes because writing them isn't considered to be a fun, cool role. If you have someone on the team who enjoys taking meeting minutes, you should definitely give them the role. And that being said, don't take their enthusiasm for granted. Every once in a while, offer to give them a break if they want it or send them a small *thank you* for taking on the assignment. I'm sure no one else will mind because they don't want the task.

And if absolutely no one wants to work on meeting minutes, then it's very appropriate to spread the work around and ask everyone to take a turn preparing the minutes.

Meeting minutes serve a valuable purpose. They tell everyone that the meeting was productive. It's important to have a record. This is another reason using the SMART acronym we discussed in *Chapter 1, Meeting Roles, Responsibilities, and Activities* is helpful for meeting minutes. In some ways, the minutes write themselves. The person responsible for minutes knows exactly what to record (Specific, Measurable, Actionable, Responsible, and Time-bound).

5 tips for a better meeting

I've discovered some of the best advice, tips, and resources for meetings by watching and listening to others. Here are some pointers you can incorporate into your next meeting:

Kristofer Cooper, Vice President and Chief Human Resources Officer at Morse Life, a recognized provider of health care, housing, and support services for seniors and their families, says preparation is key:

> *"We've implemented this meeting tip in my department and have found it very successful. It's somewhat odd and unconventional, but sends the message that participants should come to the meeting prepared. Here's the structure/tip: the team comes once a week for a stand-up meeting. All the members of the team must stand up and say what the most important event over the next week is and what they need help on. Oddly it keeps it focused and short and sweet but drives home the message that people need to be prepared. Each member of the team can challenge the other member of the team with no more than two questions."*

The agenda is your friend says Michael Haberman, SPHR, consultant, advisor, and blogger at Omega HR Solutions, which offers human resources solutions including compliance reviews, wage and hour guidance, supervisory and managerial training:

> *"One tip that I have used and seen used is to always go to a meeting with a printed agenda. There are several types of people in a meeting. Most want an agenda. The ones that don't need it will ignore it anyway. Another tip I have seen used is to make all meetings stand up meetings. Tends to keep them short."*

Susan Meisinger, SPHR, JD, former Chief Executive Officer at the Society for Human Resource Management (SHRM), columnist for HR Executive Online, consultant and speaker on human resources leadership, reminds us that successful meetings are all about the W's—who, what, where, when, and why:

> *"Regular status meetings can be an excellent tool to insure that an organization's projects and plans remain on budget and on time. They can also be an enormous waste of time for all attending if the meetings become a show-and-tell exercise, where lots of people attend and simply report on everything they've done. That's why it's important to be clear on the 'who, what, and when' of such meetings. Set up clear parameters on who should attend, requiring necessary decision makers to attend; what will be discussed— progress on milestones and identification of roadblocks and problems, not a recap of everything that's happened—and when the meetings will be held, thereby ensuring that the people who need to be there are able to plan to be there."*

Joyce Maroney is the Senior Director of Customer Experience and Services Marketing for Kronos, the global leader in delivering workforce management solutions in the cloud. Tens of thousands of organizations in more than 100 countries—including more than half of the Fortune 1000—use Kronos to control labor costs, minimize compliance risk, and improve workforce productivity. Her recommendation is to keep the meeting focused on items everyone needs to know:

> *"Rather than using meeting time to provide routine updates, the meeting manager should ask members to provide their updates to him or her prior to the meeting via e-mail or by updating a shared document online. During status meetings, the conversation should be focused primarily on items that everybody needs to know about, especially those that are off track and may affect others.*
>
> *The meeting owner should provide a mechanism to record action items, owners, deadlines, and updates so that all participants are clear on the tasks they own and any interdependencies between individual tasks. Spreadsheets are good to use for simple projects, more complex projects may require more specialized project management tools. After the meeting, the meeting owner should confirm any changes to the plan in writing via e-mail to the meeting members, especially those who were unable to attend."*

John Hollon, Vice President for editorial at TLNT.com and ERE Media, the go-to source for information and conferences in the human resources and recruiting industries, suggests setting expectations for a more productive meeting:

> *"The trouble with status meetings, whether they are weekly or monthly, is that they sometimes lack a sense of urgency that more focused daily or timely meetings have. This means that status meetings can easily get sidetracked by people who aren't focused on the task at hand and perhaps want to slowly ease into things, or worse, spend too much time engaged in personal chatter about what they did that has changed since the last meeting.*

That's why status or update meetings need to be run strictly and with a firm grip. When I chair such a gathering, I make sure the meeting starts promptly with me telling the participants what I want—a 2 to 3 minute per person update on where things stand in their area or from their perspective. I don't allow questions at this stage, but instead, scribble a few notes on each that allows me to go back and ask questions after everyone has given their update.

By doing this, you don't get bogged down in each person's brief presentation, and holding off questions and discussion until after everyone has weighed in with their update means that you can truly focus on what is most important and not get mired inside issues. And, by holding the meeting length to a fixed time period, say 30 or 60 minutes, tops everyone knows they must simply give highlights and not in-depth details.

Status meetings take discipline to keep them from becoming long discussions that take the wind out of everyone. If you truly work to make them one where everyone gets a brief update, in a reasonable time frame, you'll find that they actually will move along quicker the more of them you have because everyone will get into the spirit of the update session. That's a win-win for everyone, and keeps a status or update session from becoming just another long-winded meeting to avoid at all costs."

Summary

A status meeting is exactly that—a meeting to share the status of something. They're important for keeping the business running. If the meeting stays focused on that goal of keeping the operation informed, then the meeting stays valuable and productive. Groups can also use tools, such as meeting agendas and the parking lot, to keep the conversation on track.

How often you conduct a status meeting is based on the status you're sharing. It can range from daily to annually. The goal is to create a balance between holding them enough to get good information but not so much that participants get bored.

In the next chapter, we're going to talk about another kind of sharing meeting—brainstorming.

> 3

Brainstorming

Status meetings focus on what has happened. Brainstorming shares what could happen. The term brainstorming was introduced in the 1940s by Alex Faickney Osborn in the book *Applied Imagination*. The story is that Osborn was frustrated with his employees' creative output and began experimenting with ways to improve it. The book shared his conclusion that group brainstorming is a more efficient way to improve idea generation compared to individual thought. Osborn stated there were two principles that contribute to an effective brainstorming session. They are:

> ➤ Deferring judgment, that is, not getting frustrated when people introduce what is considered impractical or impossible ideas

> ➤ Reaching for quantity, that is, the need to generate as many ideas as possible

On the surface, this sounds like simple criteria to follow but the challenge is actually conducting brainstorming sessions where these two principles are consistently put into practice.

The goal of brainstorming

Simply put, the goal of brainstorming is to generate as many ideas a possible without excluding anything immediately. This is not as easy as it sounds because our natural tendency is to evaluate ideas at the time they are presented. But that's not the purpose of brainstorming.

In order to accomplish this goal, it's important to have the right people in the room. During our discussion about status meetings in *Chapter 2, Regularly Scheduled Status Updates*, we didn't focus much on who should attend the meeting because the participant list is often implied by the meeting itself (for example, the participants for the weekly department meeting are the department staff). With brainstorming, the participant list doesn't have to be tied to position, title, or department. In fact, it could be beneficial to invite people both directly and indirectly connected to whatever situation is up for discussion.

Brainstorming meetings must have diversity in thought. I'm not referring to diversity from a people sense, although, that is a good idea as well. Diversity in thought refers to people who think differently; everyone approaches a situation from a different vantage point.

The other dynamic that must be addressed in brainstorming meeting attendance is the possible challenges with organizational hierarchy. If a participants' boss or a member of the senior management team are in the brainstorming meeting, it can place a filter on the ideas generated by the group. A participant might feel less inclined to share a quirky or stretch idea if the boss is listening.

This brings up another important goal in brainstorming—the need for quantity. Notice that we haven't really talked about quality. Quality is important, but there's a right time to address quality. It's not the initial goal of the brainstorming meeting. The goal is quantity. That's why effective brainstorming should defer judgment; because great brainstorming sessions should yield ideas that are quirky.

Another consideration with brainstorming meetings is the location of the meeting. Brainstorming works best in places where participants are comfortable and interruptions are minimal. This shouldn't be misinterpreted as the meeting can take forever. We'll discuss how to put some structure around brainstorming later so participants can get their creative juices going and finish the meeting in a timely manner.

The ultimate goal of brainstorming is to generate ideas that create a desired result. The only way to do that is by bringing together people from different generations and cultures who use different points of view and methodologies to generate ideas. The more diversity you allow in the process, the better the ideas, and the more effective the brainstorming meeting.

Common challenges when brainstorming

When we think of the most common challenges in brainstorming, we can find the answers within one of Osborn's principles for an effective brainstorming session—deferring judgment. In the previous section, I mentioned the concept of diversity in thought. The fact that you're bringing together a broad spectrum of thought means there will be people who don't see the issue from the same perspective. You want that in the meeting. But it also means making sure that the group doesn't judge the broad spectrum of ideas that are generated.

Participants need to become self-aware of their behaviors that stifle the flow of ideas or put a halt to a person's participation. I remember being on a conference planning committee years ago where the chair would often encourage us to brainstorm ideas to make the event more profitable and better for attendees. Whenever someone brought up a new idea, there was one person in the group who would comment on it. She started her comment with, "Let me play the role of devil's advocate..." and of course, killed the idea.

Luckily, the group wasn't deterred by the "devil's advocate" line. After a while, whenever someone presented a new idea, they would immediately ask, "Does anyone want to play 'devil's advocate' with this idea?" Instead of the idea being killed from the start by someone else, the presenter of the idea secured ownership of the challenges to their view and they decided if and when the idea was no longer under consideration.

The other challenge I would call the opposite of judgment. That's when everyone thinks exactly the same—groupthink. In order to minimize conflict and reach consensus, the participants do not challenge each other or raise alternative viewpoints. Groups often make the mistake of assuming that a person challenging an idea obviously hates the idea. This assumption can often be incorrect. A person might be challenging an idea to confirm a thought process. Instead of viewing it as a way to tear down ideas, it could be a way to build support for them.

That is slightly different from something called the **Abilene Paradox**. The term, introduced by Jerry B. Harvey, is a description of what happens in group dynamics when people "go along to get along" even though they do not agree with the course of action. It is possible that brainstorming meetings can experience the Abilene Paradox if members of the group are afraid to express their thoughts for fear of being labeled a non-team player.

Effective brainstorming sessions need a balance when it comes to critically evaluating the ideas generated during the session. Time spent in a brainstorming session is time not spent somewhere else. So the meeting must be sensible and productive. Too much criticism can be detrimental; and not enough is equally detrimental. Both can impact the quantity of ideas generated which, in turn, can impact the quality of the final decision.

Before a brainstorming session

Thomas Edison was quoted as saying, "The best thinking has been done in solitude. The worst has been done in turmoil." Not everyone embraces the brainstorming meeting concept, especially if they've been witness to a terrible brainstorming meeting. To get all of the meeting participants prepared for a brainstorming session, it's best to give them plenty of time to think about the topic that will be discussed. The *Heart of Innovation* blog calls this **Braincalming**. They describe it as those quiet moments when we have time to think. It might be in the car on the commute to work, while walking on the treadmill, or in the shower. We're thinking and an idea comes to us.

Braincalming can be a welcome addition to your brainstorming activities. For those participants that want time to think about the topic before coming up with any ideas, they get to prepare.

Tip

Conducting brainstorming session

If that's not practical, the *Heart of Innovation* blog does offer a suggested activity that brings braincalming into the brainstorming meeting.

- Start your next brainstorming session in total silence.
- Conduct a welcome activity by having the brainstorming challenge written on a big flip chart before people enter the room.
- After some initial schmoozing, explain the 'silence ground rule' and the process.
- People will write their ideas on post-its or flip charts.
- The other participants, also in silence, will read what gets posted and respond accordingly.
- At the end of the idea generating time, you can do a verbal debrief.

In addition to giving participants an opportunity to think about the topic or challenge being raised during the brainstorming meeting, this also allows participants to think about the role they will play during the meeting. Individuals who are typically quiet during meetings have to realize they are being asked to speak their mind. And individuals who are comfortable speaking up during meetings might have to give other individuals the floor every once in a while. If the meeting organizer or facilitator doesn't feel that individuals will reach this conclusion on their own, then they might want to have private conversations with participants prior to the brainstorming session.

Understanding the subject and your role in the brainstorming meeting sets the session up for success. It allows people to arrive prepared and ready to participate.

During the brainstorming session

One of the most common misconceptions about brainstorming is that it's a free-flowing meeting without rules and structure. This is simply not true. Brainstorming is serious business and, in order to be effective, absolutely needs structure and ground rules.

Using Osborn's principles for effective brainstorming, there are four general rules for a brainstorming meeting:

> **There are no dumb ideas**: Again, every brainstorming session should yield a couple of quirky ideas. Ideas should not be labeled as a sign of a person's intelligence (or lack thereof). They should be considered as a sign of a person's willingness to contribute.

> **Every idea should be welcomed**: We're not at the evaluation phase of the process. Even if it's obvious that the idea will be ultimately rejected. Brainstorming is just about idea generation.

> **Positively contribute to other people's ideas**: When you can make an idea clearer or better, add to the conversation. A variation of an idea can bring strength to the original idea.

> ➤ **Focus on quantity, not quality**: We are very accustomed to the quality clichés. This is one time when we need to embrace the spirit of brainstorming and focus on quantity.

It might be tempting to include idea evaluation in the brainstorming process. In my experience, combining ideas and evaluation in the same meeting is more of a problem-solving activity than a brainstorming activity. Brainstorming is all about ideas.

In order to keep the rules, an individual should be designated as the meeting facilitator. Selecting the facilitator is an important decision and some dedicated thought should go into who will play this role.

Selecting the facilitator

No conversation about meeting ground rules is complete without a discussion about who is actually going to manage the meeting. It might seem logical to have the person with the highest job title run the session. But let me suggest otherwise.

There is a perception that the person who is running the meeting has a vested interest in having the meeting turning out a certain way. So if a department manager is running the meeting, then the outcome of the brainstorming session will be what the department manager wants. Now, this doesn't always happen but we can certainly see how the perception might exist.

The same holds true if the facilitator isn't a senior manager but a Subject Matter Expert. The participants might defer to the expertise of the facilitator. Or the facilitator might casually add their remarks into the conversation.

Brainstorming facilitators need to remain neutral. There are two ways to accomplish this:

> ➤ **Hire an external facilitator**: The advantage to using an external consultant for facilitation is they have no direct interest in the outcome. In fact, their lack of knowledge can raise some valid questions that are often taken for granted within the group. The disadvantage is cost. Hiring an external facilitator could become expensive.

> ➤ **Find someone in another department who can facilitate**: To avoid the cost of hiring an outside resource, ask someone in another area of the company to facilitate the session. Maybe you can return the favor in the future and facilitate a session for them. If you don't have people within the organization who are capable of facilitation, consider hosting a facilitation training workshop so a group can learn the skills.

If these two options don't seem practical, then by all means have someone with insight facilitate the meeting. Just remember the goal for a brainstorming meeting should be to have a facilitator who will encourage discussion and not control the conversation. Otherwise, participants could feel manipulated and the meeting will be a waste of resources.

The other advantage to using a facilitator is their ability to encourage responses from everyone in the group. We all know that, during a brainstorming session, some people talk more than others. Using a facilitator outside of the normal group can help keep the conversation balanced. They don't know the personalities and can manage participants without people questioning their motives.

Being chosen as a meeting facilitator should be considered an honor. This person is being selected for their ability to be trustworthy, objective, approachable, and firm all at the time. It's a role that should be taken seriously.

Keys to effective facilitation

Wikipedia defines **facilitator** as someone who helps a group of people understand their common objectives and assists them to plan to achieve them without taking a particular position in the discussion. It's important to realize that facilitators do not need to be the leaders of a group. They don't need to be senior management or an expert in the topic being discussed.

A skilled facilitator will conduct the research necessary to be effective, whether that's pre-meetings to learn about the industry or reviewing material about the topics to be discussed. Years ago, I facilitated a strategic planning session for an organization I was new to. The group provided me with their prior strategic plan and financials. I was able to talk with the CEO and COO prior to the event. This allowed me to learn enough to be an effective facilitator for their session.

Facilitators help people logically follow the process. Here are three ways that facilitators help the brainstorming process:

> **They create an atmosphere conducive to sharing**: Good facilitators encourage participation and bring out conversation. They know techniques to spark creativity.

> **They welcome every idea that's presented**: Facilitators are not there to judge ideas. They might ask questions to understand and seek clarification, but not to draw conclusions.

> **Facilitators keep their opinions to themselves**: While some facilitators are experts in a particular subject, they understand their role. And while some facilitation sessions later require the facilitator to render an opinion, they respect the role they are performing at that time.

Now, I'll break my own rule here and say that, practically speaking, facilitators do sometimes get drawn into the conversation, usually because the facilitator has some connection to the topic or because participants want to know what they think. If that's the case, the facilitator shouldn't jeopardize their relationship with the group and not join the discussion. But the facilitator will also want to find an appropriate way to give the discussion back to the group. Otherwise, the facilitator's role changes to the meeting leader.

One way I've found to do this is by sharing my thoughts during meeting breaks. It's not part of the formal discussion, and it's not a conversation with the entire group. Then, if the group wants to bring my thoughts into the formal discussion, that's their decision to make.

Being a meeting facilitator is tough. The hardest part is keeping the meeting moving forward without becoming part of the meeting.

Case study – brainstorm in a box

OpenIDEO is an online collaboration platform designed to turn good ideas into great ones. In 2011, OpenIDEO partnered with workplace furnishing company Steelcase to explore the topic of revitalizing struggling cities around the world in what they called the **Vibrant Cities Challenge**.

To help the group facilitate ideas on the issues of revitalization, economic decline, and restoring vibrancy to communities they created an aid called "Brainstorm in a Box". They encouraged participants to organize live brainstorming sessions with their friends and colleagues using the "Brainstorm in a Box" and then post outcomes on the OpenIDEO site.

Here's how using "Brainstorm in a Box" for a brainstorming session works:

> ➤ **Gather your participants and materials**: Send out an e-mail, organize lunch or brunch, and get your brainstorming group together. 3-5 people is a good group size. Alternatively, you could use this guide to brainstorm on your own while commuting to work, waiting for a friend, or just spending some quiet time alone. Materials to have ready include blank paper (or printouts of the following Concept Capture Sheets), post-its, and sharpies. M&Ms, Starbursts, and popcorn are also good for encouraging creativity during brainstorm sessions!

> ➤ **Pick a brainstorm topic**: OpenIDEO suggests drafting a topic in the form of a question such as "How might we...". With the vibrant cities challenge, one of the topics that groups were encouraged to brainstorm was "How might we foster a sense of local identity to strengthen our local communities?"

> ➤ **Start with a warm-up exercise**: OpenIDEO labels this as optional, but I would encourage groups to do some sort of introductory activity to get the creative brainstorming energy flowing. The activity they suggest is a good one and only takes 5 minutes:

> Let's say you're having a brainstorming session on ways to use social media to increase organ donor registrations. A warm-up activity might be to have participants name their top five brands on social media and the reason why.

> ➤ **Brainstorm**: This is where the work takes place. Brainstorm for 15-30 minutes on each topic. Make sure participants know your brainstorming rules.

> Identify the concepts and follow-up.

> In the case of the Vibrant Cities Challenge, brainstorming groups were asked to upload their ideas to OpenIDEO. If you don't have a collaboration platform, then the group will want to agree upon next steps before ending the session.

The OpenIDEO Vibrant Cities Challenge demonstrates how significant issues can be addressed in a fun way. The challenge was facilitated globally and coordinated in a central location, in this case being a software platform.

Organizations facing global challenges can use a format similar to OpenIDEO's Vibrant Cities Challenge to create their own brainstorming aid that individuals and departments can use regularly. The challenge will be creating and maintaining momentum with the brainstorming teams.

Using improv techniques to improve idea generation

We've talked about two methods to improve idea generation during a brainstorming meeting—facilitation and creating a brainstorming aid. Another way that can be used in both of these methods is to incorporate improv techniques.

Improv is short for improvisational theater, which is a form of acting where most of what is performed takes place in the moment. There's no script or outcome that the group is trying to reach. Each person improvises their participation as they go along.

Val Vadeboncoeur, writing for *The Heart of Innovation* blog, reminds us that one of the most powerful techniques in improv is the rule of "Saying Yes!" It means that you immediately accept, without judgment, whatever is being offered to you by a fellow actor. A classic improve example is if someone says "Hey! Look at that enormous pink elephant!" your response should be something along the lines of "Wow, that's the biggest pink elephant I've ever seen." Now, not only should you agree but you should also contribute. Using the pink elephant example, you could add: "Are those real diamonds on that tutu or just rhinestones?"

The last thing you want to do is say no or shut down a person's comment. Your response to the pink elephant comment should not be "Are you drunk? I don't see any pink elephant!"

Now apply a work context. A company is considering allowing employees to work from home. The conversation might go something like this:

> *"Yes, we're going to allow employees to work from home."*
>
> *"Wonderful, employees will be more productive because they can set their own work hours."*
>
> *"Terrific, employees will be happier because they can have more work/life balance."*

A comment like "But what if employees cheat on their timesheets?" would be negative and break the "Yes!" cycle. Vadeboncoeur shares his brainstorming technique using the principles of improv, which generates a lot of good ideas quickly. It's called "Yes, and...". Here's how it works:

You're part of a group of 6-8 people. One person starts by coming up with a new idea in response to a challenge or problem. Then the second person says, "Yes, and..." builds upon the initial idea. The third person builds on the second idea, beginning with "Yes, and...". The group continues for as long as the process generates interesting content and ideas.

There are also a few variations on this activity:

➤ You can start with a predetermined idea, perhaps something generated earlier in the brainstorming session, re-state it for the group, and ask someone to build on it using the "Yes, and..." technique.

➤ You can set the number of rounds for each idea in advance, for example each person will contribute once, twice, or more. Or, change the order that participants comment.

The "Yes, and..." technique can add a level of fun to the idea generation activity. It can also help to balance the contributions of participants because everyone gets a say in the activity.

Using power to control the brainstorming environment

Brainstorming relies upon participation from everyone in the meeting. In order for brainstorming to be successful, everyone needs to be a part of the discussion. In an article for Inc.com, Leigh Thompson, professor at the Kellogg School of Management and author of *Creative Conspiracy: The New Rules of Breakthrough Collaboration* shared a statistic about team dynamics that I wish was surprising: "In a typical six or eight person group, three people do 70 percent of the talking." This means that, during your next one-hour meeting, the remaining participants—those who aren't monopolizing the conversation— are contributing about four minutes each.

Thompson goes on to say, "The topper is that the dominant people do not realize this. In fact, they vehemently argue that the meetings are egalitarian. They lack self-awareness." She suggests the way for leveling the playing field is "brainwriting", which she describes as "the simultaneous written generation of ideas." Here's how it works:

1. Write just one sentence each. For the first five to ten minutes of your next idea-generation meeting, every team member writes down one good idea or one proposed solution. Thompson recommends using small index cards so people contain their thoughts to a sentence versus a paragraph. You could probably also use post-it notes.

2. Consider the idea, not the source. At the end of step 1, all cards are submitted anonymously for the whole team's consideration. They could be posted on a wall or spread out on a table. The focus is on the idea not the person who submitted it. "I have two rules: no guessing and no confessions," Thompson says. "No one signs their name and I don't want anyone guessing who said what."

3. Put it to a blind vote. Team members signal their interest in an idea by marking it with a sticker. Everyone gets a limited number of stickers and, if done right, the best ideas emerge quickly. Thompson says it encourages people to focus on the idea. "I shouldn't be voting for the CMO's idea; I should be voting for an idea that I really think is going to be exciting for our company or organization."

What I like about Thompson's approach is that it removes the connection between a person and their idea. As much as we want to align ourselves with only the ideas that are best for the organization, sometimes workplace power gets in the way. There are two forms of power that can surface:

➤ **Bestowed:** These forms of power are given to us. They're usually based upon our position or title. Or they may be granted to us in terms of who we have access to in the company or what actions we are able to authorize (based upon our position.) For example, as a human resources director, I was able to authorize payroll to cut a manual check for an employee. That was something I had the power to do based upon my title within the company. Everyone in the company knew that and, frankly, they would try to use having a cordial working relationship with me to get a check cut. I knew it and they knew it. But it didn't change the fact that my bestowed power was involved.

➤ **Earned**: These forms of power are related to who we are as an individual, or what we know in terms of expertise and information. It's less about title/position and more about us as a person; like the time I was invited to a brainstorming session on human resources and social media—it's not about my job as a training consultant but my expertise as an HR pro and a blogger. During those meetings, I was able to have a voice to suggest ideas for a new community network being developed.

All of us are placed in situations where we need to decide the best use of our power: "Should I agree with the boss's idea?" "What will people think if I make this suggestion?" To decide the best course of action, ask yourself the following two questions:

> ➤ What action would I like to take?

> ➤ Do I have the power so people will support it?

If the answer to both questions is yes, then it's a good use of your bestowed or earned power. If not, then ask yourself whether there's a way to align with a person who does have the power you need to make it happen. Here are two examples to demonstrate this.

You're in a brainstorming session. One of the other participants is the **Chief Marketing Officer** (**CMO**). The session is focused on generating ideas for a new customer loyalty program. The CMO offers some ideas based upon conversations she's had with current customers. The CMO's ideas are powerful because of the information she's been able to obtain in her position (bestowed power). And chances are others will give them consideration.

In the same brainstorming session, a customer service representative brings up some ideas to improve customer service. These are the result of taking customer complaint calls. The customer service rep certainly is in a different position than the CMO, but they both have customer insight, which makes them and their ideas powerful.

Power and ideas have a tendency to go together—as in, he who has the most power has the best ideas. But we all know that's not necessarily true. When faced with an idea, take the person out of the equation for a second and just focus on the idea:

> ➤ Is the customer loyalty program a good idea?

> ➤ Are the ideas to improve customer service good ones?

If the answer is yes, then it's easy to support them. If the answer is no, then ask yourself whether you know of others who would agree with you. I've seen CMOs change their mind when a handful of employees didn't agree with their idea. Do you have information that could influence the idea? I've also seen people change their mind when presented with historical data regarding customer buying patterns and complaint trends.

So think of the action you'd like to take (support the idea or challenge it) and then figure out whether you have the bestowed power in the form of access to data and information to change minds or earned power in terms of others who agree with your point of view.

Using technology in your brainstorming session

In this chapter, we've talked about brainstorming sessions in a way that implies we know the people we're brainstorming with. Either we work with them, volunteer with them, or we're friends with them. One way I think we can gain some really out of the box ideas is by brainstorming with people we don't know; maybe even complete strangers.

Crowdsourcing is the concept of soliciting ideas from a large group of people typically outside the company. It's often done online using social media tools. Individuals will participate for many reasons—everything from intellectual stimulation to self-esteem to possible financial gain.

Crowdsourcing activities, such as brainstorming, still need structure. And they still need someone to facilitate the flow of information.

PepsiCo's Frito-Lay division use crowdsourcing techniques when looking for ideas for a new potato chip flavor. They created a marketing campaign called *Do Us a Flavor* and awarded $1 million to the person who submitted the winning flavor.

The benefits to crowdsourcing include gaining access to a large audience that doesn't have any internal power struggles to deal with. It can offer new ideas that internal staff had never considered before. And lastly, crowdsourcing can create a sense of connection with the company brand.

It's not a method that can be used in every situation but when organizations have the time and resources to coordinate the campaign, it can generate many worthwhile ideas plus much more.

After the brainstorming session

Congratulations! You've had a successful brainstorming session and generated dozens of ideas. Now what?

First things first, the group must sift through the ideas and decide which ones are viable and which are not. While it might be tempting to do this at the same time as the brainstorming meeting, I've found it best to give people time to think about all the ideas before evaluating the list. There are a few reasons for this:

➤ Let people be happy and celebrate the number of ideas that were generated. If you create the list and cut the list in the same session, participants might leave feeling that they didn't accomplish as much.

➤ Terrible ideas will still be terrible ideas. There's no need to rush taking a terrible idea off the table. If it's not viable when generated in brainstorming, it will still not be viable a few days later when the group gets back together. In fact, it's possible that the person who originally suggested the idea will take it out of consideration in a follow-up meeting. And that's the best scenario you could ask for.

> ➤ Ideas can gain support. Once the group leaves a brainstorming session, they can't help but talk about the ideas that were generated. Good ideas keep getting discussed. People who were lukewarm about an idea initially, get time to think about it and can become supporters.

Next, remember the consensus building straw poll I shared in *Chapter 1, Meeting Roles, Responsibilities, and Activities?* You can use a variation of it to find out what ideas people loathe, which ones they can live with, and the ones they love. After narrowing down the list (this could take a while) the group needs to decide the best way to proceed. If there's only one idea to pursue, it can make things easy. But there is a good possibility there will be multiple ideas to consider.

Using the **SMART** plan format to document ideas keeps individuals accountable and the idea on target:

> ➤ **Specific**—What is the specific idea being considered?
>
> ➤ **Measurable**—What would make this idea successful? Why is it being considered?
>
> ➤ **Actionable**—What steps will help us decide whether this idea is viable? Or what steps need to be taken to make this idea successful?
>
> ➤ **Responsible**—Who are the individuals responsible for each step?
>
> ➤ **Time-bound**—What is the timeframe to completion?

This format can be used for each project. And a master SMART plan can be created to track the progress of all the ideas.

The next thing to consider after brainstorming is a long-term consideration but still important. We use brainstorming techniques to encourage creativity and generate ideas; that can't happen if the brainstorming environment becomes stale.

In an article on Lifehacker.com, Christian Catalini, an assistant professor at Massachusetts Institute of Technology's Sloan School of Management, shared research on scientists who were relocated regularly to different work buildings. The research found that they experimented more.

We might have a tendency to think that comfort and stability lead to greater creativity but that might not always be the case. Catalini admits the shake-up produced some bad ideas but also more breakthroughs. Brainstorming efforts can benefit from changing locations for meetings and mixing up participants.

The brainstorming meeting is a living, breathing dynamic in your organization. It's not just another meeting. The outcomes can change your business for the better...or worse.

5 tips for better brainstorming

Heather Bussing, an employment attorney specializing in training and preventative advice for businesses, reminds us that brainstorming meetings often become a catchphrase for other goals:

> *"Before you call a brainstorming meeting, make sure it's not really a meeting just to divide up work, or for you to have an audience while you think out loud. If you genuinely want other people's input, then think through how to make that work."*

Are there politics involved where you won't get genuine discussion? Would smaller work groups be better?

Do you have people on the team who need time to think before they respond?

> *"In other words, don't just call a brainstorming meeting because you're not sure what to do and want ideas. First, get clear on what you are trying to accomplish and the best way to get it done."*

"Think about your audience" is the advice from Elisa Camahort Page, cofounder and chief operating officer of *BlogHer*, the web's leading guide to the hottest news and trends among women in social media:

> *"My primary tip is to make sure the most senior people in the room speak last. If you start a brainstorm session with the boss-woman's cards on the table, you won't get the best, most diverse ideas from everyone else.*
>
> *My secondary tip is to make sure that when the most senior people in the room share, they don't immediately dismiss all the other input they've just heard and outline a go-forward plan they already had in mind.*
>
> *Nothing stunts future brainstorm sessions more than faux-storming that's supposed to make teams feel 'heard and included', but is really just a sham."*

Renie McClay, global learning consultant at Inspired Learning LLC suggests starting with an activity to stimulate the thought process:

> *"When brainstorming with a group it is important to set any ground rules you are interested in. For example, no stomping or evaluating ideas at this point. Just oblivious listing! The first ideas to come out will likely be the pedantic ideas that have been discussed before, let that happen. Then keep going to go for the more non-traditional and creative ideas.*
>
> *It is helpful to begin with a thought stimulator. For example, what are all the uses of a post-it? The first suggestions offered will be more traditional: writing notes on books, writing reminders, capturing a phone number, shopping list, and so on. But keep going to get the more bizarre answers. Wallpapering a room, paper weight, a flag on a world map, write a love note, and cover a whole in the wall. Accept all, no evaluating, the more 'out there' the better. The purpose is to stimulate creative thought and to give permission for crazy ideas."*

Fran Melmed, owner of Context Communications Consulting, recommends supplying participants with the tools to encourage creativity and ideas. And those tools don't have to be expensive!

> *"There are several fundamental challenges to running an effective and participatory brainstorming meeting. One of the biggest challenges is that while brainstorming is meant to be egalitarian, those involved represent hierarchies within their organization, potentially or inadvertently squelching involvement. I recommend leveling things while injecting creativity into the process.*
>
> *Rather than opening the floor to ideas or words and jotting them down on a whiteboard or post-it notes—a standard approach that works—layout markers, colored paper, magazines, and other supplies and invite people to independently craft their thought or suggestion. Bring the group together and ask participants to share their board, and then use these presentations as a springboard for joint discussion. This approach works particularly well when visualizing a customer experience."*

Cathy Missildine, SPHR, chief performance officer at Intellectual Capital Consulting and author of the blog *Profitability Through Human Capital*, reminds us of the importance in setting expectations early:

> *"The best meetings I have been involved in have expectations SET before the meeting. By circulating an agenda, and giving individuals the opportunity to bring agenda items to the group is very important. Actually sticking to the agenda also sets expectations for future meetings so that attendees know that the items brought forward will be discussed.*
>
> *I use ground rules to manage the meeting as well, things like don't interrupt, don't talk over each other, no cellphones, etc. Effective meetings don't end when the meeting is actually over, by scribing action items and circulating those items will make sure accountability is set for things that need to be accomplished. I use that action item document to begin the next meeting."*

Summary

Brainstorming is about generating ideas. That's what makes it wonderful and challenging at the same time. It's wonderful, because it has so few rules and lots of results and is challenging because it's hard to stay focused only on idea generation.

The rules of brainstorming must be followed. If the meeting veers off course and starts evaluating ideas, making decisions, or solving problems, then it can turn into a terrible waste of time and energy, not to mention damaging the reputation of future brainstorming meetings. There's a time and place to evaluate the outcomes of a brainstorming meeting. We'll discuss in later chapters how to pitch ideas, incorporate them into strategies, and finally turn them into projects. For now, we're going to talk about what could be considered a very scaled down version of a brainstorming meeting. In the next chapter, networking meetings are when we get together with another person to share and swap ideas. Since we all need to have a strong network to be successful, let's talk about how to do this meeting the right way.

▶4

Networking Meetings

Every time I go to a conference, whether it's being hosted by a company or professional organization, I'm reminded of the importance of networking. I meet many wonderful, smart people and I want to stay in touch with them.

One of the best books I've read about networking is *Never Eat Alone* by Keith Ferrazzi. It's somewhat ironic that I read the book while traveling (alone) from a conference. But I digress. Before I share my takeaway from the book, let me first explain what networking isn't:

> ➤ It's not handing out your business card to everyone you meet.

> ➤ It's also not giving your resume to everyone you meet.

> ➤ It's not about calling to ask for favors.

> ➤ It's not something to cross off your 'to-do' list (as in "I networked today.").

Networking is about building relationships. Let me say that again. Networking is about building relationships. And, that's what Keith Ferrazzi's book talks about ... how to build relationships. For me, I think of listening, smiling, sharing, offering assistance, being helpful and connecting. Networking is about giving, not about getting.

Ask yourself, "*What have I given to my network lately?*"

Networking goals

Networking is a two-step process: the first step is **building relationships** and the second is **leveraging the relationship**.

Building relationships

We all meet people that we find interesting and smart. We enjoy their company and want to stay connected with them. We might not speak with them every day, but we want to have access to them—call to ask a question or send them a quick e-mail. Basically, these are people we want to build relationships with.

I can't tell you who to build relationships with. Only you know the answer to that question. I can tell you that trying to build a relationship with a person because they're rich, famous, and/or powerful can come across as opportunistic. Here are a couple of examples:

> ➤ "You have one of the most popular blogs on the internet. I'd like to network with you."

> ➤ "Your company is very successful. I'd like to create a partnership with you."

These examples tell someone why you want to connect with them. They don't explain why they should connect with you. It immediately creates the impression that only one person will benefit from the relationship. Here's another way to phrase those same examples:

> ➤ "Since we're both bloggers, I thought it might be valuable to connect."

> ➤ "As a fellow business owner, I'd like to see if there are partnership opportunities."

Now you've provided someone with the feeling that both participants stand to gain from the relationship.

The size of a person's network is not a reflection of the quality of their network. It's also not a reflection of their willingness to use their network or their influence within their network.

Everyone has a network. Instead of speculating about a person's network, it's best to build relationships with a person you genuinely are interested in and then worry about their network later.

Leveraging the relationship

Once you build a solid relationship with someone, then you're positioned to actually leverage the relationship. If you don't take anything away from this chapter, please remember this. *Networking is about two-way communications and dialogue.*

Contrast this to the concept of cold calling. Cold calling is defined as contacting another person without notice. It's about one-way communication. The person initiating the phone call wants to convey a message.

I'm bringing up cold calling because I believe many people confuse the two. A person will say they want to network when, in reality, they want to sell you something. The word networking sounds nicer than sales. In today's business world, cold calling is very difficult and often doesn't yield a positive outcome. The reason? Because calling a stranger and asking them to drop everything to do something that will benefit you—and only you—isn't networking.

Here are a few more examples of what networking isn't:

> ➤ Cold calling a top influencer in your industry to introduce yourself and ask them to give your business a shout-out on social media.

> ➤ Sending an e-mail (with a copy of your resume) to a recruiter you met at a conference three years ago to let him know that you are planning to change jobs and would appreciate it if he kept you in mind for any future openings.

> ➤ Asking a consultant in your competitive set to share with you their format for client proposals.

Examples of what networking is (or could be):

> ➤ Sending an e-mail to a top influencer in your industry to introduce yourself and see if you can schedule a call to learn more about their business. Hopefully, the influencer accepts—the invite can benefit both of you.

> ➤ Contacting a recruiter you met years ago, apologizing for not staying in touch and asking if the recruiter would accept your resume. Not exactly a mutual exchange at this point but good recruiters are always looking for top talent.

> ➤ Inviting a fellow consultant for coffee and a discussion about opportunities to form a strategic alliance. It might not lead anywhere but a good consultant will listen to opportunities.

Networking is about mutual exchanges. You will ask of others, and they will ask of you. Three of the most common exchanges during a networking meeting involve job search, requests for information, and business connections.

Your business card is a networking tool

One of the essential tools in networking is your business card. Since the goal of networking is to build relationships, you want a way for individuals to stay in touch. Business cards should be viewed as marketing collateral to be designed and used effectively.

Always have a business card available. I am amazed at the number of people who do not carry business cards with them. You never know when you're going to meet someone who might offer you a dream job or assignment. It's not necessary to carry hundreds or even dozens of cards, but tuck a couple away in your wallet so you don't miss an opportunity.

Include best methods of contact. Notice I didn't say *all*. With technology and social media, there are lots of ways to be contacted. But we all have our preferred channels. Those are the ones you want to share. It's about quality not quantity.

Have a professional e-mail address. One might think we're past this conversation, but I continue to see *sugardaddy87@aol.com* and *sexymama79@hotmail.com* e-mail addresses so obviously not. Unless there is a business reason for this, use an e-mail address that is suitable for any audience.

List a reliable phone number. Whether it's a landline or cell phone, the number listed should be one that is regularly in use. And if voicemail is attached to the number, it's a voicemail account that gets checked for messages.

A mailing address is optional. Over the years, I've found less correspondence happens via the postal service. So don't hesitate to omit your mailing address. There was a time when that would have been in appropriate but not anymore.

Business cards should contain current information. The cost of business cards has really decreased over time. In fact, there are free business card websites. (Just do an internet search for options.) There's no reason to have an outdated card. You can even have two cards—one for business; another for personal.

Ask before giving. Several sales professionals have told me that the most appropriate way to give someone their business card is by asking for the other person's first. Usually, the other person will reciprocate. This way you don't appear to be pushy and the focus is on learning about the other person.

Job search

If you've ever looked for a job, then you know that staying top of mind when colleagues hear about openings that you're a good fit for is essential. I'm living proof of that: my first job in human resources was based upon what I knew, and every other job after that was based on who I knew.

I'll never forget sitting in my office one day and the phone rang. It was a colleague of mine who had just heard about this fabulous opportunity. He wanted to let me know about it in case I knew someone who might be interested. As he was explaining the role, I thought to myself, "This is a really cool job." Jokingly, I told him it was a terrific position and I might be interested in it. He very seriously said, "You would be perfect. Let me know if I can recommend you."

How did the story end? Well, he did recommend me and I did get the job. It reminds me that you never know who is thinking about you.

Finding a job using your network

According to *The Wall Street Journal*, as many as 80 percent of job openings are not advertised. This statistic has been around for years and, from my experience, has quite a bit of truth in it. Even if it's not exactly 80 percent, the number of jobs being advertised in the newspaper is dwindling. You can see it by just picking up the paper.

Many organizations place emphasis on employee referrals as part of their recruitment strategy. It continues to be a very cost-effective recruiting method. Recruiters are hearing about candidates from people who know them—their friends and co-workers. And trust me, employees will not recommend their friends if that friend isn't going to do a good job because the person who ends up being accountable is the person who made the initial referral.

LinkedIn and other professional social networks

Technology has had a definite impact on the way we do business and the way we communicate with others. The idea that our network is contained to individuals we have physically met doesn't exist anymore. Social media allows us to build an online personal brand, network with individuals around the globe, and possibly even get jobs using those connections.

There are many social networks, but the one that is very prominent in the business world is LinkedIn. In 2014, LinkedIn had over 300 million registered users in over 200 countries. More than 3 million companies have LinkedIn company pages and 94 of the Fortune 100 use LinkedIn for their recruitment efforts. As you can see, social media has significantly changed the recruiting landscape.

When we think about networking, it's important to consider not only in-person interactions but also online. In many cases, the same principles about networking and networking meetings apply. Just because the interaction is happening online doesn't mean you should simply send a note asking for a favor. (That's the equivalent of cold calling.)

While in this book we're not going to discuss the specifics about how LinkedIn or any other social network works, but it is important to recognize that social networks are a mainstream part of business. Interactions we used to conduct in person now happen online, and we should treat them with the same respect.

The other step in the recruitment process that relies heavily on relationships is references. In a traditional hiring process, there's a point where the company will ask for professional references. Realistically, we all want our references to say we're nothing short of perfection. (I'm being a bit dramatic here, but you get my point.) The people who should be your references are those who you've built a relationship with and can accurately and positively speak about your work.

Job seekers learn about open positions today through their friends and colleagues. They get introduced to companies by the same friends and colleagues. Networking means building a relationship with people who will get to know you and your work so they feel comfortable recommending you.

Requests for information

Another type of networking meeting is the one where you're looking for information. These are often known as *pick your brain* conversations. I might call someone and ask if I can "pick their brain" about a topic. Some examples might include asking someone:

➤ How to use social media

➤ Feedback on a presentation you're developing

➤ Tips for starting as a new consultant

➤ Resources for first-time authors

➤ Ways to improve your blog readership

When asking others to share their experience and expertise, it's important to remember that you're asking someone to share their experience and expertise. I don't want to rant about the social graces here but one of the most common mistakes people make when networking is they lose sight of what they're asking for.

Most business professionals I know are very open and giving with their time and expertise. In exchange, it's important to give them the respect that the request deserves. If you're going to pick someone's brain about a subject, consider these ideas:

> ➤ Think about what this person does for a living. I must say I'm thoroughly amazed at the number of people who will call asking for something pro bono that others pay me to do. Some of you reading this know exactly what I'm talking about. I'm not saying you can't or shouldn't still make the request but make sure you realize what you're asking for.

> ➤ Example: You're volunteering for your local professional association. They are putting together a program for small business owners. The program committee is looking for speakers but has a very small budget and probably can't afford to pay speaker fees. You tell them you know a fabulous speaker and decide to call your friend, who is a professional speaker. It's certainly okay to contact your friend about speaking. They might be willing to do the presentation. Just remember, this is what they do for a living.

> ➤ Find a way to thank the person. If you want to ask someone a whole bunch of questions or ask for a favor, thank them for their time and willingness to share. Buy them a nice dinner, send them a gift after the meeting, or create a way for them to promote their business. Recognizing the gift of their knowledge is absolutely essential, especially if you ever want to ask them for anything again. Now you might be saying, *this is a no-brainer.* You would be surprised at the number of people who do not do this.

> ➤ Using our speaker example above, let's say you reached out to your speaker friend and they say yes. The program committee could offer to allow the speaker sell their book in the back of the room because they waived their usual speaker fee.

> ➤ Business professionals are willing to share their knowledge with others when asked in a considerate way and thanked for their contribution. The acknowledgement doesn't have to be ridiculously expensive; it does have to be thoughtful and sincere.

Business connections and partnerships

The third reason that network meetings occur is to conduct business. This doesn't only apply to consultants or freelancers. Business professionals network in an effort to create opportunities for the organizations they are affiliated with.

Recommendations and referrals

A referral is when you give (or in this case receive) a business lead from someone else. It's a little different from a recommendation, which is a positive affirmation of someone's work. Recommendations can sometimes lead to referrals.

When you give a referral, it's a big deal. Many times, when you give someone a referral, you already have a relationship with the company that needs something. Maybe they're a client or a friend's company that needs some work you don't provide. I know when I give someone a referral, I want to know the other person is going to treat my client well. Because, of course, I want to keep that company as a client.

So you want to know that, whatever business you refer, the person or company taking the job will do top notch work. And, when done properly, a referral can provide the best networking opportunity. What better way to endear yourself to a colleague than by handing them potential business?

Getting a referral is an equally important responsibility. If you are the person who receives the referral, you need to remember that someone has put them self out there on your behalf. The client has been told fabulous things about you and they will expect nothing less.

Recommendations and referrals are very powerful. They play a huge role in purchasing decisions. Make sure the people who get your referrals deserve them and work hard for them. They should treat your clients just as well as you do, and treasure the referrals you receive. Someone opened a door for you. Be grateful. Thank them!

Strategic alliances and partnerships

Sometimes in our business responsibilities, we need other people to help us complete a project. I'll share with you a couple of examples where I've experienced this:

Once I was hired to work on a project where I was asked to design a few training programs. Shortly after I started the project, my client wanted to expand the scope of work and accelerate the timeline. Of course, on one hand, I was thrilled that the client wanted to add to the project. But the new timeline meant I was going to need help. To solve the challenge, I reached out to other consultants that I had relationships with and asked if they would like to work with me on the project. It created a win for them, win for me, and a win for my client.

In another situation, I was awarded an annual contract to perform various human resources projects for an organization. One of the projects was a compensation study. Since, my specialization isn't compensation, I reached out to a consultant who works exclusively on compensation projects. After our initial project together, we've had several other opportunities to partner when compensation was involved.

Healthy business competition

Admittedly, I'm a very competitive person. My father was extremely competitive, and I learned it from him. But over the years, I've tried to direct my competitive nature in a healthy way.

As the owner of a small human resources (HR) consulting firm, I know there are other owners of small HR consulting firms that offer the same services. When bidding on business, some days I'm selected for the assignment. Other days, another firm is selected. And some days, I partner with another firm to work on a project. That's because our combined talents are what's best for us and the client.

In theory, is that other consulting firm a competitor? Sure. But they're also a potential collaborator. That's why it's important to network with your competition.

Should you do your business intelligence and pay attention to what the other firm is doing? Absolutely. My guess is they're paying attention to you. But that doesn't mean everything someone else does will be right for your company—and vice versa.

Over the years, I've discovered the best way to deal with competition is to point it inward. When I meet people who are doing really exciting things that inspire me, instead of focusing my energies on squashing them ... I use that energy to make myself better. There are two reasons for doing it:

> ➤ I get better at something.

> ➤ I can eventually collaborate with that awesome person.

Obviously, there are moments when the situation calls for one winner for a piece of business. And that's fine. When it happens, being a gracious winner and/or loser will say volumes about you. Are you allowed to celebrate the win? Of course! And your competition (for lack of a better word) will be happy for you, because now you're inspiring them to be better.

That's what competition is all about. It's a balancing game. It's about knowing the difference between situations that only allow "winners and losers" versus opportunities to create a "win-win". If you play your cards wrong, it can alienate people. And when you need collaborators, none will be around.

But, if you play the cards right, you can "win" beyond your wildest dreams. That means having a network that includes your occasional competition. And, isn't winning what competition is all about anyway?

Volunteerism

A very common way business professionals thank their communities and profession is via volunteerism. Conversely, volunteerism can lead to relationships that will yield business.

In my experience, volunteer efforts are a wonderful way to meet people and build business relationships. If a person is trying to expand their network, volunteering is a good way to do it for a few reasons:

> ➤ **Cold calling someone for networking purposes isn't acceptable**: Maybe at one time this strategy worked but in today's business world, the way to build business relationships is by meeting people.

> ➤ **Volunteering allows people to have a common bond**: Sometimes it's hard to start a conversation with a stranger or acquaintance, especially if you're trying to get to know them. Whatever effort you're volunteering for becomes an immediate conversation starter.

> ➤ **Your strengths will shine through your volunteer efforts**: Volunteering is a great way to showcase your strengths. If you do something well, consider sharing it with organizations that need the skill. People will notice.

> ➤ **The community benefits from your participation**: While I've been talking about volunteering from the context of building your network, don't forget that volunteering is just a good thing to do for the community.

Being in the business world is a never-ending realm of networking meetings. These interactions involve giving and getting information to make our careers and our companies more successful.

Types of networking meetings

Let's talk about the best approaches and the advantages and disadvantages to each.

- ➤ **Group networking events** are gatherings which either allocate time for networking or devote the entire agenda to networking. Professional associations will often have a networking hour prior to their regular membership meeting. Conferences will often schedule networking time for attendees. There are also organizations that promote themselves as networking groups, specifically for business people to share business leads and referrals.

    - ➢ **Advantages**: There's an opportunity to re-connect with people you already know as well as meet new people. These are an excellent forum for people who are comfortable meeting complete strangers and can easily start conversations. And it's easy to leave conversations that don't appear to be going anywhere.

    - ➢ **Disadvantages**: It is very difficult to have a long, detailed conversation. You have to rely on small-talk to get the conversation going, which can be difficult if you're not a fan of chit chat.

- ➤ **Individual meetings** are face-to-face appointments, usually between two people who already know each other. Business professionals in similar industries or professions will often network with each other.

    - ➢ **Advantages**: These are great for times when you want to have a private conversation or a long, detailed discussion. They're ideal when a person wants to ask for a favor.

    - ➢ **Disadvantages**: These are susceptible to becoming one-way conversations. Also, if individuals do not know each other well, there can be moments of awkward silence.

- ➤ **Synergy calls (or networking calls)** are the often-used term for people to connect via phone versus in person. These calls could be the first contact individuals have with each other. They could also be follow-up calls after a brief initial meeting.

    - ➢ **Advantages**: The calls are often not time-consuming.

    - ➢ **Disadvantages**: They may not give the best first impression. Sometimes you don't get the benefit of seeing body language. Poor cell phone coverage can create frustration (and can lead to dropped calls).

While individual in-person meetings and synergy calls might appear like the same thing, it's important to decide the best way to present yourself. You are networking for a reason. Think about that reason and the best way to accomplish your purpose.

Common networking challenges and how to overcome them

The two components to networking are building the relationship and leveraging the relationship. If you don't build the relationship, there's nothing to leverage and it's not networking. One of the first challenges people make has to do with the person themselves. Someone meets an individual and makes an immediate assumption that either:

1.   This person isn't worth the energy it takes to build a relationship or,

2.   They don't know anyone's worth value.

These are totally incorrect assumptions. You'd be surprised at who knows who in your community.

When I first moved to South Florida, a friend told me to pay attention to how money moves in the community. If you have to create a networking strategy, she suggested that being where the money goes is effective. It doesn't always mean the largest companies in your city. Think of the charities and non-profits that attract attention—they're getting money too. That's where the power players are probably volunteering.

The next biggest challenge in networking occurs in the relationship. Networking takes time. Good business relationships do not happen overnight. People need to know you and trust you. Networking will not be effective when it's viewed like the Janet Jackson song *What Have You Done for Me Lately?*

One-sided conversations

All meetings should be an exchange—a two-way conversation. This couldn't be truer than during a networking meeting. Andy Porter, vice president of human resources and organizational development at Merrimack Pharmaceuticals in Massachusetts, offered a tongue and cheek description of meetings in a blog post on Fistful of Talent. "During this meeting, you'll see all the tricks you've come to associate with Charades such as vigorous hand waving and facial contortions, incoherent drawings on the white board, and people generally making themselves look like assess." Unfortunately, there's a bit of truth in this description.

Sometimes individuals are so wrapped up in themselves and their story that they dominate the conversation. I completely understand that the person is excited about the job or the opportunity. It's not networking when only one person controls the conversation. That's storytelling. Or a lecture. Or both.

There's no easy way to get away from a one-sided conversation. When I find myself in those situations, I take myself through this mental flowchart:

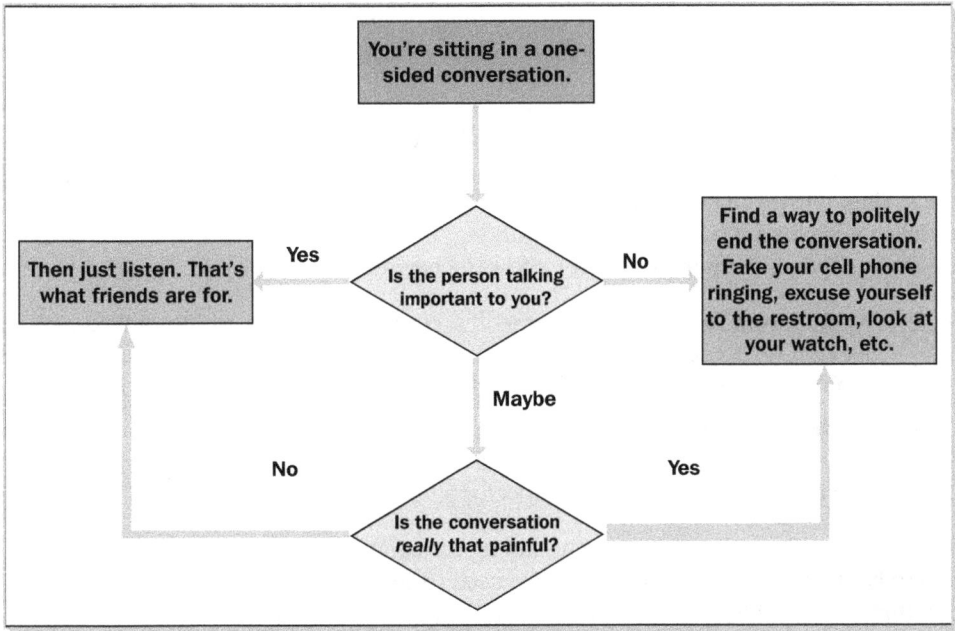

It really comes down to my relationship with that person. And that's what networking is all about—relationships. The stronger the relationship, the more important the person is to you. And the more important they are, the more we're willing to tolerate an occasional one-sided conversation.

All take and no give

Networking meetings are about giving. When I share information with someone, it doesn't mean they owe me. It's possible that I will ask someone for information, and they've never asked for anything in return. I might start out a business relationship by giving more than I'm getting. You could also find this to be the case on social media platforms. You're sharing more of other people's work than they're sharing of yours.

The spirit of networking isn't about keeping score. Some people refer to it as *paying it forward*. It's the expression used for describing when the beneficiary of a good deed repays it to someone other than the original benefactor. According to Wikipedia, the phrase may have been coined by Lily Hardy Hammond in her 1916 book, *In the Garden of Delight*.

In thinking about it, I believe we have to separate networking and paying it forward. Networking is about mutual exchange. Paying it forward is a gift with no expectation of return. In fact, the expectation is that you will gift someone else.

If done correctly, networking does have a *return the favor* element to it. We often feel obligated to do something nice for someone when they've done something nice for us. Granted, it might not be right away and there's no scorecard to make sure the exchanges are always in balance. But I'm challenged to think of one situation where someone is very willing to be called upon repeatedly for business, information, and jobs without some level of future expectation.

I'll confess, I know people who only call me when they are looking for a job. Now maybe they think I haven't put the pieces together and don't realize that. But as soon as I get a note saying, "Hey! I've been thinking of you. Let's find time to have some sushi.", I know they're looking for a job. This is not networking. If I choose to help them, it's really a gift or a favor, depending upon how well I know the person.

> ➤ **We do favors for people we know**: If a complete stranger asks for a favor, I'm not sure we process it the same way as when our best friend asks for a favor. This implies that a little mental benchmarking takes place when a favor is requested.

> ➤ **We do favors for people we like**: Yes, admit it. Whether we know the person or not. If someone you don't really care for asks for a favor, you are less inclined to help than if someone you like asks for a favor.

The challenge with networking is maintaining the balance. Networking is something we need to be successful in our careers. So we need to get something out of it. But to get something, we need to give something away. Successful networking involves looking at the big picture, not the short-term.

As you're out there building your networking circle, the last thing to remember is that networking is forever. A *huge* mistake many people make is they don't start building a professional network until they need one (translation: lose their job)—and then it's too late. You need to network every day, all day, and all the time. You never know who you might meet and when you will be presented with an opportunity just make sure that you're ready.

Before you go to a networking meeting

We've been talking about networking at a high level so far—we've discussed the purpose of networking meetings, types of networking meetings, and some networking strategy. Now it's time to actually participate in the networking meeting.

The type of meeting you attend can help you choose your strategy. Going to a networking meeting doesn't mean you have to ask for something. But it might be helpful to think about the possibilities. Here are a few situations I've been exposed to:

> ➤ At a group networking meeting:
>> ➤ You meet someone new and decide to schedule an individual meeting or synergy call to learn more about them.
>> ➤ You see someone you haven't seen in ages and decide to set up a call or meeting to catch up.

> ➤ I've also seen current or past clients at group networking meetings. We'll say hello, and they'll ask me to give them a call after the meeting regarding a new project.

➤ At individual meetings:

> ➤ Someone asks for your help to find a job or supply some information (or vice versa).
>
> ➤ You meet with a colleague to discuss a new business venture.
>
> ➤ You set a meeting with someone you recently met to learn more about their business.

➤ On synergy calls:

> ➤ Someone you know calls you about a new business venture. If you're interested, they'd like to set up a face-to-face meeting (or vice versa).
>
> ➤ A person you don't know wants to initiate a conversation. The hope is that it will lead to some sort of business relationship.

Unless you're attending a group networking event that's being organized by someone else, there are a couple pieces of networking etiquette that should be followed:

➤ **Be punctual.** I realize emergencies happen, and traffic is uncontrollable. But we have cell phones today. Networking is not an impromptu event. It's a planned and scheduled meeting. Needless to say, it's frustrating to schedule a call or meeting with someone only to have them not show, or arrive long after the scheduled time.

➤ **If you can't make it, ask if you can reschedule.** As a consultant, I completely understand when another consultant asks to reschedule because of a last minute client request. I appreciate that clients come first—mine do too—and a last minute "gotta reschedule" is fine. I've had it happen to me plenty of times. But the no call, no show is totally not professional or acceptable. It's disrespectful of a person's time.

➤ **Tell people the purpose of the call.** If you're inviting someone to a synergy call, tell them that's the purpose of the call. I recently had someone leave me a message they wanted to book me for a speaking engagement. When I called back, they said they wanted to "explore synergies". In other words, what can I do to help them? No joke. I'm sure there are lots of people who refuse to engage in these synergy calls. And if that's their position ... I say fine. No one should resort to lies and trickery to get someone on the phone. It's very inappropriate.

➤ **In addition, if you're planning to ask someone to do something during a networking meeting, let them know ahead of time.** You can say, "I was wondering if I could buy you lunch. I'm working on a new company website and know you have some experience with building websites. I'd like to pick your brain if you don't mind." This tells the person what the conversation is going to be about, and they can come to the meeting knowing what will be asked of them. And, as thanks for their time and information, they get a free lunch.

Networking meetings are still meetings. The people who attend them should think about why they're going and what they hope to accomplish.

During the meeting

As I'm writing this chapter, I can't recall a time where a networking meeting has had a specific agenda beyond knowing why you're meeting. But there are a few essential steps you can do during a networking meeting to make sure the time spent is productive:

> ➤ **Find out about the other person—what they do and what they're working on.** The purpose of a synergy call is an exchange. I can't begin to tell you the number of times people call me or meet with me, tell me what their company does and never once ask what I do or the projects I'm working on. Those are usually the people who also don't let me get a word in edgewise so I can tell them. That's not an exchange. Make sure that everyone has a chance to share.

Tip

How much do you need to know?

Whenever I'm preparing for a meeting, I do research about the other person and their organization. This raises the question—how much research or information is enough?

In my opinion, I don't expect people to know everything about me or my business. That's why we're networking in the first place. The purpose of the meeting or phone call is to give both of us the opportunity to "fill in the blanks".

So as you're doing your meeting preparations, consider the balance. Know enough to have a couple of questions handy. This tells the other person that you've done your homework and you're showing a genuine interest in them.

> ➤ **Tell the person how they fit into your plans.** Obviously, there's a reason for the meeting. Let the other person know how you see them fitting into your project or organization. It might not be clear to them. For example, after explaining your background, talking about your company/products/services, tell the person how you might see them being a partner to your organization. Simply explaining what your company does and asking, "Whaddya think?" doesn't give the other person a clear picture of what you want.

> ➤ **If you put a request on the table, be willing to listen to one.** Keeping with the spirit of networking being about exchange, remember that, if you ask for something, the other person might want something too. Prior to making the request, think about what a person might want in exchange. Is that something you can agree to? Is it something you'd like to offer at the time of your request?

> ➤ **Don't expect an answer right away.** If you're asking for something specific, give a person time to consider it. For those times when giving a person time to consider isn't an option, let the person know prior to the meeting that an immediate reply will be expected.

> ➤ **Close with a way to stay in touch.** Not every initial networking meeting will yield an outcome. Sometimes the whole purpose of the call is just to get to know someone, then find a way to stay connected. One way I stay in touch is via LinkedIn—it's a professional network and, since this is a professional meeting, it's the perfect platform.

All of us are business people trying to make the most of our time. We understand that building a network is a part of being successful, regardless of our job title, company, or industry. And we don't want to waste time doing it. Conducting productive networking meetings will help us be successful networkers today and in the future.

Saying no

Being a successful networker means you will get requests (while it might be overwhelming at times, it's a good thing):

> ➤ "You know lots of people. Can you help my friend find a job?"

> ➤ "We just launched a new website. Would you mind taking a look and sharing your thoughts?"

> ➤ "We're creating a program for business executives to network and learn more about industry analytics. Could you send some information about our event to your network?"

Just because someone makes a request of you, it doesn't mean you have to do it. Even if it's your best friend, you don't have to say yes. Well, maybe there are people you feel you must say yes to, but you get my point. It's simply impossible to accept every request.

Saying no is one of the most difficult things for business people to do. Probably because it's been engrained in customer service training programs to avoid saying no to customers. We want to be accommodating even when it means considerable inconvenience to us. Don't shy away from networking because of the requests others make. Instead learn how to say *no* comfortably.

Lynne Curry, Ph.D., SPHR suggests asking questions before jumping to say yes. The questions should be about the work or task being asked of you and the time commitment.

> ➤ What would be involved in the project?

> ➤ What would I be responsible for?

> ➤ What's the time commitment?

Asking questions lets the requestor know that you are carefully and thoughtfully considering the request. It also can give the requestor a "heads up" that you might decline the offer.

After getting the answers about the work and the time involved, ask one last question, "When do you need an answer?", I used to put undue pressure on myself by giving myself too quick of a deadline. I thought everyone wanted a response right away. At the point I started asking when my response was needed, I was surprised at how much time I had. I made better decisions because I had the time to properly consider the request.

Take the time to consider the request. I must admit there have been times when I wanted to quickly say yes, only to realize the best answer was no. And the reverse is equally true. I've left meetings thinking "no way" and, with proper time to consider all the benefits, I changed my mind.

Curry suggests when saying no, say it directly.

> *"While you can give a brief, convincing explanation so the requester understands the reason for your no, avoid excuses; others see through them and would rather be told no than suffer through a layer of phony excuses."*

You can also consider providing a partial yes or compromise. For example, a colleague asks you to serve on a volunteer board and because of work commitments, you aren't able to do it. You can reply with "I'm not able to accept your gracious offer but I would be able to work on a smaller project with a clearly defined start and end date." Another option would be "I can't accept the board position but I'd love to find some way to participate. Can we talk about opportunities that don't involve the same level of commitment?".

Networking is necessary and can actually be fun. But if we overload ourselves, networking becomes a chore, and this will show in networking meetings and create barriers to building good working relationships. It could possibly create regret and resentment over the things we agreed to do. It will impact our productivity and hurt our ability to get referrals, recommendations, and references.

Connection power–how to get more of it

Every business person needs connection power. Simply put, it's the power that lies in the people you know, and your connections. A great example we all might be familiar with is the administrative assistant to a company executive. The assistant has power because of their connection to the executive. Often the administrative assistant is referred to as the gatekeeper. Sales professionals need to get past the gatekeeper in order to meet with the executive and close the sale.

This concept doesn't only apply to sales professionals. I once worked for a company where my boss' administrative assistant had an excellent read on how my boss was feeling. If she liked you, she would forewarn you about visiting the boss when he was in a cranky mood. And if she didn't care for you, well ... you didn't get forewarned, and you possibly had to deal with a grumpy boss.

The point is we can do many things on our own—but not everything. We need our connections to help us. To give us a piece of advice. To introduce us to someone they know.

Each of us needs to constantly be building our connection power. We should be meeting new people and building new connections all the time because we will lose connections as well. And I don't mean because of an argument or falling out. Sometimes we grow apart because of job changes, life changes, or geography.

Thank goodness we have technology tools today to help us maintain those connections over the years and the miles.

Technology and networking

There are many social networks that focus on professional networking. One of the more popular ones is LinkedIn. The idea is simple: create a profile with your experience and expertise, and then connect with co-workers and colleagues. LinkedIn also allows you to join groups and interact with like-minded professionals.

The reason I want to mention social networks is because I've found them very useful for staying in touch with people from my previous jobs. It's so easy to say "let's stay in touch" but the reality is we get busy. Sometimes we forget to update contact information and before you know it, we can't find that connection anymore.

Social media has made keeping the connections easier. You can see when someone changes jobs or gets a promotion and wish them well. Some social media networking sites allow you to leave recommendations – a great way to let a person know what you think of their work. I wouldn't say it's effortless but social media allows you to stay connected in an unforced way.

Now, while I'm a fan of using technology to stay in touch, I do want to caution professionals about overusing technology. Don't waste your networking meeting chatting or texting on your phone. Here's a true story to illustrate:

> *"During a conference, I ran into a colleague who I hadn't seen in ages. We were both on a tight schedule but wanted to spend some time together. So we decided to catch up over a glass of wine. During the entire time we were together, she was texting the person she was planning to meet for dinner. Not details about where to meet or what time… jokes and conversations they could have had during dinner. Needless to say, we didn't do much talking – or networking."*

In an interview for *The Build Network*, Gary Vilchick, chief financial officer of Veracode, says when he's in meetings, he views it as a responsibility to participate. "To do that well, it means you're following the conversation closely and you're thinking about every point along the way where you may be able to step in and add some value to the conversation. If you're multitasking, your ability to do that drops dramatically." Vilchick provides an example, "This time in the quarter, one of my responsibilities is to review sales orders and make sure they're structured appropriately. For the last few days of the quarter, it means I have a tablet with me when I go to a meeting, checking the e-mail flow so that [when] a sales order comes through, I respond to it immediately. But I also realize I'm giving up something in the process, because I'm not listening as intently. It's not ideal."

I get it. We want to believe we're multitasking experts. Our companies expect us to be multitasking experts. The reality is … we're not. When we're multitasking, something isn't being given our full attention. And when we're networking, the "thing" not getting our full attention is a person. If you've ever been on the receiving end of a person multitasking while you're talking, you know—it's annoying. And dare I add, rude.

You never know when you might need the help of a connection. Remember every impression. That last interaction could decide if someone is available to assist in the future.

After the networking meeting

Even when there are no follow-up items from a networking meeting, it's important to follow-up. This sends the message to the person you just met with that their time and expertise were important. It lets them know that you value them and their time.

Following-up

I mentioned in the previous section that I like to use social networks to stay in touch with former colleagues. Another good use of social networks is staying in touch with new connections.

Let's say you meet someone at a networking event. If you'd like to stay in touch with them, when you swap business cards, ask if you can stay in touch via LinkedIn, or follow up after the event with a LinkedIn connection request and personalized note like *Great meeting you at the ABC event this week. I enjoyed our conversation and would like to stay in touch.*

Be forewarned. Some individuals will not connect with acquaintances on LinkedIn. That is their prerogative. Most individuals who are trying to build their network will connect with individuals that they have met and had a productive conversation. (Please note the word productive in the previous sentence. If you spent the entire conversation asking what the person could do for you ... chances are they will not accept your connection request.)

Another very common way to stay connected is by adding the new contact to your online address book or **Customer Relationship Management** (**CRM**) software. Be cognizant about where you keep contact information. In some cases, your new contact's information might be added to the company e-mail blast. I'm all for marketing your company but when the first piece of follow up after a networking meeting is a sales e-mail ... it doesn't look like you're serious or professional. In fact, you look like a spammer.

When and how to ask for a favor

At some point, you will have to ask one of your connections for a favor or to do something for you. It's going to happen. You will have people asking you for favors. But that's okay because, someday, you'll need one too.

Years ago, I saw a poll in a publication called *SmartBrief on Leadership*. The poll question was:

> *"What best describes your approach to doing favors for others in the workplace?"*

82% replied, "I help out everyone who asks for favors whether I know they'll reciprocate or not."

I'm sorry, but I don't believe it. This isn't about SmartBrief; they asked a legitimate question. I'm just not buying that 82% would help everyone who asked. No strings attached. I'm all for being nice and paying it forward, but I really struggle with believing this one.

I totally believe that people want to do all the favors people ask of them. I really do. The reality is we can't—there just isn't enough time in our busy lives. So we have to develop some sort of criteria for who we say yes to and who we have to turn down. What's unfortunate is when the person saying no is perceived as not being helpful or not being a team player.

The hard part of asking for a favor is where the responsibility of the favor is being placed. Typically, it's on the person who is being asked. If you want to do it, you say yes ... and if you don't, you say no. When in actuality, the responsibility should rest with the person making the request. People should stop and ask themselves, "Do I know this person well enough to ask for this favor?" and "Is my request reasonable?" Instead, many people just ask with the sole intent of getting the task completed.

Favors should be considered valuable commodity and requests should not be taken lightly. As a responsible networker, you want to evaluate requests carefully and thoughtfully. More importantly, you want to wisely make your request for a favor.

5 tips for better networking

Lauren Berger, CEO of InternQueen.com and author of *Welcome to the Real World* recommends pushing yourself outside your comfort zone for better networking.

> *"Set a goal. Networking meetings and events can be overwhelming. Before you go, decide how many new people you are going to introduce yourself to and how many business cards you are going to walk out with. Push yourself out of your comfort zone and make sure you reach your goals. Also, make sure that your business cards are clean, organized, and easy to reach. Women—wear a purse you can put on your shoulder—you don't want to be walking around with too many things in your hands!"*

Steve Browne is executive director of human resources at LaRosa's Inc. For over 60 years, LaRosa's has been the #1 family pizzeria and Italian restaurant. Steve shares his secret for remembering names during networking events.

> *"To be successful at a networking meeting work on remembering people's names. People like to have their names remembered. When you introduce yourself, say the person's name three times while you make the introduction. It's like this..."*

> *Hi, I'm Steve, and you are?*

> *Hi, I'm Susan.*

> *Well Susan, what brought you here to this event?*

> *I wanted to meet other professionals in HR.*

> *That's great Susan. What kind of HR role do you have?*

> *I'm an HR Director for a manufacturer.*

> *That's interesting Susan. What does your company manufacture?*

So, now you know that Susan is in HR for a manufacturer and she wants to meet other HR folks. This exercise works and makes you a more effective networker yourself be being able to make meaningful connections personal. "

Dawn S. Bugni, MRW, CMRW, CPRW is a career strategist and master resume writer at The Write Solution. She reminds us of the ultimate networking skill—listening!

"While mastering the core of good networking,—research, plan, give more than you take, and follow-up add two words to your repertoire: Be interested.

People probably won't remember much about you if you fire hose information "at" them during networking events. You can't tell absolutely everything about you in the first sentence (also known as an 8-10 minute monologue, with no breaths, breaks, or periods.) And, you can't create an instant bond with information overload. You'll overwhelm the listener and quickly fade from memory as you walk away.

Instead, ask questions that can inform and enlighten you toward your career goals, but give the listener an opportunity to talk about themselves. (Who doesn't like that?) Be interested. Learn from other's stories. Of course, given the opportunity, tell your own story. Then put all that planning and research into play and succinctly convey your unique value proposition. But remember, sometimes, the best way to learn, and create a lasting impressing, is to be interested in what someone else has to say. "

Heather Huhman, career expert and blogger at Glassdoor, the world's most transparent career community, shares three tips for networking online.

"Networking not only happens in person but online. Being able to send a networking email is an essential skill in today's technology driven workplace. Here are my three tips for sending a well-written networking email:

1. *Start out strong. You need to write an introduction explaining who you are (if they don't know already) and why they should read on. If you've never met the person you're writing to, the best way to start is by sharing something you have in common. This can be a mutual friend, interest, or something else. If you have met the person you're writing to, start out by introducing yourself again. Then touch on something you talked about in your initial conversation.*

2. *Keep it concise. Most people don't have time to read lengthy e-mails that aren't directly related to their work. In a networking e-mail, you need to get to the point and get there quickly. Once you've made an introduction, explain what you want right away. Make your request simple. Ask for a bit of information or advice at the most.*

3. *Wrap it up. Just as quickly as you began your e-mail, you need to conclude it. Wrap it up by thanking them for their time and providing a call to action. Ask them a question or suggest a way to meet in person. But again, make it simple. "*

Hannah Morgan, career strategist and founder of Career Sherpa.netuses an activity called the Networking Bucket List with her clients.

"I was asked to make a list of three people I would like to get to know better; people I admired or respected. Geography was not a restriction. I was supposed to reach out to them and cultivate a relationship. This "networking bucket list" was well outside my comfort zone (it still is!)...and worth every moment invested.

As you consider who to select for your top three contacts, do some prep work:

Ask yourself why you want to meet each person. Dig deep, beyond the obvious (that they are famous or well-recognized).

Research each person online to identify their most noteworthy accomplishments.

Construct a list of well-thought-out questions you want to ask each person. Select some that are specific and some that are more personal and insightful. Perhaps some of these will give you ideas:

> *What part of this job do you personally find most satisfying? Most challenging?*

> *What trends do you see in the future that will have the greatest impact on your industry?*

> *What keeps you awake at night?*

> *What's the best gift you've ever given?*

> *What's your favorite movie of all time?*

> *Who do you admire most and why?*

Now... pick up the phone! Yes, the phone.

Briefly introduce yourself and immediately explain why you would like to meet with them. Smile, speak clearly and confidently, and most importantly, keep your introduction and ask under minute. You won't always get a yes, however, if your reason for asking for the meeting is sincere and well thought out, you will get more yes answers than "no" replies.

Who are your three bucket-list contacts? Yes, carrying this out is difficult. And if you do decide to take action, you – and your career – will grow. Imagine what you'll learn. Who knows, it might lead to your meeting someone really spectacular."

Summary

Always be networking. It was the advice my first manager gave me. Networking can be a challenge at first but, the more you do it, the better you get at it. The more you meet with people, the easier it becomes to see who is sincere about networking and who's not. The more you network, the more you will learn about the people you can depend on and the more they will learn about you.

In this first section on information meetings, we discussed status meetings, brainstorming, and networking meetings. These types of meetings are about giving and sharing different types of information.

The next section of the book will focus on feedback meetings. We'll cover training, employee performance, and focus groups. Performance conversations aren't punishment. They are designed to be helpful and improve performance. In the next chapter, we'll discuss training meetings as a way to offer feedback.

> 5

Training Meetings

Our thoughts about training usually conjure up an image of people in a classroom setting with a whiteboard or PowerPoint. While formal classroom training is valuable, the majority of training takes place in a much more casual setting. On-the-job training (OJT) or just-in-time training happen frequently in business. That's what this chapter is about—informal learning.

Informal learning still has many similarities to the formal classroom environment, which we will discuss here.

What is a training meeting?

By definition, training is the act of teaching a person specific information or a particular skill. We might have a tendency to think of training as a formal classroom experience with a group of people and an instructor. But training can take place in a one-on-one session such as on-the-job or just-in-time training. It can also happen during a regularly scheduled status meeting as in, "Let's give John from accounting 15 minutes during our next staff meeting to train everyone on the proper way to file expense reports."

Training is different from development, which is focused on teaching someone a skill or information, usually for a future job. Often we hear the terms "training and development" in the context of training employees for both current and future work responsibilities.

Before we can move forward with the subject of training, we have to decide whether the topic that needs to be conveyed is actually a training issue. Not everything can be addressed with training.

Typically, the training process starts with a discussion like this:

> ➤ Senior leadership asks someone to implement a training program.
> ➤ A manager needs to correct a performance issue with an employee.
> ➤ The company is making a change that involves a new process or procedure.

Whether it's training for one person or one hundred people, in order for training to be effective, it must be connected to a business metric. Some common business metrics include: sales revenue, employee turnover, manufacturing defects, customer complaints, and so on. Whenever you conduct training, you want to know what the business metric is prior to the training and after the training to gauge the impact of the training event. Even with topics that might appear on the surface as not quantifiable, there's a metric that can be attached. It takes some extra searching. For example, the metrics for anti-harassment training might be the percentage of participants who have taken training or percentage of participants who completed training within the first month of hire. This aligns with the company's goal of maintaining business compliance.

Another example is stress management training. It's possible that conducting this type of training could reduce sick days, complaints to human resources about being "stressed out", or comments in exit interviews about stress levels. Again, look for the connection between the goals of the business and the training topic.

If a business metric doesn't exist, then it's not training. It could be conveying information but it's not training. Remember the training provides a person with information or a skill. That information or skill is then used in the employee's current job.

An example would be if the vice president of operations comes into your office and says, "We need time management training for our supervisors. They just can't seem to get anything done."

Can you offer a time management training program? I'm sure of it. You could create one yourself or call a consulting company to do it for you. It could be a fabulous program. The supervisors tell you they loved it. The real question is will it fix the problem? We don't know.

Time management could very well be an issue, but in relationship to what? Is it because they can't deliver projects on time? Or because a customer complained about a delivery being late? Training must tie to a business measurement.

After identifying the business metric, it's time to determine whether training is necessary. Here are three questions you can ask to determine whether training is the answer:

➤ Does the person have the skills to do the task?

➤ Does the person have the desire to do the task?

➤ Is the person allowed to do the task?

If the answer to all three questions is yes, then training is not the answer. It could be an equipment problem.

If the answer to the first question is no, training *may or may not* be the answer. The answer could be coaching. An answer of "no" to question 2 means you may have a motivation problem. An answer of "no" to question 3 might mean a policy or procedural issue.

Let's use the time management example again. Maybe the reason supervisors aren't able to deliver on time isn't because they have poor time management skills but rather it's because the copier has been broken for the past two weeks.

Another reason the supervisors might not deliver on time is because the regional manager has told them it doesn't matter how good the project deliverable is, the vice president isn't going to approve it. The supervisors aren't motivated to finish a project that won't get approved anyway.

Lastly, what if the reason that the supervisors can't get the project completed is because the regional manager changed the scope of the project three times in the last week. The supervisors have no clue what they need to be working on.

So again, while the company could very well need time management training, it's important to ask a few questions and confirm before jumping into the commitment for training.

The goal of a training meeting

We've established that the definition of training is to teach someone a particular skill or specific information. So obviously, that's the goal. We've defined what training is. However, while we're talking about goals, I feel compelled to also expand on what training is *not*, because it can impact the goals of the training meeting.

Communication versus training

Training is not communicating a policy or procedure. It's easy to fall into the trap that training is any form of communication, so let me provide an example to illustrate.

The accounting department creates a new policy regarding the proper way to file expense reports. They decide to hold a meeting to communicate the new policy. While that's good and communicating the policy should be done, it's not training.

Now, if the accounting department tells everyone to come to the meeting with their last two expense reports, adds a discussion, and creates activities giving employees the opportunity to see a demonstration of the new policy in action and practice the policy in a safe environment, then that's training. But holding a meeting where one person communicates a new policy or procedure, everyone else listens and we all sign a form saying we will adhere to the new procedure doesn't mean training occurred.

Training implies that the subject being conveyed needs to be learned. Using our expense report example again, if accounting developed a new policy on coding expense reports, there might be time dedicated during a status meeting to explain the changes, but not a training session because everyone knows how to complete expense reports. However if the company starts using a brand new software program to process expense reports, they might have a training session because no one knows how to use the software.

It's important to note this difference because sometimes business leaders will say that they conducted training when the reality is they held a meeting. At the end of the meeting, the company has no idea what employees learned, if anything. And they get really frustrated when employees don't follow the new policy or procedure.

This is how that disconnect usually plays out: when confronted about performance issues, the employee says, "I never got any training!" The manager becomes defensive and says "Sure we did... don't you remember that meeting a few months ago?!" A-ha! The disconnect between communication and training.

Training doesn't have to be long or complex. It does need to give participants a chance to actively review the knowledge or skill topic as well as an opportunity to practice. When communicating information, the decision must be made if the content is to be communicated or trained. It not only makes a difference in the way information is shared, but how it is received. More importantly, it makes a difference how information is retained and accounted for.

Presentations are not training

The *Wall Street Journal* once reported that over 30 million PowerPoint presentations are done each day. That's not a typo—30 million.

Presentation software programs such as PowerPoint are *not* a substitute for training. They are not an excuse for instructors to not learn the training material beforehand. They are also not a stand-in for participant handouts or an alternative for taking meeting minutes. Presentation programs are a powerful way to add polish to your presentations and make them come alive, but only if solid content and presentation skills are already there in the first place.

Tip

Components in a good presentation

I don't want to single out PowerPoint because in today's marketplace there are many excellent presentation software programs. PowerPoint is probably the first one that comes to mind. With the phenomenal amount of presentations taking place it only seems logical to me that, somewhere along the way, people would spend some time to learn how to use presentation software as an effective tool. Because that's what it is—a tool.

Here are three tips to consider when developing a presentation:

- **Everything you say does not have to be on a presentation slide**: Intentionally plan your presentation so there is a balance between your speaking and the visual presentation. The author and speaker Guy Kawasaki suggests the 10/20/30 Rule. No more than 10 slides, that last no more than 20 minutes and contain no smaller than 30 font.

- **Highlight key takeaways**: Barbara Roche from The Wharton School of the University of Pennsylvania recommends using a kicker box, a framed text box in a different color, to emphasize an important point. If you need more space, try a jolt slide, which has a different background. When placed in the presentation deck, it will "jolt" or stand out to viewers.

- **Include images and animation strategically**: The brain processes visual information faster than text and approximately 65 percent of the population are visual learners, according to the website http://www.studymode.com/. It only makes sense to bring eye-catching visuals into our presentations. The audience wants them!

The key to developing an effective presentation is to put yourself in the seats of your audience. That is, if you had to sit and listen to you, with your presentation, would you be sitting up attentively listening and taking notes? Or would you be slouched over creating your grocery list or checking your Facebook account?

Keep in mind the "less is more" philosophy when it comes to presentations. And, if you aren't going to put time and thought into your presentation, then maybe consider not using it at all!

Is a training meeting the best approach?

But there's a next step that's important to the training process—does it need to be a meeting? Given the number of meetings out there, it's amazing to me how many people don't ask this question. We've decided training needs to be conducted. What's the most effective way to deliver the training?

There are two key elements to consider when trying to decide whether the training you're planning should be conducted during a meeting: message and medium.

Message is the point you're trying to get across. What do you want people to come away with from your training? For example, if you're a restaurant manager trying to teach your servers how to open a bottle of wine, a training meeting would be perfect. Employees can see a demonstration and have the chance to open a bottle of wine to practice.

On the other hand, if you want all of your employees to learn the basics of a social media platform, it would be possible for you to ask them to view a video, create an account, and connect with you prior to the next team meeting. Did the employee learn something? Yes. At the point they connect with you, they've learned how to set up an account. But it didn't take a meeting for that type of learning to happen.

Training meetings are perfect for topics that involve complex discussion or multiple steps. The training agenda encourages discussion and practice. While it can be done, straightforward subjects or activities might not require a meeting. It might be possible to use another method, which brings me to the second consideration.

Medium is the communication tool you use to get that point across. It might be PowerPoint, video, lecture, and so on. A new hire employee needs to learn the organization's ethics policy. The company has prepared a pre-recorded webinar with the CEO and human resources director talking about the policy and common scenarios the employee might face. Both during and at the end of the webinar, the employee answers questions regarding the information presented. The employee is learning and the company is getting confirmation that the employee understands the material. But a meeting did not occur.

A nonprofit animal shelter invites a veterinarian to speak on the signs to look for in feline leukemia. Did learning take place? Yes. The staff in attendance learned the signs they need to be aware of when working with cats. And in this case, a meeting did take place.

Now, is it possible that the animal shelter staff could have read a book or watched a video and still learned the information? It may be possible. But let's say the veterinarian is the local expert on the subject and it was the group's only chance to hear from the expert. That would be a good reason for a meeting. Or, if the information needed to be presented to everyone quickly versus letting each person learn at their own pace by reading a book.

So for those times when physical presence or timing is key, training meetings are a good option.

The last element to consider when it comes to whether or not to hold a training meeting is what I'll call the entertainment factor. Bringing people together can be fun. You can add non-meeting elements to the agenda such as teambuilding and recognition. So if the message is a bit on the dull side (you know what classifies as dull in your industry), it might make sense to create a training meeting even if it's not necessary and insert some other things into the agenda to make it more engaging.

The caution with doing this is that the fun part of the agenda cannot overshadow the training part. It's not a fun meeting with a little insertion of training. It's a training meeting with a little infusion of fun. If the fun, entertaining part overshadows the training, it's possible that people will leave the meeting happy but with no clue what they were supposed to learn. The conversation goes something like this:

Employee: "Wow! What a great meeting. You should have heard him/her."

Manager: "What did they talk about?"

Employee: (Insert sound of crickets here.)"They were just so funny!"

I've actually seen this happen. The company needs to train employees about very serious topics. But they wanted to also give the employees an enjoyable training experience. So the trainer they hired was humorous and entertaining. He was also very smart and knew the subject matter well. Don't confuse being funny with not knowing the material. But the problem occurred when the trainer spent more time trying to get laughs than convey the important material. Subsequently, the employees did attend training but didn't learn everything. The company was forced to hire another trainer to conduct more focused sessions a second time.

Choosing to conduct a training meeting is an important decision. Most companies already have plenty of meetings. A training meeting adds another meeting to peoples' busy schedules. Calling a training meeting when it's not needed can cause people to tune the message out. So instead of employees learning, they are walking in/out of the session, texting their friends, or planning their next vacation while the training is supposed to be taking place.

As much as we want to think it's only the content that counts, message and medium allow the presentation to be engaging and understood.

Training meeting challenges

We've talked about what training is and isn't. We've learned that training isn't just a presentation. For the purposes of this chapter, I think it's important to recognize the difference between being a trainer and conducting training, because sometimes it can get in the way of training.

In the business world, there are training professionals; people who go to school to study how people learn and how to develop specific content for specific learning experiences. This chapter really isn't directed toward those people. Although if you're a training professional reading this, I hope you get a few tips you can use and share.

There are also people without formal training education and background who are asked to conduct training. It happens all the time and can be very successful. A person can be asked to put together a training session and do a great job conducting the training, without being a professional trainer. We're going to discuss exactly how to do that in this chapter.

It's necessary to highlight the difference because organizations need to know when to use a training professional and when not to. Every training opportunity is not a reason to hire a training consultant. Here are a few questions to ask when trying to make this decision:

➤ Does the subject matter require an outside resource?

➤ Does the organization have the capabilities to create and deliver the training in-house?

➤ If you do have the capabilities, can your internal team deliver the project within the necessary time frame?

➤ Lastly, can the company afford to do the project over if employees don't learn the material?

Even when the company has the expertise and the resources, using an external consultant isn't always the answer. Sometimes highly sensitive or confidential topics need to be trained using internal staff because of their delicate nature. And for the same reason, certain sensitive topics are best handled with outside resources. When deciding whether to use internal or external trainers, it's worth asking the question.

It's equally important for people who have given a presentation or conducted training at some point in their career to recognize when they need the services of a training professional. I'm not trying to burst anyone's bubble. Just because everyone says at the end of a training session "You did a great job", please don't make the assumption that you're now a "professional trainer".

Now that being said, I do think those compliments drive home an important point about having excellent platform and delivery skills. There's nothing more painful than listening to a training session with so many "ums" and "OKs" that text betting starts on how many will be uttered by the end of the meeting. People with good platform skills help us listen better and encourage interaction necessary for learning to take place. That's a very important piece of the training experience.

Tip

Things to consider when speaking

Since this section addresses giving presentations, I want to take a moment and offer some tips for becoming a better speaker. While giving a presentation and training are two different things, you do have to speak during training and having good platform skills is important.

- **Know the subject**: This is half the battle. When you know the topic, your confidence comes through. The audience will see you know your stuff. Don't agree to speak about subjects you're not comfortable with.

- **Practice**: It's not necessary to memorize every word. But do review your presentation. Some tips that I use are review the presentation standing up, say the presentation out loud so you can hear how phrases sound, do the presentation in front of a mirror to help with posture and body language and lastly, time your session so that you know whether you have too much or too little information.

- **Arrive early and get comfortable with the room**: Before the audience arrives, stand at the front of the room. Say a few sentences. If there's a microphone and podium, test them out. Don't just stand there for 30 seconds. Get comfortable being at the front of the room.

- **Get experience**: Regardless of the audience size, the way to become proficient speaking in front people…is by speaking in front of people. When given the opportunity, don't shy away from it.

If you are tasked with conducting training activities within your organization, people tell you that you're good at it, and you enjoy the experience, there are organizations that are dedicated to training and the inter-related disciplines of **Human Performance Improvement** (HPI) and **Organizational Development** (OD). There's even a training-related certification that demonstrates mastery of learning performance. I would encourage people with an interest to study training as a professional discipline.

Before someone can stand up in front of a group of people, there needs to be some devoted thought about the audience, the goals and objectives of the presentation, the learning content, and the means to measure comprehension. I've seen people who don't prepare for a session because they rely too heavily on their platform skills. Was the presentation successful? I guess that depends on what you call successful. If people leave the room saying it was great, but can't tell what it was about, then I'm not sure the speaker hit the mark.

One of the biggest challenges that can impact a training meeting is when someone who thinks they're a trainer or someone who relies too heavily on their delivery skills doesn't give the proper attention to the *other* aspects of the training experience.

Training, facilitating, and presenting

The Langevin.com blog has a great definition for the difference between training, facilitating, and presenting:

> ➤ Training is for learners to acquire knowledge and skill for use in their current job.

> ➤ During facilitation, participants are guided through a process, which might include generating ideas, analyzing the ideas, solving a problem, or making a decision.

> ➤ A presentation is a session where information is delivered to the audience to inform, persuade, inspire, or even entertain.

By now, we've established that presenting is not training. But it's also important to note that facilitating is not training. Sometimes the element of facilitation can be included in training but that's a conscious decision with the training design process.

Presenting, training, and facilitation each involve different skills. A great presenter might not be a great trainer. A great trainer could be a not-so-great facilitator. And a great facilitator... well, you get my point. We've talked about tips for presenters. Here are some tips for those times when you need to facilitate:

Tip

Conducting a great facilitation

Facilitation is the art of helping a group through a process. Good facilitators are able to engage the group without becoming the focus of the conversation. Here's how they do it:

- **Listen**: The first step in getting the group to participate is letting them talk. Facilitators start the conversation and then encourage the group to take over.

- **Ask questions**: When the conversation isn't clear, the facilitator can guide the conversation. Example questions include: "Can you expand on that idea?" or "What's your reaction to XX?"

- **Invite and encourage participation**: When the topic is becoming one-sided, a facilitator can bring others into the conversation. "Sara, would you like to add something to the discussion?"

- **Allow respectful debate**: Sometimes disagreement is healthy and productive. Groups need to share differing opinions to ultimately reach consensus. Facilitators know when to step in and when to allow the conversation to continue its logical conclusion.

- **Keep conversation on task and on time**: Facilitators can manage the conversation by organizing the discussion. "The conversation has moved away from XX. How does this relate to the original topic?"

- **Know when to stay silent**: In theory, facilitation is about talking and conversation. But a key element to conversation is knowing when to keep quiet. Facilitators need to recognize when they should let the group think.

"Flipping" training

A new trend in training brings changes to the presentation and facilitation discussion. It's called "flipping" and basically reverses traditional training methods. The idea being that activities such as reading and lecture would be done outside the classroom, and interactive exercises and discussion would be done inside the classroom.

At present, the discussion is contained to education and academics. Homework for students would be activities they can do on their own like watching a presentation or reading a chapter. Then class time is spent doing activities or having discussions to reinforce the materials.

It makes me wonder whether this is becoming the new way to conduct training. I could see businesses embracing the idea of less meeting time, with the thought that the time spent in the actual training meeting is action-packed. Participants might love the idea of listening and reading at their own pace, prior to attending training. It would also mean a whole new way of designing training and that the people asked to conduct training would become more of a facilitator and less of a presenter.

This figure, taken from an infographic created by Knewton, an infrastructure platform that allows companies to build learning applications, does a good job of comparing the traditional and flipped classroom models:

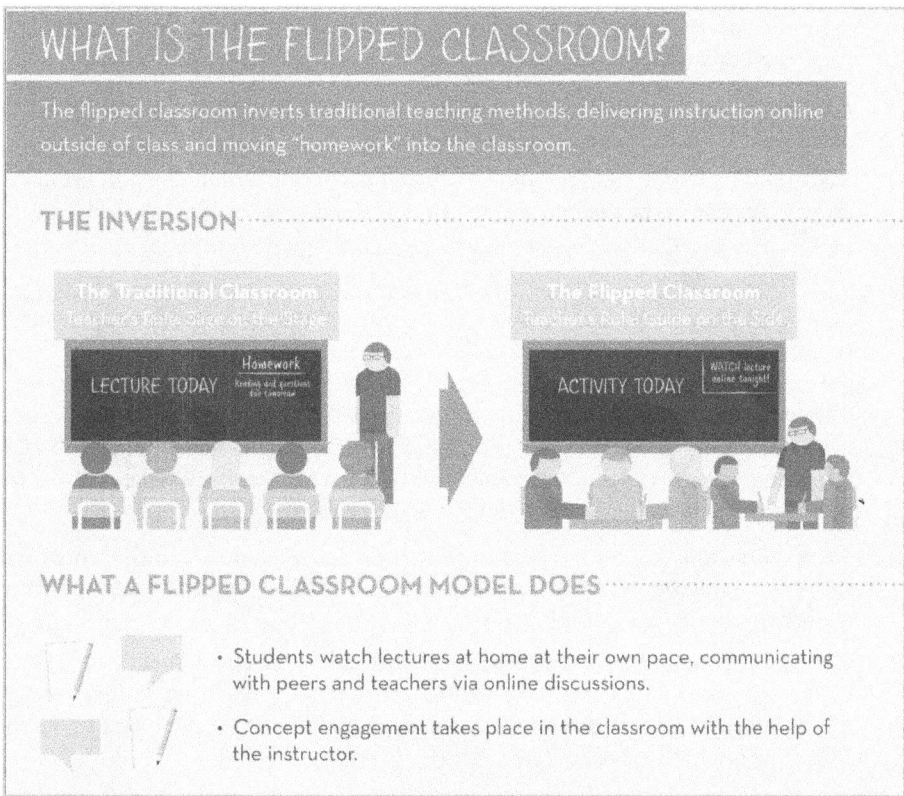

WHAT IS THE FLIPPED CLASSROOM?

The flipped classroom inverts traditional teaching methods, delivering instruction online outside of class and moving "homework" into the classroom.

THE INVERSION

The Traditional Classroom
Teacher's Role: Sage on the Stage

LECTURE TODAY   Homework
Reading and portions
for tomorrow

The Flipped Classroom
Teacher's Role: Guide on the Side

ACTIVITY TODAY   WATCH lecture
online tonight!

WHAT A FLIPPED CLASSROOM MODEL DOES

- Students watch lectures at home at their own pace, communicating with peers and teachers via online discussions.
- Concept engagement takes place in the classroom with the help of the instructor.

Before training occurs

Planning and logistics are important for all meetings but especially for the training meeting. External factors can have an impact on the meeting, which will impact the outcome. The person conducting the training meeting should take an active interest in meeting logistics.

As a training pro, I'm reminded of it every time I plan a training session. I often say, "The mind can absorb only what the rear can endure." Think about it. It's true. Logistics is the first key to any meeting's success. Here are some logistics issues to think about when planning a meeting:

➤ **Logistics letter**: When people need to travel for your meeting, consider drafting a single logistics letter providing information about how to get from the airport to the hotel or office, restaurants in the area, and so on. Sending a dozen short e-mails with information is not an acceptable substitute. Yes, the information is disseminated but it's a pain to organize! One page with everything on it—very simple and participants will love you for it.

➤ **Pre-reading or pre-work**: Tell participants in advance if they are to read or review something beforehand. Sending an article or PowerPoint prior is not an automatic directive to read something. Set a clear level of expectation.

➤ **Welcome**: Prepare a welcome for the event. Even with groups that meet on a regular basis, the welcome can also serve as a way for the group to reconnect since their last meeting.

➤ **Agenda**: Do not assume that everyone printed and brought a copy of the meeting agenda with them. Make copies for everyone.

➤ **Visitors**: When you have people who travel in for your event, keep in mind they might not know the city or the building. The host location should sensitize themselves to their visiting colleagues and what might seem to be obvious questions.

➤ **Newbies**: They might not be new to the location but newbies are people "new" to the meeting or event. For example, I used to attend a regular meeting where the executive team sat in the same seats. Creatures of habit I guess. When someone new joined the meeting, we would make sure they knew that. Another important thing about newbies is that they can be a valuable feedback source after the meeting. Consider reaching out to them for feedback—they have a fresh perspective you probably won't get anywhere else.

➤ **Views**: I recently went to a meeting where a large pole blocked my view of the speaker. Shame on me for sitting behind a pole! Shame on the event for putting a chair there in the first place!

➤ **Comfy chairs and working equipment**: Uncomfortable chairs make people cranky. Cranky people do not make for good meetings. And, if you need equipment during the meeting, make sure it works. Have a backup plan just in case it breaks down. Murphy's Law is always an option at any meeting.

> ➤ **Wireless**: This is the 21st century. Everyone wants access to Wi-Fi. If you have visitors attending your meeting, set up a guest account and password. Tell people how to access Wi-Fi prior to the meeting starting. Put the passcode on the agenda. My guess is bad/lack of wireless access rates is the most popular complaint in the list of meeting complaints.

> ➤ **Refreshments**: Despite what anyone might tell you, refreshments are important. I'm totally convinced refreshments tell people how much you care. For short meetings, a few beverages or at least pitchers or bottles of water should be present and for longer meetings, snacks and possibly meals need to be considered. Even if you decide not to provide refreshments and you personally can live with skipping lunch, please keep in mind not everyone is the same. They might have health issues they need to address by eating regularly scheduled meals.

Setting up the meeting room

Speaking of chairs and meeting room logistics, a decision you need to make when conducting training is how the room should be set up. The layout of the room should align with the content of the training. Depending upon the topic you're training, some room layouts are better than others. Here are a few of the most common layouts, their advantages, and disadvantages:

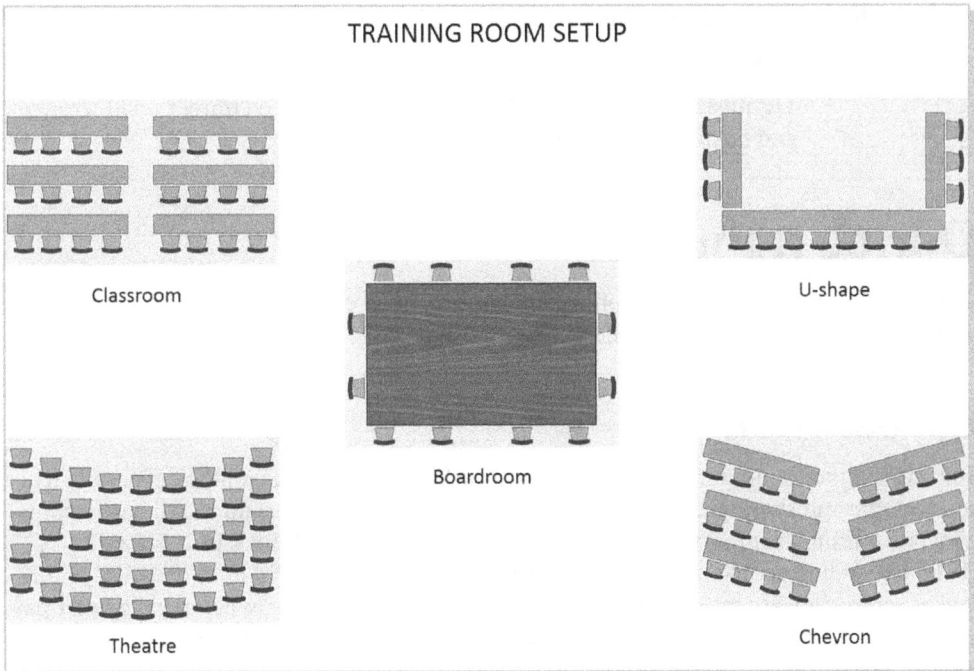

TRAINING ROOM SETUP

Classroom

U-shape

Boardroom

Theatre

Chevron

- ➤ **Classroom**
  - ➤ Advantage: Gives learners space to take notes, great for lecture situations
  - ➤ Disadvantage: Provides minimal interaction among participants
- ➤ **Theatre**
  - ➤ Advantage: Allows large groups to participate
  - ➤ Disadvantage: Not conducive for sessions that require learners to take notes or do any standing activities
- ➤ **Boardroom**
  - ➤ Advantage: Great for small groups
  - ➤ Disadvantage: Doesn't work well for group breakout activities; it also can imply positions of power based upon where people sit
- ➤ **U-shape or horseshoe**
  - ➤ Advantage: Works well in programs that will have discussions, also in programs where demonstrations are expected
  - ➤ Disadvantage: Space intensive, not always conducive for group breakout activities
- ➤ **Chevron, cabaret, or half circles**
  - ➤ Advantage: Learners can easily work in small groups
  - ➤ Disadvantage: Discussion and movement between trainer and learners can be difficult; it requires certain table sizes

During training

Whether you're training one person or one hundred, you can use the following five-step outline to conduct your training meeting.

Introduction

Starting out the training meeting, you have several goals including making everyone feel comfortable and sharing the goals of the meeting. First, it's important to tell participants why this training is important to them. This is also known as **What's in it for me? (WIIFM)**. When people have a clear understanding of why they're in attendance, and it makes sense, they are more likely to participate. Most of the time, when people don't pay attention in training, it's because they don't understand the reason they need to learn the topic or skill.

Discovering participant expectations

Depending upon the topic, it might be important and valuable to learn what participants expect from the training session. I say "might" because if the training is compliance or mandatory, then participant expectations might not have the ability to influence the training content.

However, if participant expectations are important for your training session, there are a couple ways to find out:

> Survey participants prior to the session. You can do this by phone, in-person, or via an electronic or paper survey.

> Include it in introductions. Ask participants to share one thing they hope to get out of the session.

A word of caution: when you ask participants what they expect to get out of training, then you have to be prepared to address it, whether that's by adding it to the content or telling participants that won't be covered (and hopefully telling them where they can find that information). If you ask people to share their expectations and you don't deliver them, participants will be disappointed.

I'm not mentioning this because the goal of training is to get good evaluations. The goal of training is to convey the information that participants need. Sometimes participants do not know what they need. They look to training to help them figure it out. That's why WIIFM is important.

The bottom line is: don't create expectations you can't deliver.

The next item to accomplish during the introduction is finding out what people already know about the topic. There are three reasons you want to understand this:

> **To focus on the right information**: If all of the participants already know a piece of information, you don't have to spend as much time on it. It can be covered quickly, leaving more time for other parts of the training. An example would be if you're conducting a training meeting on the steps to create a mail merge within a word processing program. The participants are all familiar with the proper way to create the database file, so instead of spending a lot of time on it, a brief review will suffice.

> **To clear up any incorrect information**: Sometimes participants will have information about the topic but the information is incorrect. During the review, you can determine whether participants have the correct information and address any misinformation.

> **To solicit the knowledge of others**: Often organizations will conduct recurrent or refresher training. These are short programs designed to remind people about a subject. Customer service is a great example. A training meeting might be focused on telephone standards to deliver good customer service. Employees who have been through prior trainings can be a source of information. Instead of training to them, train *with* them.

Discussion/demonstration

This step is the actual training. It's when the learning happens. You can conduct this step in two different ways depending upon the purpose of the meeting.

If the meeting is about something that people do, then it's best to conduct a demonstration. One way to know whether the topic is something people do, is to think of it in terms of "how to". Some sample topics would be:

> ➤ How to mail merge documents
>
> ➤ How to answer the phone
>
> ➤ How to properly complete an expense report

When it's necessary to give a demonstration, be sure you are prepared and have everything you need for the demonstration. This includes following a logical sequence when doing the actual demonstration. There's nothing more frustrating than watching someone conduct a disorganized, ill-prepared demonstration.

Another step to remember is to make sure all of the participants can see what you're doing during the demonstration. It can help to explain the steps while you're doing them to make sure participants are making the connection.

The other topic is about what people know. It could be considered information or facts. The best way to conduct the training meeting is with discussion. Example topics include:

> ➤ best-selling products in the store
>
> ➤ Employment application instructions for callers
>
> ➤ Proper communication during a hurricane threat

These are topics that don't necessarily need a demonstration. For instance, you can share the process that applicants should follow to apply for a job with the company without anyone physically completing an application. But participants might have questions about the process. There could be a discussion about what to do "if" this happens or "if" that happens. The point is to convey the information and encourage discussion about how to use it effectively.

Testing/practice

Whether you conduct a discussion or a demonstration, it's necessary to test participants and ensure they've learned the topic. If you have a discussion, then you can test participants on the information. This can be done formally using a pen and paper test or informally with a verbal question and answer session. The topic might dictate the best approach. Compliance-related training might require a formal testing procedure. You should know what your organization requires.

If you conduct a demonstration, you can ask participants to also do a demonstration. This allows you to physically see that the person can do the task. When it comes to participant demonstrations, here are three things to keep in mind:

> ➤ **Allow the most inexperienced person to go first**: Having the most experienced person go first creates an intimidating training environment. When the least experienced goes first, there's an opportunity to build confidence for everyone.

> ➤ **Don't interfere**: It might be tempting to help the person giving the demonstration. Resist the urge. Taking over the demonstration takes away their confidence and sends the message they're doing it wrong. Your role is to provide support.

> ➤ **Ask the participant to describe what they are doing while they are doing it**: Just as you explained the steps while doing the demonstration, ask the participant to do the same thing. It confirms that the participant knows the steps even if the demonstration is a bit awkward.

Tip

Training "homework"

One of the best ways to reinforce learning is to have participants immediately apply what they have learned on the job. A popular method of accomplishing this is by giving participants "homework", that is, an activity they should complete that allows them to use the content they received during training. Should you decide to add a "homework" element to your training meeting, here are a few things to remember:

- Get support from the participant's managers. This is time above and beyond what has been requested for training.
- Create a mechanism for feedback. Once participants complete the assignment, how do they share the experience? And what do they do if they have questions along the way?
- Establish consequences for noncompliance. Set a deadline and hold participants accountable. The activity wasn't designed to be optional.

Including activities outside of training is a great way to keep participants engaged with the content. However, like all training content, it must be thought out to be effective.

Feedback/debrief

After the testing/practice step, conduct a debrief or feedback session. Debriefs are an opportunity to discuss those things that went well and what can be improved. Research from The Group for Organizational Effectiveness shows that teams that conduct debriefs perform an average of 20 percent better. The debrief itself can be as simple as:

> ➤ What did you do well? Or what went well?

> ➤ What would you do differently? Or what would you change?

After discussion and testing, you can ask the group what topics were easy to remember and why. Another question would be to find out how people remembered a topic—what strategy did they use to recall. On the flip side, you can ask the group what topics were a challenge to remember and what methods they might use in the future to keep them at the top of mind.

After a demonstration, the feedback process has a bit more structure. Here are the three steps:

1. **Always ask the participant(s) for feedback first**: Always ask them to tell you what they did well first. As humans, we sometimes get too focused on what went wrong. It's important to celebrate our successes, especially when we're learning something new. Allow the participant an opportunity to share what they feel they did well. Don't rush an answer. Even if it means allowing time for a little silence.

    When it comes to the participant providing feedback on what they would change, encourage the participant not to view their actions as "wrong". This is a training environment and should be a safe place to practice. That's why the demonstration was done.

    The reason you allow the participant to provide feedback first is because, as a general rule, the participant will be far more critical of their performance than anyone else. This positions the rest of the group to be supportive versus critical.

2. **Then allow the group to respond**: Most groups will not focus on the negative feedback because the participant has already mentioned it. The thought is "They know it; I don't need to bring it up." The group will offer supportive comments. Why? Because they want supportive comments when it's their turn.

3. **Finally, as the trainer/meeting organizer, give your feedback last**: This is a great opportunity for you to support the participant. You can add any positive feedback the participant didn't cover, offer suggestions for next time, and express your confidence in their ability.

Wrap up

To wrap up the training meeting, review all the key points of the topic. Make sure participants clearly understand what is expected of them back on the job and tell them what to do if they have any questions after the session.

Tip

Dealing with difficult participants

Most employees like training. They view it as an investment into their future. But every once in a while, an employee will bring negativity to the training environment. If you're directing the training, it's important to deal with these difficult participants, so they don't spoil the event for everyone.

Here are three of the most common types of difficult participants and how you can handle them:

- **Know it all**: This person believes they should be conducting the training. They feel they're already the Subject Matter Expert. You can sometimes identify a know it all during the introduction step of the meeting when you ask how much people know about the topic. Sometimes you can effectively bring a know it all around by tapping into their expertise.

- **Center of attention**: This person wants to comment on everything. They want to share one of their stories, ask a question about their situation, and so on. This type of person can quickly take the training off course. As trainers, we want people to be engaged but not to the exclusion of others. Often a subtle change in body language such as avoiding eye contact or standing in a different part of the room can correct the situation.

- **Naysayer**: This individual will focus on distrust and negativity. They will focus on what won't work or can't happen. It will be your job as the trainer to keep the group focused on the positives. If you can see that the group is responding favorably to training, you might be able to pose a negative question or comment to the group. For example, if a naysayer says, "No one is going to follow this new process", ask the group "What do you guys think? Will people embrace the process?"

Modern perceptions about power and training

As a training professional, I've always thought of training as a requirement. Companies need to provide training to employees in order for them to be successful. But in recent years, I've seen a shift in the way companies and individuals view training and who has power when it comes to training.

Training as a reward

More companies are using training as a way to reward and recognize employees. It can be done by sending an individual employee to a conference or workshop. Another approach is to bring a consultant into the organization for a day of training. Instead of companies saying "We have to conduct training", they're saying "We want to conduct training."

Employees are responding well to the change. Young professionals are eager to learn and have expressed a desire for training over benefits such as cash bonuses and company cars. People want ways to constantly improve versus instant gratification incentives. They understand that training gives them knowledge that no one can take away from them.

Organizations are using training and development as a means to demonstrate how much they care about their employees. It's a benefit to both the company and the employee. They're letting employees know that the investment being made by the company is because they want employees to be successful.

On the flip side, employees are telling employers, "Training is valuable to me now and in the future. If you want me to stay, train me."

From a power perspective, training is becoming a negotiable item for job candidates and employees. Top talent will demand that the company should invest in their professional development. In addition, companies are treating training as a special event, putting dedicated thought into who attends and what information is shared.

Individuals owning their professional development

As companies shift to thinking about training as a reward or special event, they are also shifting the way they view skills and professional development. Companies are willing to invest in training, but they want employees to take on some development responsibilities as well.

I believe part of this shift has to do with the number of people working in a virtual environment. Working outside of a traditional office involves doing a lot of things independently—resolving your own conflicts, figuring out the solutions to your problems and creating your own work. It also involves thinking about your future and generating your own professional development plan.

In a traditional office environment, your boss might tell you what skills to develop. When the boss doesn't see you all the time, they might—scratch that—they will rely upon you for input. That's where knowing yourself comes into play. You want to be confident in the things you do well and cite specific examples of when you've used that skill.

In today's business world, we have a tremendous amount of influence over our career path. Companies are looking for employees to take control over their professional development. As such, we have to be prepared to discuss what skills we'd like to develop. It might be something that will help you do your work easier, better, or faster. It could also be a skill you would like to acquire for the future.

Tip

How do you like to learn?

Once you and your manager agree upon that skill or quality you want to develop, think about how you want to go about learning it. We all have preferred methods of learning. Do you ever hear someone come back from a workshop only to say, "What a waste! I could have learned everything I needed to know by reading the book." This is why understanding how you like to learn will be very valuable.

Audio learners like to learn by listening; this could be at a lecture or podcast. Visual learners want to see in order to gain understanding; charts, graphs, diagrams, pictures, films are all visual learning mediums. Visual learners might also like to learn via books. Kinesthetic learners prefer to have a hands-on learning experience. They enjoy the opportunity to practice the activity, conduct an experiment or maybe even role play.

No style of learning is better or worse. It's understanding the best style for you that makes the difference. For instance, if you're a visual learner then the last thing that might interest you is attending a lecture. And, if you did attend the lecture, you might not learn anything.

You might also find that you gravitate toward different learning styles depending upon the subject. An example might be learning how to create a spreadsheet pivot table (by doing it, which is kinesthetic) versus learning the history of blogging via a lecture.

Being in tune with not only the subjects you want to learn but your preferred learning style creates greater opportunities for you. It allows you to allocate your resources (time, money, and so on) toward those experiences that will help you learn the most.

As individuals, we are in control of our professional development. And what better way to drive your career than by establishing your own development plan—on your terms.

Technology in training

One of the subjects that regularly comes up when planning training is whether or not to allow participants to use their smartphone devices (for example, iPhone or Android) or computers (a laptop or tablet) during training. I totally understand the question. It's about the learning experience. Training is about knowledge transfer and retention.

However, the answer isn't about the equipment; it's about holding the people who use the equipment accountable. I'm perfectly fine with participants having their phone and/or computer in the room. One of the new trends I'm seeing is participants using the devices to take notes. There are many excellent note-taking apps available. Another trend is participants taking pictures, video, or recordings during a meeting. It's a way to record information.

Instead of holding the equipment hostage, it's time to hold participants accountable for using that piece of equipment properly. And I'm holding them accountable for the material covered in the meeting.

Participants need to manage their equipment. This includes setting expectations regarding response time. Some things need to be answered right away. Many things do not. I once facilitated a customer service focus group in which participants said a normal e-mail response time is 24 hours, not 10 minutes. As a technology user, it's your responsibility to know the difference and the expectation.

Businesses still have to operate during training. It's naïve to think participants won't have to answer a single e-mail or take a call during training. As a trainer, it's my responsibility to design training with adequate breaks so participants can comfortably reply to operational issues and still focus on the material. Participants can let their departments know they will answer questions during breaks or they can send a quick note during training that they will call in at a certain time.

If it's an absolute emergency, a participant can step out of the room and answer a question. Then return to training. Folks, I hate to say it, but this isn't rocket surgery. It's all about managing technology. *Don't let your technology manage you.*

At a higher level, companies that offer technology tools need to also explain expectations when they issue an employee a smartphone, tablet, or laptop. I'm sure there are managers out there who honestly believe when the company handed them an iPhone they now need to answer everything in 10 minutes. The company didn't tell them that, but they've made that assumption.

With all the technology tools available, if businesses haven't done so, they need to set technology expectations. In turn, managers should appropriately use the tools provided to them. That way, the company will continue to operate and users will effectively use available technology. It's a win-win.

After training occurs

The first rule of wrapping up a training meeting is to end on time! I know this is also a sign of conducting a great meeting, but I wanted to expand on this.

It goes without saying that ending a meeting late isn't good. People have other obligations and running over the allotted time is disrespectful. It also impacts decision-making. Let's say the meeting is supposed to end at 5:00 p.m. It's 4:50 p.m. and the meeting isn't close to being over. The meeting changes—the trainer will start skipping over topics to get done on time, which means participants aren't learning what they're supposed to. Or the trainer keeps people late because they don't want to schedule an additional session. Participants start thinking about all the places they're supposed to be or the work they have to catch up on so, again, they're not learning.

Ending too early can have a negative impact as well. If you're supposed to end at 5:00 p.m., ending the meeting at 4:30 p.m. is okay. In fact, it's possible that ending at 4:00 p.m. is okay if you've accomplished everything on the agenda. But if people are told the meeting will end at 5:00 p.m. and it ends at 1:00 p.m. that looks like a planning failure. Participants will leave wondering what the trainer didn't tell them.

Tip

Time management for trainers

One of the most difficult aspects in training is estimating time. Rushing participants will impact learning and having people sitting around twiddling their thumbs will derail momentum. Here are a few things you can do to manage your time during training:

- **Start on time**: It's tempting to start late and give people a chance to show up. This can negatively impact training in two ways: first, it sends an immediate message to the people who did arrive on time that they're not important. And secondly, you might need that time along the way.

- **Allow time for questions**: I try to figure that training will get off track one time. So I build a sidebar conversation into my training. For a one-hour training session, it might be a 5-minute sidebar. If it doesn't happen, participants finish a few moments early and that's fine. If it does happen, we finish on time.

- **Let participants decide on breaks**: I like participants to feel invested in the time we're spending together, so I let them decide when we take breaks and the length of those breaks. Of course, some people will joke about skipping breaks to get finished early. That's an opportunity for me to remind them that we have plenty of time to do both. Giving participants a say in the timing allows me to move them along if I see we're falling behind schedule. We make those decisions together.

- **Practice timing of activities**: Once you've put together your training agenda, don't guess at the time it takes to complete an exercise. Take a dry run of the activity or ask a friend/colleague and time them. It will give you a good estimate.

Evaluation

We've talked about creating a feedback mechanism within meetings to determine whether participants learned the topic. Another component to feedback is the training evaluation. This gives participants an opportunity to evaluate the learning environment. It's different from the feedback during the session. I know it might sound silly, but you do need to get feedback about aspects of the training such as logistics. If the chairs are hard, the seating is cramped, lighting is poor, and the room is cold... guess what? *It impacts training.*

But it's equally important to get some feedback about the training session from other stakeholders—for example, the subject matter experts who provided input during the design process, the instructional designers who wrote the program, and the trainers/facilitators who delivered it.

It's also critical to get feedback from the participant's managers—find out their perceptions now that one of their employees has attended training. Did the employee come back from training excited and energized to use their new knowledge or were they indifferent to the time spent in training?

Get feedback about the trainer/facilitator. There's a time and place for "edu-tainment" (translation = education + entertainment) and there's not. I can't begin to tell you how many times I've asked participants about a facilitator and received the reply, "He's so funny!" I asked what the topic was and got crickets. Having the right person deliver the content in the right way is essential.

Tip

Future training topics

We talked earlier in the chapter about setting expectations. One way to give participants a voice in training is by asking about future training topics on the evaluation form. This gives people the opportunity to share what they'd like to see in the future. The answers can be tracked for trends. If all of a sudden, the responses mention time management or a specific software program that gives the organization something to consider.

Being able to solicit feedback about the training process helps build good training programs. It gives companies valuable information to use before, during, and after training sessions. It allows adjustments to be made that will enhance the session for future participants. And all of these actions lead to one thing—more effective and impactful training that will deliver outcomes to benefit the organization.

5 tips for better training

Better training meetings take practice. Here are some words of wisdom from business professionals who have conducted more than their fair share of training meetings.

Pamela J. Green, MBA, SPHR, is president and CEO of the Power Project Institute. The company partners with organizations who love their employees and recognize the power of traditional values when delivered with modern human resource practices:

"My favorite meeting tip is this and I use it as a guide when helping clients prepare for meetings with me, as well as to help their teams prepare for trainings with me:

➤ *Provide context about the purpose of the meeting in advance*

➤ *Offer an agenda in advance of the meeting (not the same day, but perhaps the day or two before, especially if someone needs to prepare)*

➤ *Send out questions for attendees to consider for discussion purposes and add to the agenda*

➤ *Set high standards, start, and end on time. If you can't end on time get the group's approval to move beyond the established end time*

➤ *Establish time frames for each meeting item, this will help you stay focused*

➤ *Assign a time keeper to keep you on track*

➤ *Create white space: a time for just open dialog, additional thoughts, and other opportunities for innovation and creativity (10-15 minutes preferred)*

➤ *Send a meeting summary and next steps whenever possible"*

Gerry Hoeffner is the president of Personnel Dynamics Consulting, a firm that specializes in change implementation strategies:

"I always look at meetings as an opportunity to move a group of people. Whether it be move them in their learning, or move them in their motivations. The purpose of a meeting is taking a group of people from one point of knowledge, opinion, emotion, or action and moving it to a higher level. I reject the temptation to just share data. If they are going to take the time to attend the meeting, they should leave better off in some form or fashion just by attending the meeting."

Alexandra Levit is a globally recognized business/workplace author, speaker, and consultant. She has been named Money Magazine's "Career Expert of the Year":

"My best advice for impromptu training is to allow yourself to be vulnerable. Employees crave genuine interaction with senior leaders, and this means taking them into your confidence when you are facing a crisis. Instead of locking yourself in your office or a conference room, open the doors. Allow an employee or two to shadow you through the problem-solving experience. Explain to him/her why you are making certain decisions, and ask for input. This real-world type of experience is much more useful than trying to explain a concept theoretically without any substance behind it. Your employees will hopefully learn so efficiently that they will be able to manage a similar situation themselves next time."

Vito Scotello, SPHR, is the Director of human resources at Norwegian Cruise Line, the innovator in cruise travel:

> *"When I studied and taught organizational communication, a key pitfall that we were warned to avoid was 'False Consensus'. Twenty years later in the business world, I see its prevalence more than ever.*
>
> *False Consensus occurs when there is the appearance of agreement on a plan or decision, but that agreement is not real or is only superficial. The result is that decisions that you thought were final are brought up and discussed again and again. Or, people with assignments postpone their efforts or only minimally comply. Why does this happen? One reason is that in an environment where "time is money" (in other words, the place we all work), more effort is put into being efficient than is put into being inclusive. We march through an agenda and claim victory, when the actual result is something less.*
>
> *This can be avoided, but it requires time: time spent before the meeting, getting support; time spent before the meeting, preparing your thoughts and words; and, time spent during the meeting, listening to the ideas of others. Getting everyone's input and buy-in will actually cut your time and increase your success. If you understand that meetings and decision making take time, 'I agree' can be more than just something said."*

Trish Uhl, is a Certified Professional in Learning Performance (CPLP) and founder of Owl's Ledge, a consulting firm specializing in performance and project management:

> *"Subject Matter Experts (SMEs), such as supervisors and managers, often find themselves playing the role of "accidental trainer". To assist front line employees in learning, try using what I like to call the "motivation mashup." The concept is to motivate people (that is, move them to action) and provide them with simple instruction so they could filter through their own experiences and make decisions.*
>
> *SMEs faced with a training situation can apply this concept by providing the trainees with:*

> ➤ **Mastery:** *Humans have an intrinsic desire to "go deep"; most tend to like working hard at getting better at something. Accidental and professional training practitioners need to stop pushing content and start instigating challenges. An example would be to provide the trainees with a real-world challenge along with a few suggested tactics, then allow trainees to work through the challenge on their own or in small groups (the formal name for this is "action learning."). Guiding and supporting trainees through mastering the challenge allows them to explore both the rewards and consequences of their choices and actions. Provide them a safe environment in which they can succeed or fail forward.*

➤ ***Purpose:*** *Many humans have a natural desire to engage their emotions and passions and show up to work as integrated—alive!—human beings. Do share the WIIFM with trainees but also establish a vision for them of how through their own actions they can strive to be their higher selves. Paint a picture of who they can become if they take responsibility for their own training, put the instruction you've given them into action, and exhibit the desired behaviors on the job. Speaking to purpose goes beyond functional role; it targets people's aspirations."*

Summary

Training meetings are some of the most important meetings a business schedules, and you don't have to be a professional trainer to conduct a training meeting. Proper planning, organized content, and attention to the detail can make your training meetings effective.

Training meetings sometimes get a bad reputation because they are called for the wrong reason. Training should connect to a business goal or metric. Participants need to understand why they are there and get the opportunity to practice what they've learned—both during training and on the job. This helps people retain the material and make training a success.

The same holds true for our next chapter on employee performance meetings. Managers do not need to fear this meeting. It's a natural part of business. We will see how to structure those sessions for results.

> 6

Employee Performance Conversations

Employee performance meetings happen all the time in business. Well, they should happen all the time in business. We're not talking about meetings that address employee discipline or terminations. Your organization has a policy for that and managers need to follow it.

Employee performance meetings are about helping employees succeed. They are the regular conversations that take place in an ongoing manner. These discussions tell employees what they're doing well and possibly what they need to improve upon.

I've said that no news is good news is not a management philosophy. Managers have to talk with employees about their good performance as much, if not more, than improving their performance.

The goal of performance conversations

The direct goal of a performance meeting is simple: to support or improve performance. I've seen many cases where the only time a manager would talk about performance is when something was going wrong. I've also seen many situations when the only time a manager would mention performance was during the scheduled annual performance appraisal.

Both of these approaches are wrong.

If the only time a manager speaks to an employee is when something is wrong, then employees won't want to speak with them. This potentially means that companies are missing out on great ideas because employees don't spend time with their managers. One example would be the impact on workplace safety. Employees don't share potentially unsafe working conditions or possible improvements because conversations aren't taking place.

In addition, if employees aren't talking with their manager, then the company doesn't know what they're doing well. Organizations should want to know what employees enjoy about the company and their work as part of a retention strategy.

The timing of the meeting is equally important. The purpose of conversations like this isn't to punish the employee. It's to change their performance. Employees should know what's expected of them and they should already know what they've done. That's why you don't want to delay the conversation. If an employee hears about a good job they've done for a project at the time, it means much more than if the employee is told six months later.

Many performance conversations are held within a regular status meeting, which we discussed in *Chapter 2, Regularly Scheduled Status Updates*. When managers have their weekly one-on-one with their team to talk about projects, it's the perfect time to bring up performance.

Tip

One-on-one meetings

If having regular one-on-one meetings with team members isn't happening right now, it might be something to explore. I've spoken to many managers who like the ability to schedule quality time with employees, and employees appreciate having dedicated time to speak with their manager.

The biggest benefit I hear is that scheduling regular one-on-one meeting can reduce the number of interruptions during the workday. If people know that a one-on-one meeting is scheduled, they will hold their questions/comments for the meeting.

An indirect outcome of performance meetings can be to help employees achieve their goals. When an employee's performance is improved, it should lead to the employee being able to accomplish their goals. This is especially true when coaching someone to take on a new role. As they attain new skills, they are getting closer to their new role.

Setting relevant goals

If one of the reasons that you're having a performance meeting with someone is to help them achieve a goal, it's important to set relevant goals and manage them properly. This is the appropriate time to talk about performance expectations. If employees have questions, suggestions, or a unique perspective on performance goals, this is the perfect time to address it—not when something has gone wrong. The conversation could become defensive and this will not help anyone:

> ➤ **Set goals that align with the department and organization**: An individual employee's goals should align with the department's goals, which should align with the company's goals. Employees need to clearly see how their performance contributes to the organization.

> ➤ **Set goals that are important**: If someone creates a goal based upon what the cool kids are doing, it's not really their goal. Goals must be important to the person accomplishing them; otherwise, getting commitment will be a challenge.

> ➤ **Create a realistic number of goals**: Most people can't accomplish dozens and dozens of goals. It's better to have a small number of goals and achieve them than hundreds of goals, most of which are left undone.

> ➤ **Establish a manageable timeline for achieving your goals**: I'm totally convinced that part of the reason people don't accomplish their new year's resolutions is because they try to start a handful of things at the same time. You've probably seen this too—people who quit smoking, start a diet and exercise program, and a Spanish language course all at the same time. Let's face it…that's too much change at one time. Schedule an achievable number of goals over a span of time.

> ➤ **Agree upon the measurement of success**: Every goal should be measured. It's important for both the employee and manager to know what accomplishing this goal will look like. And that the employee and manager agree on the definition.

> ➤ **Be open to flexibility as conditions change**: As dedicated as we may be toward accomplishing our goals, sometimes external forces decide to wreak havoc on our lives. Instead of beating ourselves up that our goals aren't progressing, we should step back and re-evaluate the goal. It could be that the goal is fine; we just need to give it a little bit more effort or maybe the goal needs a little tweaking.

Comparing performance to the company standard

Since I've already mentioned performance appraisals, let me take a moment to clarify that the goal of a performance meeting shouldn't be the same as the goal of the annual performance appraisal meeting.

The goal of the annual performance appraisal meeting should be to spend a little time talking about past performance and goals accomplished, then a lot of time talking about future goals and performance. The things discussed in an annual performance appraisal meeting shouldn't be a surprise to either the manager or the employee.

I like to think of the annual performance appraisal meeting as wrapping up all the performance meetings that happened during the year. One is not a substitute for the other.

The one thing that both meetings should have is a clear way to measure performance. Companies should not compare employees to each other. Let me repeat—managers should not compare employees' performance. Asking an employee, "Your co-worker Bob is doing great and meeting his goals. Why can't you?" doesn't help the employee improve their performance. Managers should, instead, compare employee performance to the company standard. Here's another example: let's say Matt is a sales manager. His performance goal is $1million annual sales. The company decides to rank all the managers in order of sales. Matt is at the bottom of the list. How much did Matt sell? $10million. Yes, Matt exceeded his goal ten-fold but is labeled *the worst sales manager*. The problem isn't Matt. It's the goal.

If the company standard is to sell $1million, then Matt exceeded the company standard and his performance review should reflect that. Now, if every sales manager is exceeding goal then it might make sense to change the standard to a higher number. But when discussing performance, it should always be compared to the company standard—not to co-workers.

Common challenges when discussing performance

It might be tempting to think the biggest challenge with employee performance meetings is the employee. But in reality, it's the manager. Specifically, the manager's reluctance to discussing performance.

When performance is good, often managers think there's no need to take time out of everyone's busy day to talk about it. The thought is that employees should know their performance is good. And while that might be true, it can be very beneficial to discuss good performance anyway. Reinforcing good performance brings more than a confirmation. It provides recognition and creates engagement.

On the flip side, when managers need to discuss a not-so-good performance situation, they might have a tendency to ignore it because some managers have the impression that discussing performance is a form of punishment—both for them and the employee. So they rush through the conversation to make it less painful and it doesn't accomplish the goal.

Good managers are comfortable with discussing performance. In this chapter, I'll give you a template that you can use when planning a performance conversation (regardless of good or bad performance).

The second challenge that managers bring to the performance meeting is the timing of their discussion. A manager is busy with their job so they're trying to find time to meet with the employee. Sometimes, they forget or say to themselves, "*I'll address the issue if the employee does it again.*"

The problem with that thinking is, the longer you wait, the harder the conversation, because the employee will think their behavior is acceptable since no one addressed it.

Tacit approval

I used to work for a boss who had me issue the same memo every year about the subject of tacit approval. The word tacit means *expressed without words or speech; implied or indicated but not actually expressed.* It represents silent consent and acceptance.

Every year, it was the exact same memo. The words didn't change. The memo was designed to remind everyone of their responsibilities as well as the basic principles of business. Believe it or not, some ten plus years later...I still have it. Here are a few key takeaways I see every time I take the memo out and read it:

> **Tacit approval condones poor performance**: In our workplaces, tacit approval is given whenever someone fails to speak out about existing conditions. Tacit approval leads everyone to assume that the status quo is acceptable, will be tolerated, and allowed to continue.

> **Tacit approval undermines company standards**: Not only does tacit approval work against improving performance, it makes it unlikely that standards will be met. Let's use a simple example, such as when a supervisor doesn't say anything about an employee who's wearing something more suited for clubbing. What's going to motivate the employee to wear the proper attire in the future? The supervisor's silence implies that it's okay to wear unprofessional clothing. Other employees will see this and, before long, the office has turned into The Viper Room.

> **Retraining becomes a challenge**: Trying to re-institute a policy after allowing it to spiral out of control requires a major retraining effort not to mention an internal public relations campaign. To avoid this situation, the supervisor should be vocal, but not in an overbearing, sarcastic or caustic way. A timely comment can bring general awareness and serves to remind everyone of the policy.

> **Tacit approval can lead to a double standard**: Let's say an employee doesn't arrive to work on time. The employee must be coached on the need to be punctual. Failure to say something would be silent approval of tardiness. But this also means the manager needs to be punctual as well. The hypocrisy of enforcing one standard while demonstrating another will cause resentment and even more problems.

> **Passing the buck becomes common**: Someone in another department has an inappropriate screen saver on their computer. Because this employee is in another department, the manager figures it's not their responsibility and doesn't address the issue. Even though they realize the screen saver could offend a co-worker or customer. The assumption that someone else will handle it is misconceived. Meanwhile, the employee has the silent approval from a member of the management team.

Tacit approval takes many forms and arises for a variety of reasons. It can often result from fear of conflict or rejection, laziness, or misguided intentions. All that really needs to be done to eliminate tacit approval is to recognize the reasons tempting us to overlook a situation that we know needs our attention.

We must become comfortable with raising issues that need attention, in spite of our apprehensions. If we speak up, then before long, the reasons for remaining silent will cease to exist. Our reluctance about speaking up to correct an issue becomes less important. Our focus shifts from whether or not to speak up to taking action to improve a situation—which is where it's supposed to be in the first place.

Another challenge during performance meetings is the ability to show empathy. By now, we all know that empathy and sympathy are two different things.

- ➤ **Sympathy** is feeling sorry for someone else
- ➤ **Empathy** is the ability to understand someone else's feelings

Unfortunately, there are managers who believe that they cannot have a performance conversation with an employee and demonstrate empathy. Maybe they've been told it's necessary to have a poker-face when talking performance, especially poor performance because of potential legal risks.

Yes, there are times when you have to consider risk and legalities. Remember, we're not talking about performance meetings where someone's job is on the line. If you're considering terminating someone's employment, then you need to speak with human resources, your boss, or your company's friendly employment attorney for guidance.

Okay, back to empathy. Managers should use empathy to let employees know that they understand what the employee is feeling. If it's a positive conversation, let the employee know that you share their enthusiasm. If it's a less-than-positive conversation, tell the employee that you understand how difficult the situation feels.

Empathy is very easy to define and very difficult to actually do. When planning your performance meeting, try to think of a time when you've been in a similar situation. Now, I must admit, there have been times when I could not relate to the other person's situation. I've never been in anything like it. But I could relate to the feelings—anxious, excited, frustrated, embarrassed, and so on. That's how the connection was made.

Before meeting with the employee

Some meetings need very little pre-planning. This isn't one of those meetings.
For an employee performance meeting, logistics are incredibly important.

When to hold the meeting

First, choosing the right day and time for the meeting is key. Think about the message you're trying to convey and select a time when you believe the employee will be able to receive the message well. For example, holding a performance meeting at 4:30 p.m. on a Friday afternoon right before the employee is leaving for a vacation is probably not a great idea. The employee's thoughts are focused on a bunch of other things.

Also, if you know that the employee isn't really a "morning person" then a first-thing-of-the-day meeting might not make sense either.

Carmela Sperlazza Southers, a senior consulting partner with The Ken Blanchard Companies, suggests meeting where the employee is most comfortable. "Let the direct report choose the best time. As humans whose energy varies during the day, there are times best suited for problem solving, routine reports, crunching data, or reflecting and envisioning the future. As a leader, let your team member choose the best time for your one-on-one call. Have them choose a time when they aren't rushing for a deadline or needing to be alone to focus."

Southers continues to say that, as a manager, you're responsible for making sure one-on-one meetings happen. The goal is to have the meeting be a welcomed time for connection, reflection, and investment in future success and not seen as a distraction or interruption of real work.

Where to hold the meeting

Unless you're congratulating someone for a huge success, holding a performance meeting over a meal can create some uncomfortable moments. There's an example in the film *Jerry Maguire* where the title character is fired in a crowded restaurant by his former protégé. Again, we're not talking firing here but delivering less than celebratory news in a public place can feel like getting fired.

The same holds true for a glass windowed conference room inside the office. Every employee can see the conversation even if they cannot hear the words. That can make an employee feel like the entire company knows what's taking place and it can give onlookers the opportunity to make up their own account based upon the body language they see.

Years ago, I went to work for a company that had a nice conference room in the building. One day early in my tenure, I booked the conference room for a department lunch. The employees didn't want to come. I was completely flabbergasted. Why wouldn't employees want to come to lunch? What had I done? Then they told me, "We don't want to meet in the conference room. That's where people get fired."

Over time, managers had created a work environment where all bad conversations happened in the conference room. The good conversations happened in their offices. So this beautiful conference room never got used.

It became my mission to change the perception of the conference room. I bought lunch for my team every week on the condition they ate it in the conference room. After a while, we had a celebration for someone's promotion in the conference room. Eventually, the conference room shed its label of the firing room.

Ultimately, find a place that is suited to private conversations. Regardless of the talk, everyone appreciates a meeting with few distractions and detractors.

Who to invite to the meeting

There might be times when you'd like for the performance meeting to include other people. This does get a bit tricky. Inviting someone to a performance conversation can immediately send the "witness" flag and you don't want an employee coming to your meeting on the defensive.

Before inviting someone to the meeting, think about the reason. For instance, my boss once invited me to a performance meeting where another vice president was present. What was the reason for this? The other vice president told her about something good I had done, so they were there to thank me.

If the other person plays a key role in the conversation, then it might be helpful to have them there. If their role is to play witness, then you should probably speak to someone in human resources about the meeting.

Plan the conversation

Prior to speaking with the employee, you want to do your homework and gather all of the necessary details about the employee's performance. (We'll talk about the actual structure of the conversation in the next section.) Here's the three things you should know:

> **Describe the employee's performance in specific terms**: Be prepared to very clearly articulate the performance behaviors. If the purpose of the conversation is to support or change behavior, then the only way that will happen is by specifically detailing the actual performance.

> **Know when the performance has taken place**. It may be a single date or a span of time but, either way, you'll want to communicate when the performance took place. The performance meeting should be close in time to when the behavior took place.

> **Understand the impact of the performance on the rest of the team and the company**: This is important. You want employees to know why their performance matters. The way to do that is by sharing a connection between their behavior and the success of the team.

Whether you're on the giving or receiving end of a performance meeting, the conversation can be a bit scary at times. The conversation will go much easier if you take time to plan out your thoughts, consider the different responses that could arise, and how you would answer them.

During the employee meeting

You've done all the preparation, found a good location, and confirmed the date and time with the employee. Now it's time to have the conversation.

Scheduling the meeting

There's an old saying that "timing is everything." If, on the day of the meeting, something goes terribly wrong at work, and it doesn't even have anything to do with this meeting (for example, a big problem in the operation or a major customer issue), don't hold the meeting. Reschedule it for another time. After all the work you've put into the meeting, don't allow external factors to distract you from the conversation.

How to start the meeting

When we are meeting to convey a good message, the words seem to be a bit easier to find. However, I'm often asked how to start a difficult or challenging conversation. It might be a sensitive topic, performance matter, or personal issue. In my experience, managers often want to either:

> **Tap dance around the topic with small talk**: This includes conversations about football, movies, pets, and so on, and then launch into the performance discussion. This can send mixed messages to employees about why they are there. It's better to keep the message on point.

> **Get straight to the point**: This can come across as a bit harsh. It might send the message that the manager is uncomfortable and wants to get the discussion over as soon as possible.

Finding the right words can be a challenge. Here are a few suggestions for starting a performance conversation:

"I'd like your permission to discuss a sensitive subject.

I have some things to say that I imagine will be hard to hear. I think it's important that you know, and that's why I want to have this conversation.

I wish I had better news to share. I'll tell you straight out, answer your questions, and explore next steps with you."

Each of us has moments when we're looking for a better way to say something. You might find a variation of the above statements works for you. If you're still struggling, ask a colleague how they start a difficult conversation. Try their words. You can also get those "perfect phrases" books for suggestions. The point is, find the words that you're most comfortable with because when you do, it helps express sincerity, authenticity, and empathy.

Conducting the performance conversation

Here's an outline you can use during your performance meeting with the employee. You can create a one-page form with this outline and use it to plan your conversation or print it on an index card so you have all the steps handy:

> **Let the employee know the purpose of the meeting**: Don't minimize the importance of this conversation by spending a huge amount of time talking about the latest reality television program and a little on the topic of performance. This is an important matter and should be treated that way.

> **Share what you have observed**: Offer specifics about actual behaviors you've witnessed. If someone else witnessed the behaviors, try to have that person there. Employees don't like the line "Someone told me you did this...". If you're trying to support or correct behavior, be able to specifically discuss behavior.

> **Give employees time to respond**: It might be tempting at this point to keep talking but resist the urge. Allow the employee to answer. You might learn a few things about what's currently taking place in the business.

> **Explain how their performance impacts the team**: Employees might not realize how their behavior impacts the organization or the team. It's important to draw a connection between their behavior and impact to the company. If impact can't be explained (positive or negative), then an employee will question why their behavior matters.

> **Reinforce the expected behavior**: It's possible an employee will not know what they should be doing, or could have questions about the existing standard. Come to the discussion prepared to explain the current company standard and how an employee can achieve and even exceed the standard.

> **Solicit solutions from the employee on how to improve the situation**: This is so important! Let the employee tell you what they're going to do in the future. It creates buy-in. If you tell an employee what to do, they haven't bought into it. Give the employee time to think about possible solutions.

> **Convey the consequences**: Let the employee know what will happen if the situation is -and isn't -resolved. You'll notice I haven't written one word about disciplinary action. Sometimes the consequence is an employee will not be eligible for a transfer, or they will not be able to participate in flexi time. Maybe the next step is discipline. Regardless, make sure the employee is aware of next steps.

> **Agree upon a follow-up date**: Remember, no news is good news is not a management philosophy. After agreement has been reached, set a follow-up date to discuss progress.

> **Express your confidence**: Since the goal of this conversation is to support or improve performance, don't be afraid to tell an employee you're confident they will achieve their goal.

The conversation needs to stay dedicated on helping the employee be successful. Don't let the conversation become personal and emotional. If the discussion is focused on performance, then it's a win for everyone involved. We'll explore two examples of performance meetings (one positive, one not) in the following sections.

Example – positive employee performance meeting

> **Manager**: "Hi Jim. Thanks for meeting with me today. I want to talk with you about an important matter, the Wilson account. Last week, you did an awesome job handling the client after our production error accidently sent them a past due notice.
>
> Your customer service skills were very effective. Proactively contacting the client, explaining the situation, and following up to make sure the client didn't have any additional concerns."

> **Jim**: "Thanks! The company's customer service training was helpful. One thing you should know. In dealing with this situation, I did discover a small glitch in our accounting system that's creating the past due notices to be generated. I've already told someone in accounting."

> **Manager**: "I didn't know that. Thanks for sharing and telling accounting. Obviously, when we are able to effectively deal with customers—whether it's our internal or external ones—it only makes our jobs easier. And our customers happier.
>
> After handling this situation, do you think we need to put any other steps in place to deal with the billing issue?"

> **Jim**: "You know, I've thought about it and can't think of any."

> **Manager**: "Very well, if this occurs again, please let me know so we can escalate the situation. Let's plan to touch base next month just to make sure there are no outstanding items with the Wilson account.
>
> Thanks again Jim."

Example – improvement-needed performance meeting

> **Manager**: "Hi Jim. Thanks for meeting with me today. I want to talk with you about an important matter, the Wilson account. Last week, we had an issue with them when our production error accidently sent them a past due notice. I received a call from the client upset about the incident."

> **Jim**: "I forgot to call them. Sorry. I did discover a small glitch in our accounting system that's creating the past due notices to be generated. I've already told someone in accounting."

> **Manager**: "I didn't know about the accounting glitch. Thanks for sharing and telling accounting. It's important for us to remember that when we deal effectively with customers, it helps everyone on the team. We can spend more time doing activities to improve our business versus putting out fires. And our customers are happier.
>
> What can you do if this situation occurs again?"

> **Jim**: "Definitely give the customer a call as soon as I realize the error."

> **Manager**: "Yes, and if you have any questions about whether or not to contact a customer, I'm always available to discuss the situation."

> **Jim**: "Okay, I will bring my questions to you and not make assumptions."

> **Manager**: "Thanks. Please remember that in matters like this it's your responsibility to proactively contact the client, explain the situation, and follow-up to make sure the client doesn't have any additional concerns.
>
> Let's plan to touch base in a month to make sure everything is fine with the Wilson account. If you have any questions in the meantime, please let me know.
>
> Oh, and thanks again Jim for handling the situation with accounting and accepting responsibility for this issue. I know you have the ability to handle these kinds of situations in the future."

Tip

Dealing with emotional responses

If for whatever reason, the conversation becomes emotional, it's important to remain empathetic without letting the conversation go off track. Remain calm, listen to the employee, and if necessary, ask for more information to help the employee stay engaged.

Now, I do realize every conversation might not go as smoothly as these examples. But don't underestimate the power of planning. Whether the conversation is positive or not so positive, planning the conversation keeps the discussion on topic and productive. This is the key to achieving the goal of the meeting, which is to ultimately reinforce or change behavior.

Using workplace power during the meeting

Many times, the individuals involved in a performance meeting are a manager and their direct report. If this is the case, managers have a tremendous amount of power in the conversation:

> **Legitimate power**: This is the power associated with their position title.

> **Coercive power**: This is the power to impose punishment.

> **Reward power:** This is the ability to give rewards.

Managers must remember the amount of power they have during the meeting and show restraint at certain times. It can be tempting to use the performance conversation as what Andy Porter, Vice President of Human Resources and Organizational Development at Merrimack Pharmaceuticals calls the *preaching session*. This is when the manager tells the employee what they should do to fix the issue.

It might sound mean or seem unhelpful to not tell the employee what they need to do to correct an issue. Managers have experience. They might know exactly what needs to be done. But telling an employee doesn't help the employee buy into the plan. Managers should use the discussion as a means to help employees reach the decision on their own.

What if the employee comes up with a bad idea?

This is going to happen. At some point, an employee will come up with an idea that you either know won't work or it just sounds crazy. Now is when you want to dig out those problem-solving tools we discussed in *Chapter 1, Meeting Roles, Responsibilities, and Activities* and ask some questions:

"How do you see this solution working?"

"How would you define success with this idea?"

"Do you need any support in order to implement this solution?"

"If the solution doesn't work, do you have a plan B?"

Be open to hearing the employee out. It's possible that they might have a viable solution that works for them, albeit it might appear unconventional to you. The goal is for the employee to take responsibility for the situation, so we have to be willing to allow them their own unique ways of solving challenges.

The other thing to be open about is that the employee might need to fail the first time. Years ago, knowingly watching an employee fail was considered an absolute terrible thing to do. The business world has matured and today, we are much more willing to embrace failure as a means to overall success. Some people even subscribe to the idea of seeking out failures as a way of learning.

Sara Blakely, founder of Spanx, which manufactures pantyhose and undergarments for women, credits failure as part of her success. At dinner each night, her father would ask "What did you fail at today?" It wasn't to make her feel bad or to lose confidence. It was to stress the importance of trying and stepping outside of your comfort zone.

Performance discussions and appraisals

The other reason that managers should practice control during performance meetings is the performance appraisal. This book isn't going to address specific performance appraisal processes but we do need to acknowledge that there can be a connection between performance discussions and performance appraisals.

The performance appraisal process is maligned on a regular basis. I believe one of the reasons everyone hates performance reviews is because the company hasn't defined them properly. Ask yourself: what's the purpose of a performance review in your organization?

If a company defines the performance review as a summary of the performance discussions that have happened during the year, then it sends a message that performance meetings aren't to help the employee. They're to document performance for the annual review.

Add to that the fact most organizations tie annual performance reviews to merit increases and it's no wonder that employees get defensive during a performance meeting.

Organizations need to create a mechanism to discuss performance with employees and give them the chance to correct behavior. None of us is perfect. We all make mistakes. The performance meeting is one of those opportunities to help employees correct a situation.

Redefining the performance review

Companies that really want to take performance meetings to the next level should think about redefining the performance appraisal process. One complaint I constantly hear about performance reviews is that they are the "necessary evil" in the merit increase process. To really make performance reviews about performance, organizations should consider separating the review from merit increases. Yes, performance does play a big part in compensation. But it's not mandatory to talk about performance and pay at the same time. Honestly, it's not.

And I know that managers might not want to admit this…but how many times has a manager "finessed" the performance review to align with the pay increase they want to give an employee? I know—it's shocking! (Please note a small amount of sarcasm in my last sentence.)

Performance reviews should be focused on performance:

> **Past actions**: I believe this should be a small part of the review conversation. Why? Because it's the past and both the employee and manager know what happened. If a manager is doing their job and providing regular feedback, spending an hour talking about what everyone already knows makes no sense.

> **Future goals**: This is where the manager and employee should spend the majority of time. What are the goals of the company and department? How does the employee fit into those goals? Identify the challenges and resources the employee might face. Agree upon what success looks like.

If done right, the company performance management process does not have to suck the life out of the business. That's really not its intention. But in order for it to be successful, the company must clearly define what the performance process means and focus the time spent solely on accomplishing that mission.

When performance reviews are properly defined, it keeps the intent of the performance meeting focused on the employee's success. That's how companies improve productivity, employee engagement, and the bottom-line.

Technology versus a face-to-face meeting

Two factors drive the decision for using technology during a performance meeting. The first is location and the second is the message. There are some very well designed enterprise software solutions with the capability to share performance feedback. If your organization has those tools in place, you should explore how the software works.

But let's assume your company doesn't have that technology available. The first consideration, location, refers to where you and the employee are located. If you're both in the same building, then having a conversation in-person is relatively easy.

If you and the employee aren't located near each other, then there are voice over Internet protocol (VOIP) services that allow you to have a conversation where each person can see the other. This is optimal because the employee can not only hear the sound of your voice but see your body language and facial expressions. Employees are able to hear and see your empathy and support.

The second consideration, message, refers to what you're trying to convey. Complicated, complex, or emotional topics are better face-to-face or voice-to-voice because there's an opportunity to ask questions and seek clarity. This doesn't just apply to negative feedback. Managers should be careful not to fall into the habit of sending positive feedback via e-mail and negative feedback in voice-to-voice. Positive feedback should be given the same consideration.

Technology can be a valuable tool in delivering feedback if the proper technology is used for the right message.

After the meeting is over

Performance meetings are one of those occasions where there should always be a follow-up meeting. A performance meeting should never end with a "Hope we don't have to meet again about this" statement. You should always meet again.

The follow-up meeting will be to either address why the matter hasn't been resolved or to congratulate the employee for overcoming the challenge. If the matter has not been corrected, then your organization probably has a process in place for escalating the matter. You would want to speak with your supervisor or human resources to find out what that process looks like in your company.

But if the matter has been corrected, it's time to celebrate! Providing reinforcement is an important part of correcting behavior. An employee wants to know their manager has seen the change in their behavior.

There's one other reason that managers should have follow-up conversations with employees after they correct a situation. The employee has found a solution and the company should want to know the solution.

Here's an example: a manager speaks with an employee about their punctuality. The employee has been showing up for work five minutes late every day this week. Now, five minutes seems petty and the manager certainly doesn't want to give the employee a written warning over five minutes. But the manager is concerned that, if they don't address it, those five minutes could turn into fifteen. So they speak with the employee and the employee says they're going to set an extra alarm on their clock in the morning.

The manager was concerned about this approach but decided to support the employee and scheduled a follow-up meeting for two-weeks later. The first couple days after the meeting, the employee was still late. But then, all of a sudden, the employee started showing up on time.

During the follow-up meeting, the manager asked, "How did you do it? Did setting a second alarm help?" The employee said, "Initially, I set the second alarm next to the first alarm. That didn't work at all. But then, I moved the second alarm across the room so I had to get up to turn it off. That's what did it."

If the manager had never conducted the follow-up meeting, they might have always thought the idea of setting the second alarm was an epic failure. After getting feedback from the employee, they can see how the idea was executed and, if faced with the same situation again, be in a position to help another employee.

The steps to conduct a follow-up performance meeting are fairly straightforward:

➤ **Establish the purpose of the discussion**: Provide a recap of the situation and what was agreed upon.

➤ **Describe the positive behavior or performance**: Tell the employee what you've noticed.

➤ **Explain the importance of this behavior**: Remind the employee how the behavior impacts the team, the department, and the company.

➤ **Ask the employee for the reasons for his or her success**: This isn't a bragging opportunity for the employee. You want to know what the employee did to correct the behavior. It's now a proven solution to a problem, and you can use that information in the future.

➤ **Listen actively and empathetically**: The employee will appreciate it.

➤ **Thank the employee and express your confidence in continued positive performance**: Leave the meeting on a positive note.

The meeting outlines in this chapter can be printed on paper to plan out the discussion. They can also be copied to an index card and used as a guideline during a phone call or put in a notes application on a smart device for reference.

5 tips for better performance conversations

These business professionals share their tips for conducting a productive employee performance conversation:

Lori Goldsmith, SPHR, GPHR, president of Heart of HR Shared Services, a human resources consulting firm, reminds us of the purpose of feedback:

> *"One of the best things you can do as a leader is to be visible and frequently communicate the good, the bad and everything in between to your employees. Especially when it comes to employee performance meetings, don't wait until the 'dreaded meeting' and shy away from giving negative feedback. Realize that if you are not developing your employees to reach their full potential, you are doing a huge disservice to the entire team and to yourself. Ignoring an issue won't make it go away. Prepare for the meeting and practice. Be genuine, firm and fair."*

Dominique Jones, vice president of human resources at Halogen Software, a market leader in cloud-based talent management solutions, shares the importance of regular discussions:

> *"One-on-one meetings between managers and employees are so important but often don't happen on a regular basis or when they do, they're not effective. What is needed is a bit of structure for guiding these conversations:*

> ➤ *Use a conversation starter such as "What is the most important thing we should be talking about?" "How are you doing relative to your personal plans?" "What has been working well/not so well?"*

> ➤ *Set an agenda based on goal or development plan updates, feedback received, and new learning activities.*

> ➤ *Take notes to capture discussion points and action items to set expectations and accountability.*

> ➤ *Meet regularly and track progress. Use notes from past meetings to set agenda items for your next meeting.*

> *Think about one-on-one meetings as a way to develop strong working relationships with your employees. Doing so will help you increase employee engagement while, at the same time, convey just how very important employees are to the organization."*

Jason Lauritsen, director of the *Best Places to Work* practice at Quantum Workplace, says setting expectations is key:

> *"A tip I learned from a mentor along the way was to create shared accountability in any meeting with an employee. I share with my people that I know there will be times that my instructions or my feedback might not be perfectly articulated or easy to understand. I give them permission to ask as many questions as are necessary to find clarity. Explicitly, I tell them that they can't ask me too many questions, but that when we leave our meeting, I will always assume that they are crystal clear on what we discussed. If we end up with issues down the road because they weren't clear, they will be held responsible for that. This technique ensures that my people are engaged in our meeting and it takes some of the burden off of me as their leader to try to communicate perfectly."*

Planning makes a difference, according to Christopher D. Lee, Ph.D., SPHR, associate vice chancellor for human resources in the Virginia Community College System:

> *"One of the common mistakes managers make in holding difficult conversations is expecting to hold one impactful meeting about an important and trying matter. They want to get in, get on with it, and get out as quickly and as easily as possible. After all, difficult meetings are likely unpleasant, possibly combative, often tearful, and always tough. The desire to hold a single meeting is reasonable on the surface, but in reality it is wholly not. My experience has been that the most important decision about planning and executing difficult conversations is determining whether the situation warrants a single conversation, two meetings, or three interactions.*
>
> *The manager has considered the difficult issue, diagnosed the problem, determined a possible solution, and thought about how to implement a solution. Then he or she plans for the meeting, prepares for the meeting, and enters the meeting with the goal of bringing the employee along for the ride. The problem is that the employee is often lost in a state of shock, is instantly defensive about the matter, is argumentative about the merits of the matter, and often wants the meeting to end as quickly as possible. A quick end to the meeting will let them go away and sulk, cry, prepare a rebuttal, or, even worse, find some way to retaliate against this unwanted and perceptually undeserved intervention.*
>
> *Managers would be wise to consider the importance, gravity, newness, and possibly unexpected nature of the issue at hand, and plan for two or three meetings when necessary. This will allow the employee time to overcome the shock, denial, or impact of the conversation and digest it. Then he or she can come back to really hear and understand what was said.*
>
> *This will give them the breathing room to prepare to take the positive action that the manager suggests to return them to good performance or behavior. So, the best advice for managers is to plan to hold a series of short meetings designed to help the employee hear, appreciate, and then prepare to respond appropriately to the manager's direction."*

Robin Schooling, SPHR, Managing Director at Silver Zebras LLC, a human resources consulting firm located in Baton Rouge, Louisiana, suggests a strategy for getting comfortable with delivering feedback:

> *"Whether your intent is to provide positive feedback and affirmation (keep doing X) or discuss expectations for performance improvement (stop doing Y) the most important thing to do before meeting with an employee is to prepare for the discussion. If you anticipate a difficult conversation, such as when you're addressing performance issues find a trusted peer or HR representative with whom you can role-play the possible outcomes; this allows you to anticipate various employee reactions or questions during the discussion. By approaching the meeting with clear goals and a desired outcome you can focus on ensuring understanding by the employee as well as gaining his/her commitment to either making the change or keeping up the good work. "*

Summary

Performance meetings are an essential part of business. They let people know we're paying attention and we value their work. The way we conduct the meeting not only gives people specific feedback about their performance but it tells them how much we care about their success.

While I referenced the meetings in this chapter, in terms of managers and employees, these scenarios could have easily been between the president of a nonprofit board and one of their volunteers. The same principles apply and the same outcomes are desired.

In the next chapter, we're going to talk about another kind of feedback meeting: focus groups. Focus groups are interesting because they can be used to collect feedback both internally as well as externally. Let's see how we can make focus group meetings more effective.

>7

Focus Groups

In this section of the book about the different types of feedback meetings, we've discussed training (*Chapter 5, Training Meetings*) and performance (*Chapter 6, Employee Performance Conversations*). Both these topics are important for business success. On some level, training and performance rely upon a working relationship. It could be the relationship between a trainer or subject matter expert and the participant. Or it could focus on the relationship between a manager and employee. In both cases, it's the relationship that fuels the conversation.

Sometimes we want feedback without that kind of relationship. The focus is on the information and not the person conveying the information. That's where focus groups come in. They can provide us with feedback we might not otherwise be able to obtain.

What is a focus group?

Merriam-Webster defines a focus group as a *small group of people whose opinions about something (such as a new product) are studied to learn the opinions that can be expected from a larger group*. It's a very broad definition intentionally. Focus groups have tremendous flexibility, and that's one of the reasons they are a popular way to get information and feedback.

Focus groups can be either internal or external:

> ➤ **Internal focus groups** are intended to gather employee feedback. The topics can range from employee attitudes about the company benefit package to feedback for the design of the organization's customer service training program.

> ➤ **External focus groups** are planned to get customer feedback about a product or service. It could be to receive feedback about an existing product or service, as well as a future one.

Whether the audience is internal or external, the goal is the same—to get feedback.

Focus group goals

Focus groups initially emerged in marketing disciplines as a way to get customer feedback. Prior to the focus group, companies received feedback via customer surveys or questionnaires. Focus groups became popular because they provided a level of detail that surveys and questionnaires weren't able to provide. The focus group allowed participants to explain the reason behind their **point of view** (POV). Having that extra piece of information is valuable to organizations. It can confirm or deny the company perceptions about how a topic aligns with the audience.

For instance, **Human Resources** (HR) make the decision that they are going to change the employee contribution in the company's health insurance program. Employees currently do not contribute anything for their coverage and the new program will ask them to contribute $10 per month. The company's perception is employees will understand that contributing $10 per month is still a small price to pay for great health insurance.

Another example; a nonprofit organization decides to raise membership dues by 15 percent. They have not raised dues in several years. The organization doesn't plan to add any new membership benefits. They feel members realize that the increases in regular dues should be expected.

A third and final example; an educational institution invites a focus group to discuss changing the qualifications for a course. The considered change had been requested for years and the organization resisted making the change. They have decided to consider the change only if it is supported in the outcome of the focus groups.

All three of these scenarios are real-life situations. In the first case with the Human Resources department and benefits change, the employees understood. The focus group helped HR formulate their communications strategy. It confirmed that $10 per month wasn't unreasonable but added that HR needed to put employee fears at ease that the other areas of the benefit program weren't going to drastically change.

The membership dues situation was more mixed. Many members did understand that dues do need to occasionally increase, but the organization was criticized for not adding new benefits and not listening to the suggestions of the membership. In addition, members asked for more transparency regarding the organization's finances because, if they were going to increase dues, the members wanted to know where the money was being spent.

Lastly, the educational institution change was embraced by the focus groups and the organization ultimately made the change. Initially, there was vocal opposition to the change. But something interesting happened. The focus group spoke up and explained what happened during the focus meeting and their responses to the organization. They explained the change—as a peer—to the membership. It appeared that having the focus group explain their POV (instead of the organization) calmed the opposition.

In all cases, the focus groups provided the organization with valuable feedback, which helped them to achieve their desired goal. Valuable feedback is the goal of a well-conducted focus group.

Benefits of focus groups

Here's a list of benefits of using focus groups, as seen in the preceding examples:

> ➤ **You can quickly gauge participants' reactions**: The focus group participants can tell you "Yes, we're cool with this decision." Or "Hmm, not sure about this decision."

> ➤ **Participants can interact with each other**: Group dynamics can add depth to the conversation. One participant's idea might spark another within the focus group meeting.

> ➤ **The organization creates a level of buy-in regarding the topic**: By conducting a focus group, the organization is sending the message that feedback is valuable.

Pitfalls of focus groups

There are many good reasons to conduct focus group meetings. In turn, there are some reasons that focus groups are not the best option. Here are a few reasons:

> ➤ **Sensitive topics might limit participation**: Certain topics might not be appropriate for group discussion. Participants could feel apprehensive about sharing their beliefs in a public forum.

> ➤ **One person can dominate the discussion**: An individual or small group can hijack the conversation, limiting participation and valuable feedback from others.

> ➤ **Group output is only as good as the questions**: Meeting facilitators have to be skillful in remaining objective and not showing their biases.

When focus groups are used for the right reasons, they achieve the strongest results. We've already hinted at some of the reasons not to use a focus group: sensitive topics and the potential for influence or bias. Let's discuss some of the best reasons to use a focus group.

Best use of focus groups

Focus groups have a purpose (that is, to get feedback). But every time a group meets for the purpose of getting feedback, this does not automatically mean this is a focus group. A focus group has structure and a method for collecting feedback, which we're going to examine in this section.

Organizations need to make a deliberate decision to use a focus group versus other methods for collecting feedback. Here are some other methods to consider when deciding if a focus group is the best approach.

Focus groups versus surveys

Susan Eliot, a qualitative research consultant and author of *The Listening Resource* (http://www.qualitative-researcher.com/), says that surveys might be your best option when you're looking for frequency in responses or very little depth on a large number of topics.

Focus groups are better options for discussion and complex issues. They allow a facilitator to get detailed information.

Focus groups versus individual interviews

Carey V. Azzara, in an article for Quirk's Marketing Research Review (www.quirks.com), consulted with 20 qualitative researchers to find out which is better: focus groups or individual interviews. The answer? It depends.

In-depth interviews (also known as **IDIs**) are preferred when group interaction isn't important. They are also used with success when the topic is highly personal or sensitive. An example might be if the focus group includes business competition or intelligence.

Focus groups work well if the goal is to generate some point-counterpoint debate or to have participants work in teams during the meeting.

Once the decision is made to use a focus group meeting, that doesn't mean its smooth sailing. There are key elements to focus groups that must be addressed in order for the meeting to be successful.

Common focus group challenges

Because focus groups are all about feedback, the two biggest challenges have to be addressed very early in the planning process:

1. Who will be providing feedback? (That is, participant selection.)
2. What feedback will they be offering? (That is, what questions will be asked?)

Selecting the right participants

The goal in participant selection for a focus group is balance. You want to have a variety of opinions to create a good discussion. If the group view is too similar, it might not produce any relevant information. If it's too divided, it could be impossible to see a trend or common view.

The meeting cannot have too few participants because it might lose the opportunity for discussion. Too many participants might exclude introverted participants from speaking up. There are many schools of thought when it comes to the perfect number of participants; 8-12 seems to be a very common range.

Another thing to consider is whether individuals are participating in their own time. If this is an internal focus group, chances are employees are being paid while participating in the meeting. But if the meeting is with a group of customers, it could be a challenge to find volunteers to participate. Then the question becomes, what kind of volunteers will participate?

An example might be a public organization or university looking for students or community members to volunteer their time for a focus group. Because focus group participation is voluntary, the organization could find that it's a challenge to get a diverse group of participants. Volunteers might not place a high emphasis on attending and back out at the last minute. It's possible this would leave the majority of participants having views on extreme ends of the topic, either a raving fan or a disgruntled hater.

As such, some organizations try to budget a nominal amount to provide a thank you for participation. It could take the form of a meal or gift card. This thank-you gift isn't enough to change someone's view about the subject, but it does create a level of expectation that the participant will attend.

Organizations also have to determine how many focus groups are appropriate. Most of the focus groups I've been involved with had at least two sessions. This allows the moderator to compare and contrast the feedback received.

Multiple focus groups provide the ability to orchestrate meetings by some common elements. For example, I conducted several focus groups for a major university in designing their customer service program. Some focus groups were by location—a small satellite campus—and the participants were from different areas within the organization. On the main campus, the focus groups were organized by job responsibilities.

One might think that the feedback would be very different because of the way that the groups were scheduled, but that wasn't the case. The group's feedback was very similar.

Whenever I think of focus group participant selection, I'm reminded of an old technology acronym **GIGO (Garbage In, Garbage Out)**. Not that participants are garbage! If you want good feedback, you have to put the right people in the room.

Developing engaging questions

Once the right people are in the meeting, you now have to ask the right questions. There are three few rules to keep in mind when creating focus group questions:

1. Questions should be open-ended.

    Closed-ended questions are ones that typically receive a "yes" or "no" reply. Examples might include:

    "Do you think that customers expect accurate information?"

    "Would customer service training improve the customer service experience?"

Open-ended questions give participants flexibility in their response. The same questions above can be rephrased to be open ended:

"What do the customers at XYZ Company expect?"

"If you could only make one change to improve customer service at the company, what would it be?"

2. Questions should allow participants to tell their story. The question shouldn't lead the participant to answer a certain way. Here are a few examples:

    "How and when do you use Product XX?"

    "Tell me about the positive experiences you've had with Product XX."

    "When you decide to purchase XX, what features do you look for?"

3. Questions should start with *general* and move to *specific*.

    "Think about the last time you called technical support. How was the quality of service you received?"

    "What was particularly good about your experience?"

    "How could it have been a better experience?"

All information is not valuable information. To get good feedback from your focus group meeting, the right people need to be in the room and they must get asked the right questions.

Before the focus group

At this point, you have established a clear goal of the feedback you're trying to collect. You've recruited participants and started work on questions for the session. Before actually conducting the focus group meeting, a few more decisions need to be made, which we'll discuss in the following sections.

Using an outside facilitator

In *Chapter 3, Brainstorming*, we talked about some of the pros and cons to bringing in an outside resource to facilitate. Although it's not a requirement to use a third-party facilitator for focus groups, the subject should be discussed. An outside facilitator could be perceived as not having a vested interest in the outcome of the focus group. This can position them to get information that an internal facilitator can't. In fact, depending upon who is selected as the internal facilitator, their presence could make participants feel they need to respond in a specific way—or not at all.

I know we talked about the focus groups not being ideal for sensitive subjects. If the company really wants to use a focus group meeting to discuss a topic that can be perceived as sensitive, an outside facilitator should definitely be considered. Participants might feel more comfortable sharing this type of information with a person they do not know.

Even if the topic isn't particularly sensitive, your results might benefit from an independent facilitator. Many people just won't open up to someone they know in an organization. On the downside, external facilitators do come with a cost that has to be factored into the budget.

This decision ultimately comes down to finding the person who will make participants feel at ease and be able to get the best feedback.

Meeting logistics

The whole idea behind a focus group is to gather objective feedback. The meeting location should be carefully considered. Participants will open up and share their thoughts when they feel comfortable. It could make sense to hold focus group sessions at locations that are considered *neutral ground*.

Obviously, it might be difficult to find a neutral location when conducting an internal focus group. A nearby restaurant or conference room could provide enough separation from the daily work environment.

Often, marketing focus groups will be held in a location where the client is watching the focus group taking place through a one-way mirror. While that is a specialized facility, it does raise a question that any type of focus group needs to consider—will the meeting be recorded via audio or video? If the meeting organizer decides to record the session, it's important to disclose the recording prior to the meeting and obtain the necessary permissions.

Other materials to have ready for the session include:

> ➤ List of confirmed participants and nametags
> ➤ Notepads and pens
> ➤ Flipcharts with markers

Creating a meeting agenda

To keep the focus group meeting on track, it's essential to have an agenda. With this type of meeting, where the participants and their discussion is the focus, having an agenda will allow the facilitator and the participants to stay on time and on topic. Think of the agenda with the following three main parts:

1. **Opening**: This is the time dedicated to welcoming the group, getting to know the facilitator and participants, explaining the purpose of the session, and sharing how the information will be used.

2. **Feedback**: This section will focus on the primary purpose of soliciting feedback from the participants using the questions you've developed.

3. **Closing**: This time is allocated to thanking the participants, offering a venue for further comments (if appropriate), and sharing any next steps.

Proper planning of the meeting agenda will ensure that the facilitator has time to gather all the feedback needed and not make participants feel rushed.

During the focus group

The facilitator of a focus group meeting wears lots of hats during a focus group session. It's not as easy as "ask a question and get an answer."

Tell participants the purpose

It's very important to get the focus group off on the right foot. There's a lot of information to convey to the group. I'm reminded of those restaurant servers who try to impress you by not writing down your order then have to come back and ask you to repeat yourself.

Don't try to impress everyone by remembering every little thing in your head, especially if you're collecting feedback from several focus groups for a single project. It's better to offer consistent information. Here's a sample script template you can use:

> *Good morning/afternoon/evening! I'd like to thank everyone for coming.*
>
> *My name is [INSERT NAME] and I'm the [POSITION/TITLE] at [COMPANY]. With me today are [INTRODUCE ANYONE ELSE PRESENT]. We've been asked by [CLIENT] to conduct several focus groups on the subject of [TOPIC].*
>
> *[PROVIDE SOME BACKGROUND REGARDING THE TOPIC]*
>
> *We'd like to hear from you about [SPECIFICALLY WHAT TYPE OF FEEDBACK IS BEING ASKED].*
>
> *Any questions before we get started?*

Here's an example of how a script might look:

> *Good afternoon. I'd like to thank everyone for coming.*
>
> *My name is Sharlyn Lauby and I'm the president of ITM Group, a human resources consulting firm. With me today are Leonard and Jose from my office to assist. We've been asked by ABC Company to conduct several focus groups on the subject of customer service.*
>
> *As you know, ABC Company has identified delivering world-class customer service as a strategic goal for this year. Part of their goal includes developing a customer service-training program for all employees. We'd like to hear your views on customer service both within the company and in general.*
>
> *Any questions before we get started?*

Setting ground rules

After opening the meeting, let the participants know the ground rules. This can be included in the facilitator's opening script. Here are some sample meeting rules you can adjust to fit your situation:

➤ This is a good time to mention any kind of disclosure about audio or video taping. The recording isn't to figure out who said what. It's to remember what was said. Confidentiality is the key.

➤ Even when the session is being recorded, participants should feel confident that what's said in the room, stays in the room. Participants' comments will be anonymous.

➤ Everyone should feel comfortable speaking. All ideas are important and encouraged. There are no right or wrong responses.

➤ It's okay to disagree. The goal of the focus group isn't to convince each other. It's fine if two individuals give opposite feedback. That's expected and valuable.

Taking meeting minutes or notes

Once the question portion of the meeting has started, the facilitator must find a way to keep up with the flow of information. Stopping the meeting to take notes or to ask a participant to repeat their comments will slow down the meeting and could derail the flow of feedback.

Facilitators should have a plan to address note taking. It might make a lot of sense to bring an assistant who can take notes during the meeting. The facilitator can then focus on the discussion and the assistant can concentrate on getting the content onto paper.

Exercising active listening skills

Listening is always important but, in the case of a focus group, the facilitator is responsible for listening to the participants' feedback and then communicating it to others.

As a general rule, most of us are not very good listeners. We tend to think of listening as something passive, as something we must do while waiting for our next turn to speak. In fact, most of us use the time we are silent not to listen, but to muster our thoughts for our next chance to talk. Listening is something to which most of us have given little attention.

Effective listening is an active process. Effective listening requires concentration and the exercise of specific listening skills. Listening, like any other interpersonal skill, is a behavior that can be learned, practiced, and improved.

Robert Bolton, in his excellent book titled *People Skills*, suggests that the best way to improve our listening is to focus on the three sets of skill clusters that make up effective listening:

> ➤ Nonverbal skills
>
> ➤ Following skills
>
> ➤ Reflecting skills

Attention to each of these clusters can help make all of us better listeners.

Nonverbal skills

At least half of all communication takes place nonverbally. And nonverbal communication rarely lies. If we look bored, uninterested, or judgmental; if we avoid eye contact; or if we doodle, play with a paper clip, or clean our glasses, nothing we can say will convince the person with whom we are talking that we are really interested in what they have to say.

Effective listening requires a positive posture, eye contact, the avoidance of distracting mannerisms, and appropriate nodding and smiling. More than anything else, positive nonverbal behavior will communicate the message that you are actively interested in what the other person is saying.

Following skills

In genuinely listening to another person, we are best advised to follow the direction the other person wants to take the conversation, not to lead the conversation ourselves. Yet almost anything we say has the potential of shifting the conversation back to ourselves and thus takes leadership away from the other person. There are a few techniques we can use to follow the direction of the person we are listening to.

Door openers

We can open the door to the conversation. For example, suppose someone in your focus group becomes annoyed by a comment. Perhaps they start slamming down their materials or slam shut a door. Maybe they become unusually quiet or withdrawn. Whatever the signals, you begin to sense that something has happened.

You can open the door to that conversation by simply saying something like "You appear upset. Would you like to comment on some of the discussion thus far?" A door opener begins with some kind of description of the behavior you are responding to and then invites the other person to assume leadership of the conversation.

It is possible that the other person may decline to walk through the door you have just opened. You'll have to decide if you want to try a couple more times or simply drop the matter. But if they choose to respond, it will be in a way that puts them in charge of the conversation and allows you to begin actively listening to what they have to say.

Minimal encouragers

You can follow the conversation by using such simple statements as "Go on," "Tell me more," "That's interesting," and "Right". Sometimes even sounds such as "yea," "uh-huh," and "mmm hmm" can be used to send the message that we're paying attention.

Open- and closed-ended questions

We defined these earlier in the chapter. Information can, of course, be obtained from both open- and closed-ended questions. Closed questions are appropriate for confirming specific details.

> *"When did you call our help desk?"*

> *"How many phone calls did you make to resolve your problem?"*

Facilitators should be careful not to ask too many consecutive closed-ended questions. It can be perceived as shifting the focus of the conversation from the participant to the facilitator because the facilitator is asking all the questions.

Keep in mind that open-ended questions can still be answered in ways that provide little information. However, in general, the more you find yourself asking open-ended (rather than closed-ended) questions, the more the other person will be in control and the more time you will have to listen actively to their feedback.

Reflecting skills

The purpose of these skills is to reflect back to the other person that you have heard and understood both the literal and the emotional levels of their feedback. There are two primary reflecting skills.

Paraphrase

To check your understanding of the ideas, information, or suggestions of participants, state the idea in your own words or give an example that shows what you think the participant was talking about. A good paraphrase is usually more specific than the original statement. Consider the following example:

> *Participant: "ABC Company delivers terrible customer service."*

> *Paraphrase A: "You think their service isn't good?"*

This is too general. If the participant agrees with it, you still do not know what the participant meant by *terrible*. You merely have the illusion of understanding.

> *Paraphrase B: "ABC Company doesn't have properly trained Help Desk personnel."*

This response is more specific. The participant might answer "No, their Help Desk staff is knowledgeable. Their billing department sends very confusing invoices and is not receptive to answering questions." This second paraphrase leads to a clarification of the way the participant is using the word *terrible*.

You can sometimes get some clarification by asking, "What do you mean?" or by saying "I don't understand." However, you will get more information when you paraphrase, because you show what your present understanding is and thus enable the other person to address their clarification to the specific misunderstanding you have revealed.

A good rule to follow, before agreeing or disagreeing with the statement, is to make sure that the remark you are responding to is really the message the other is sending. Paraphrasing is one way of testing this.

Perception check

To check your perception of the feelings of someone else, state what you perceive that person to be feeling. In the following examples, a good perception check conveys the message:

> *"I want to understand your feelings. Is this the way you feel right now?"*

> *"My sense is that, right now, you are feeling angry. Am I right?"*

> *"My perception is that, right now, you are feeling really motivated. Is that correct?"*

Notice that a perception check first identifies the other person's feelings in some way—"angry" or "really motivated"—and second does not express disapproval or approval of the feelings. It merely conveys, "This is how I understand your feelings. Am I correct?"

Your perception of another person's emotions often results more from what you are feeling, are afraid of, or are wishing for than from the other person's words, tone, gestures, facial expression, and so forth. Our inferences about people's feelings can be, and often are, inaccurate. Perception checking aims to convey that you want to understand the other person as a person — and that means understanding their feelings — and helps you avoid actions that you later regret because they were based on false assumptions.

Soliciting questions

Sometimes a participant will offer feedback that needs further explanation. The facilitator will want to use probing questions to seek clarification. There are a few questioning techniques that can be used to clarify an initial response:

➤ **Extension**: Using open-ended questions, the facilitator can ask a second question to glean more information.

Participant: "My last experience with the Help Desk was terrible."

Extension question: "When was the last time you called the Help Desk?"

➤ **Compare and contrast**: The facilitator uses similarities and differences to get additional information.

Participant: "My last experience with ABC Company was terrible."

Compare question: "If you compare your experience with ABC's Help Desk and Accounting department, which one provided faster customer service?"

Contrast question: "How did the customer service at ABC differ from the service at XYZ Company?"

➤ **Multiple choices**: The facilitator provides a laundry list of choices for participants to choose from.

Participant: "My experiences with ABC Airline are terrible."

Multiple-choice question: "What are the top five airlines you've flown with over the past year?" or "How would you rate these five airlines (insert the list here)?"

Facilitators have to make sure that they use probing questions to seek further information and not make assumptions about the feedback. Also, facilitators must remember to not interrupt the participant, even when they know where the participant is going with the story. It's common for focus group facilitators to hear the same feedback multiple times. The facilitator must listen to the fifth time a story is told with the same intensity as the first time.

Another place where probing questions can prove useful is in those situations where the room goes silent. No one has a response for the question. There are many reasons this might occur:

➤ It's the beginning of the session and participants are uncomfortable talking.

➤ The topic is sensitive.

➤ Participants don't understand the question.

➤ Participants are tired of the subject and would like to move on.

Restating the question or asking a probing question can keep the conversation moving. The other skill that can help is silence. Some research indicates that a two-party conversation can tolerate only four seconds of silence before one of the people feels the need to say something.

Clearly, the purpose of silence isn't to make someone feel uncomfortable but it is to encourage discussion. When we think of communication skills as tools, we have a tendency to use nonverbal skills the most and silence the least. It's important to remember that silence may be very appropriate and could be a very useful tool in good communication.

Staying on time

Use the resources available to keep the meeting on time. A skilled facilitator will create an open and comfortable atmosphere, but you don't want the meeting to become too casual. Participants might become too chatty and begin to tell lengthy stories that may or may not be completely relevant to the topic at hand.

If you start to see participants fidgeting, glancing at their smart devices, or looking for a clock, it might be a good time to take a time check. The facilitator can take a moment to tell participants where they are in the meeting agenda and gauge their responsiveness to the amount of time left in the meeting.

Ultimately, achieving balance between collecting the necessary feedback and respecting the participant's time must be accomplished.

How workplace power can impact a focus group

Focus group meetings can be tricky both as a facilitator and as a participant. The whole purpose of the meeting is to collect feedback. But if participants think there is someone in the room who has the power to bestow rewards or to punish, they might be reluctant to share their honest opinions. In fact, depending upon the group dynamics, participants might feel compelled to give answers that align with those of a person with greater power.

Another form of power that can influence a focus group meeting is referent power. This is defined as the power of friendliness or popularity. Sometimes participants will not want to disagree with their friends or a fellow participant who is considered to be one of the *cool kids*.

If a facilitator suspects the group dynamic is impacting the feedback, they can turn to some of the probing question techniques mentioned earlier in the chapter. It might be possible to ask participants to compare, contrast, or laundry list their responses in a way that does not come across as confrontational or disagreeable with others.

In addition, facilitators need to be careful to keep their own perceptions about power in check. If the meeting facilitator is internal, participants can have perceptions about the facilitator's ability to keep information confidential and their perceived informational power in using the feedback collected.

Facilitators also have to make sure they are consistent in their use of probing questions. Asking too many probing questions of one participant and too few of another can be perceived as one person's feedback being more valuable.

That's why inviting the right people to a focus group meeting is so important. Power challenges can be alleviated by dividing influential participants into separate sessions. You don't want to skew your results before you even get started.

Ending the focus group meeting

After all the questions have been asked and the group has provided their feedback, it's time to bring the meeting to a close. The facilitator should use this time to highlight some of the key findings from the meeting and thank participants for their contribution. This is a good time to mention the value the participants have brought to the organization. If necessary, the facilitator can reiterate the promise of confidentiality and how their responses will be used.

After the focus group

The most important deliverable from the focus group meeting is the executive summary or feedback report. Some focus groups will transcribe the entire session and that can be useful in the context of raw data; the summary report will offer the high-level insights the organization needs to take action. The report should focus on three areas:

> **Frequent responses**: This refers to feedback that is repeated by several people during the focus groups

> **Emotional responses**: Participants' opinions that are particularly intense, angry, enthusiastic, and so on

> **Specific responses**: Stories that have an incredible amount of detail and specificity

Drawing attention to these areas can help the organization develop a sound action plan. This leads me to the last thing that must happen after a focus group—taking action, even if it's the conscious decision *not* to take action. There is nothing worse than asking people their opinion and doing nothing with it. It makes participants feel their time and feedback was abused, and this will hurt future efforts to get feedback.

Using today's technology in focus groups

Today's technology has created the opportunity for focus groups to go online. They differ a bit from the face-to-face focus group in that the session takes place over a span of time (usually a few days). The facilitator initiates a discussion and gives participants a window of time to respond. The benefits of this approach include cost savings: no facility rental, no refreshments, no travel expenses, and so on. It also means you can invite participants from virtually anywhere. Participants benefit because they have more flexibility with their time as well. Depending on the topic, it's also possible that participants will feel more comfortable about opening up (versus during a face-to-face meeting).

Another potential form of focus group could be found in the idea of crowdsourcing. This is when a person or organization solicits feedback, usually with a social media platform or online community. The downside of this approach is that it's highly unstructured and may or may not produce reliable results. The upside is that the respondents are a highly-diverse audience and might provide valuable feedback that could have never been realized in a structured focus group environment.

The good news is that with these technology-based options, organizations can include them and in-person focus groups to get the best of both worlds.

5 tips for better focus groups

Focus groups are an incredibly flexible meeting. As such, here are five tips (and a bonus suggestion!) for conducting better focus groups.

Joe Gerstandt, speaker and advisor specializing in authenticity, diversity, and inclusion, emphasizes the importance of commitment:

> *"In my experience, any and all social/group processes tend to suffer from lack of clarity. I think that leaders tend to overlook the importance of providing real clarity about what we are doing (are we sharing information, are we brainstorming, are we making a decision, if we are making a decision how are we making that decision, etc.) as a group and how are we expected to participate (what kind of input do you want from us, is it expected/safe for us to disagree, what does respectful disagreement look like, etc.) as individual members. When I am trying to help a group meet differently, I focus a lot on clarity and also the commitments that we make to each other on the front end (and I think that "commitment" is an important word...things like:*

> > ➤ *I commit to starting on time. If I cannot be here and be ready to fully participate at the scheduled time, I will not come.*

> > ➤ *I commit to being present. No laptop, no phone, no side conversation, no doodling. I will be physically, mentally, and emotionally present and it will be apparent to my peers.*

> > ➤ *I commit to assertive communication rather than aggressive, passive, or passive aggressive. I will share my point of view without dominating the conversation or disrespecting my peers."*

Lance Haun, editor with *The Starr Conspiracy*, a strategic marketing and advertising agency, points out the pitfalls of groupthink:

> *"When you're in a focus group, the biggest tendency is for people to agree with one another. That's just human nature. People generally want to be liked and since focus groups often bring together people who don't know each other very well, people are generally more cautious in that environment, too. Unfortunately, that's the last thing you want from a good focus group.*

> *Whether you're a facilitator or a participant, there are a few things you can do to combat this. One way is to take a "Devil's advocate" position if people are coalescing around an idea. Bring out the good points of the alternatives and see if anyone in the focus group reacts. Sometimes people need to hear contrary views from someone else in order to disagree. If you're a facilitator, you can do even more. For instance, you can prep people for a focus group by asking them about their views before they start. Then, you can use those notes to start conversations that are more open.*

In the end, the goal is to have a more natural conversation and to truly discuss the topic at hand. While you can't get everyone familiar with each other beforehand, you can prepare people to have an open discussion."

Rebecca B. Ross, SPHR, is a senior human resources leader. Her recommendations focus on participant engagement:

"Consider adding an element of fun or competition to help make dry subjects more engaging, which will improve your results. I experienced the power of this when I co-facilitated five focus groups of employees to roll out a new mission statement. We offered $100 to any participant who could recite the old mission statement from memory (our point was that the old statement was too long and not at all memorable, so a new mission statement was needed). After the five focus groups, no one had been able to recite the mission in full, which helped participants see the need for change. It also generated interest, laughter (when participants tried and failed to recite it), and curiosity from participants who wanted to know what happened in the other groups. When we were finished with the groups, we still wanted to give away the $100, so we picked one of the participants' names out of a hat. We announced the winner by e-mail to all participants, thus providing a fun follow-up and a subtle message that we were serious about wanting to give away the money.

In addition to making the topic more engaging, keep in mind the role introverts can play in the meeting. Diversity of thought can be extremely valuable in a meeting. Hearing a variety of opinions can often lead to a better decision or outcome. The leader of the meeting should be aware that introverts in the meeting can provide valuable insights, but they often function differently in meetings than extroverts do. Don't assume that they don't have anything to say because they haven't said anything. Introverts often won't speak up unless there is a silent pause in the discussion. Thus, in meetings where there aren't lulls in conversation, it is often helpful for the leader to ask someone who hasn't said anything in a while for his or her thoughts. Be aware of anyone who is dominating the conversation, and try to encourage others to speak or even ask the dominator to yield the floor so that the group can hear from others. Introverts also tend to be better able to express their thoughts when they have had time to consider the topic, so sending materials in advance, such as meeting agendas, pre-reading, or questions, can be helpful. If, despite all of your attempts, the introverts simply don't say anything in a meeting, contact them afterwards to ask for their thoughts."

Gary Sapir, SPHR, president of Integrated Performance Resources, Inc., an organizational development and performance improvement consulting firm located in Boca Raton, Florida, shares an activity to build trust during focus group meetings:

> *"And yet another use for Post-It Notes!*
>
> *Trust and confidentiality are at the core of any successful focus group in order to promote an open and honest sharing of ideas, concerns, challenges, suggestions, etc. Ask a group of employees to step into a room and share their honest opinions and you may deal with deadly silence until the group understands and believes the promise of confidentiality and anonymity as it relates to sharing information about "who said what".*
>
> *I use three colors of Post-It Notes to start focus group discussions in order to promote a sense of confidentiality and to demonstrate my intention of capturing ideas but not the names behind the ideas. The color green is used to elicit and record positive ideas and suggestions for improvement; red or pink is used to capture concerns, challenges, and needs for improvement; yellow is used to promote questions or comments regarding the previously generated Post-Its.*
>
> *As a facilitator, I start by asking questions or offering a topic of discussion and ask participants to use the Post-Its in front of them to respond. I place a bunch of completed Post-Its on a flipchart or whiteboard so no one can recognize who wrote what and then I read the notes and ask for discussion around the topic. Notes containing similar comments are grouped together so the group and I can quantify trends. The owner of the note is never identified, just the feedback. Extremely sensitive topics may require that the follow-up discussion also be open to the use of Post-It Notes. Most often, after a few rounds of using the notes, we are able to promote open and free communication and drop the use of the Post-Its."*

Trudy Wonder, director of market trends and strategy at Ultimate Software, a leading cloud provider of people management solutions and recognized as one of *Fortune's 100 Best Companies to Work For*, says a good focus group starts with the facilitator:

> *"Looking for open, candid feedback? Get someone else to facilitate your focus groups! Participants will be much more comfortable –and honest – if the leader is someone who's not in their management chain, or even in a leadership position. Best bet: someone from a different area (or, an external resource, such as a communications consultant), who's seen as unbiased and objective but comfortable moderating these sessions.*

A good facilitator has to:

➤ *Manage the interactions to make sure no one dominates the discussion and everyone has an equal opportunity to participate.*

➤ *Listen carefully and be prepared to ask follow-up questions to generate deeper discussion of an issue. Some people may be bashful to speak up, so don't be afraid to gently call on them for their valued views.*

➤ *Be flexible, to follow an unplanned line of discussion that may provide meaningful insights.*

➤ *Capture all viewpoints to accurately summarize what was discussed.*

Once the facilitator has been chosen, here are some additional tidbits to consider:

➤ *Online or in-person? Although the Internet and social media have taken electronic discussions to new highs, nothing beats the energy and dynamics you'll get when you have everyone sitting together, face-to-face, in your meeting room. The interaction is more spontaneous and generates better exchanges than even the latest online tools, which may be a great adjunct to your focus groups, but not a replacement.*

➤ *Too long or too short? A good focus group will run between 90 minutes and 2 hours. Less than that, and you have to ask yourself if the focus group was really necessary, because the participants will! Too ensure that you don't run over your time limit, be prepared to limit discussion on any one question. PS: When inviting people, be sure to explain the topic(s) you'll cover. This gives them time to think and arrive better prepared to participate.*

➤ *Size matters! Keep your focus groups small; 10-12 participants tops. Too many people may not leave sufficient time for everyone to add value to the discussion. But if your group is too small, you'll lose the group dynamics and interaction that make focus groups so effective. Provide simple refreshments as an added enticement, to ensure people attend. And be sure to ask for RSVPs in advance, so you can invite additional people to achieve your "critical mass."*

➤ *How to turn negatives into positives. If your participants are critical about something, let them explain why. Then, ask a follow-on question: "How would you fix that?" or "What could we do to turn that around?" People are pleasantly surprised at the opportunity to offer constructive feedback; here's your opportunity to get it!"*

Tip

A bonus suggestion

And here's a bonus suggestion from Communications Consultant Mike Zimet, president of Dialogue Solutions and a veteran focus group facilitator. This is one of his favorite techniques, so he said I could pass it along:

Want to learn what's foremost in people's minds? Don't rely on past surveys or hunches. Instead, start with a broad, provocative question, such as, "If you could change one thing (about the company), what would it be?" Responses will often provide strong clues as to what people's most pressing issues are. That gives you context as well as a springboard for the discussions to follow. Even if their answers aren't directly related to your topic(s), you'll better understand what colors participants' opinions and attitudes.

Summary

Getting feedback from employees and customers is essential to business success. The focus group meeting gives us a format for collecting feedback in a logical, methodical way. The results can be used to develop action plans that will help move the organization forward.

We've now covered two of the three types of meetings: informational and feedback. In the third and last section on different types of meeting, we will focus on decision-making meetings.

Let's begin with how projects get started. It usually happens with a pitch. That's what we will talk about next: how to conduct a pitch meeting.

> 8

Pitch Meetings

In order to get ahead in business, we have to tell people what we do and want we want. Successful people do not sit around and wait to be asked these questions. That's why pitches are important. Simply put, pitches are brief verbal summaries, plans, or ideas.

One of the most common uses of the term pitch is the elevator pitch. This is a concise verbal summary of what someone does for a living. Business professionals use the elevator pitch to explain what their company does—"We design and deliver management training programs." Consultants might use a similar tactic in their elevator pitch—"I provide consulting services in the area of mergers and acquisitions."

The idea being, the elevator pitch provides some initial first impression of the product or service the company produces. A good elevator pitch gives potential customers a vision of what they would get if they bought your product or service, or even what they could expect if they hired you as a consultant.

On the flip side, a poorly crafted pitch will leave people confused. If I told you that ABC Company does "collaborative development of a comprehensive suite of innovation practices to dramatically increase rates of success in innovation delivery and adoption", do you know what ABC Company does? Or how about this one: XYZ Firm "develops affordable real-life solutions for important issues faced by most businesses in today's fast-changing marketplace".

Now, before you accuse me of making these descriptions up, I want you to know they are real. All I did was change the name of the company.

Pitches are necessary in business. Especially the elevator pitch, since it's often the first type of pitch we use. Everyday, we meet people both internally and externally. The first question that comes up is "What do you do?" Think about your reaction to these two responses:

"I leverage technologies to create interactive solutions for my clients."

"I design interactive games for use in business training programs."

Obviously, the second one paints a clearer picture. While I might not know anything about how games are being used in business, I now know there's a connection and can ask probing questions to get a better understanding – "What kind of games?", "Who are some of your clients?", and so forth.

How to develop a pitch

Developing a concise pitch can be hard. There are three main elements:

1. Describe who you are and what you do.
2. Tell them your mission or goal.
3. Explain why you're unique.

The words do not need to be fancy. One of the best examples I've seen over the years comes from author and consultant Wally Bock. He offers a product called the Working Supervisor's Support Kit. Here's how he describes it: "My Working Supervisor's Support Kit helps bosses do better." I get it. Buy this kit, give it to my supervisors, and they will get better at managing the workforce. Simple and direct. It clearly articulates the value proposition.

Take a few moments to think about your elevator pitch. Every business person should help "increase rates of success" and "develop real-life solutions". That's a no-brainer. Make sure it clearly tells potential customers what you do.

Action Point

Activity: Develop your elevator pitch

Use this space to jot down some keywords and phrases for your elevator pitch. This will help you focus the next time you have a meeting.

- Describe who you are in one sentence. (Example: I'm a training and organizational development consultant.)
- Explain what you do in one sentence. (Example: I design and deliver management-training programs.)
- What's your mission or goal? (Example: To help my clients manage their workforce better so they can be more productive and profitable.)
- Name one reason why you're uniquely qualified to accomplish this goal. (Example: My programs are built around the principles of behavioral science, meaning they are supported by empirical data and research.)

What's a pitch meeting?

We've discussed how the elevator pitch helps explain what you do. A well-crafted elevator pitch should lead to a meeting. A pitch meeting will help you get something you want (that is, achieve your goal). There are two types of pitch meetings:

> ➤ An **external** pitch meeting is when someone from outside the organization meets with a company to sell (that is, "pitch") something. It could be a product or service. Depending upon your role, you could be the person pitching the product or service or the person receiving the pitch.

> ➤ An **internal** pitch meeting is when a group of people within an organization meet to hear about a product, service, or idea. While pitches are often sales oriented, there can be non-sales pitches. I might pitch the idea of conducting an employee opinion survey or sending our company phone contract out for bid.

At some point, the conversation might turn to finding a vendor and listening to sales presentations, but the pitch is about selling the idea or plan.

For the purposes of this chapter, let's assume you're the person doing the pitching during a pitch meeting.

The goal of a pitch meeting

Obviously, the goal of a pitch meeting is to get or achieve whatever you're pitching. But sometimes *not* getting what you wanted can be equally beneficial because your pitch started a conversation.

Years ago, I pitched the idea of casual attire in the workplace to my boss. When I initially pitched it, she thought I had lost my mind. It was immediately struck down. However, a couple of years later, the company decided to implement casual Fridays. Even though my pitch wasn't embraced at the time, the conversation never ended. People would bring it up here and there. Employees started sending articles about casual attire to human resources.

The pitch planted a seed. It started a discussion.

The biggest challenge when pitching an idea

Keeping in mind that the goal of a pitch meeting is to get what you're pitching, one of the biggest challenges during the meeting may be that the person able to say *yes* (the decision-maker) isn't in the room.

Just for a second, let's draw a distinction between getting approval and getting buy-in, because they are different. Approval is the act of the decision-maker saying "yes, proceed with your idea". Buy-in is the act of getting someone to say "yes, I can support your idea". However, the idea hasn't been approved yet.

Getting buy-in isn't confined to senior leadership. It also includes colleagues and employees. This is especially true when the thing you're pitching could be perceived as unpleasant. Several times in my career, I've been intentionally hired to make change happen, knowing that some of the necessary change would be difficult. And how those changes are implemented defines us as a manager and leader.

To demonstrate the point about buy-in and leadership, here's an example from a volunteer board I was part of years ago:

Every year, the board formed a nominating committee to vet and present incoming officers. One year, the chair of the committee—let's call him Bob—decided to change the process. Bob made the change without getting any buy-in from the rest of the committee, who then proceeded to get upset about the changes.

The nominating committee started sharing their thoughts about what Bob was doing with the rest of the board. As a result, the board voted to formalize the nominating committee process, hence overruling all the changes Bob wanted to make.

Were Bob's ideas bad or wrong? Honestly, we'll never really know. We do know that the way Bob decided to create change was considered disruptive by the board, and the board took action to stop it. Not only did Bob not get the changes he wanted, but his working relationships were impacted as well.

So getting buy-in can help solicit your pitch. If challenges develop after the pitch is approved, then you know you have people who agreed to support the plan. The process of soliciting buy-in can also give you some insight where people might be apprehensive about your proposed pitch.

Now let's re-examine the scenario with Bob and the nominating committee. If Bob would have reached out to the other committee members before making any changes, shared his frustrations with the process, and offered some potential alternatives to address the issue, maybe he would have garnered the support to make those changes happen. In addition, his relationships with others wouldn't have been strained. In fact, it's possible that Bob would have reinforced his relationships with the other board members and they would have supported his ideas even if they didn't agree with them because Bob had taken the time to ask for buy-in.

There is a downside to getting buy-in: it can take time. Sometimes a lot of time. In fact depending upon the situation, it can seem like a waste of time. Which I think is why some people don't do it. I have to say I've never found getting buy-in to be a waste.

What is a waste is not taking advantage of opportunities to build relationships with people in your organization who you know, at some point, you will have to get buy-in. Remember the networking meetings we talked about in *Chapter 4, Networking Meetings.* You would be amazed how much easier those buy-in conversations go when you have shared some prior experiences or discussions.

How to create support for your idea

A pitch meeting is about change. If you're pitching something, chances are you're pitching a change of some sort. It could be to switch copier vendors or to change a policy or procedure. Change is not an easy subject. However, I do know one thing: the better the buy-in, the easier the change.

A couple of years ago, I had the pleasure of interviewing Dr. John Kotter on the topic of organizational change for my blog, *HR Bartender*. Dr. Kotter is the Konosuke Matsushita Professor of Leadership, Emeritus at Harvard Business School and author of several books on creating effective change and buy-in. Here are a few excerpts from the interview:

Dr. Kotter, from an organizational perspective, why is getting buy-in so important?

> *"Buy-in is critical to making any large organizational change effort happens. Unless you win support for your ideas, from people at all levels of your organization, big ideas never seem to take hold or have the impact you want. Our research has shown that 70% of all organizational change efforts fail, and one reason for this is executives simply don't get enough buy-in, from enough people, for their initiatives and ideas."*

Are there ever circumstances when a person shouldn't seek buy-in?

> *"In some situations, you face someone I call a 'No No.' This term is based on a character in my book, "Melting", which is a fable about life in a changing and turbulent world, set in a penguin colony. No No is one of the main characters, and you can imagine how he reacts to any new idea. He not only shoots them down, but is very effective at convincing others to join his side. If you face a group of No Nos—or even just one— seeking their buy-in just won't work. They will continually disrupt conversations and delay action, doing everything they can to discredit an idea and derail processes that attempt to create real change.*

> *No Nos are more than skeptics. If there aren't too many of them, skeptics can actually be helpful: they can keep naïve impulses in check and, once they have been convinced their opinions are wrong, can become an idea's biggest champions. But No Nos won't be convinced. The only way to effectively deal with them is to distract them so they cannot create too many problems, push them out of the organization, or expose their behavior so natural social forces (that is, other people who want change to happen) will reduce or stop it. My books "A Sense of Urgency" and "Buy-in" have more information on dealing with No Nos."*

What do you say to the person who is reluctant to use buy-in because they don't want to hear criticism or negativity?

> *"I tell them that avoiding attackers doesn't work, nor does quashing their attempts to block support from others. It's far better to respectfully engage these adversaries and stand your ground with simple, convincing responses. By 'inviting in the lions' to critique your idea, and preparing yourself for what they'll throw at you, you'll capture busy people's attention, and that's very important. Conflict engages. If people have no opinions, no objections and no emotions, it usually means they don't care. And you'll be hard-pressed getting their help when you have to actually implement your idea. But conflict shakes people up and gets them to pay attention in a novel way. This gives you the opportunity to say why your idea really is valuable and explain it in a way that wins over hearts and minds – securing their commitment to implementing the solution.*

The next time you're in a meeting where someone is advocating for an idea, see if some conflict emerges. If it does, watch the group and see how people sit up and how the energy level rises. Disagreement may seem like a bad thing—but it grabs people's attention. "

What's the biggest mistake people make when trying to get buy-in?

"There are a few of them. First, they don't prepare enough. People often misunderstand 'preparation' to mean just knowing their own idea forwards and backwards. But rehashing what you already know won't help you avoid sounding defensive, frustrated, or even disrespectful when fielding question after question on your proposal or idea—all things that can derail a conversation and hurt your cause. We often don't even know we come off this way until someone tells us.

People really need to practice before they attempt to win buy-in from a large group. This means grabbing a colleague to role play, attack the proposal, and practice real-life responses. Try testing your ability to defend your proposal live with select people who will be sympathetic, but who can really listen and provide honest feedback.

I think another key mistake is thinking that you can win people over with lots of data, logic, and reasons why the attacks on your idea are wrong. Almost all education teaches us to think in this manner, but this approach can kill the crucial attention span I mentioned in my last answer. We've all seen eyes glaze over or people surreptitiously typing on their smartphones as meetings drag on and on. You really need to respond to dissenters with simple, clear, common sense answers—this will slowly but steadily win an audience's minds and their buy-in. And you have to complement this approach by responding in a respectful manner to those who disagree with you, no matter how much you want to fire back with fighting words. Enthusiastic support from large numbers of people is rarely the product of a nasty fight. If you treat the ones who attack your idea with respect, you'll draw more people emotionally to your side. And emotions—what we often call 'the heart'—are essential to changing behavior. "

From your experience, what surprises people the most about using buy-in to create an organizational change?

"I think people are surprised at how well it works. A lot of people who reach senior leadership ranks have been schooled in traditional management training. They recognize a need to change, pick a task force of people (maybe the head of HR, a couple of mid-level managers, a senior VP) to oversee the change effort, assign the team their roles, and instruct them to make it happen. They don't always articulate an opportunity for their organization and then communicate it widely to obtain a broad-based sense of urgency, from employees, to pursue an exciting opportunity before pressing ahead. When they do, they're often shocked to see how quickly changes can start happening. In our client work, we've found that choice motivates people to be far more committed to driving change than being told they have to do it. It engages people who are passionate about making their organization better, harnesses their enthusiasm, and empowers them to drive change. It's something that seems very simple, but it's rare for organizations and senior leaders to work this way. "

When you're pitching a new idea or plan, you want to know that the right people are in the room, and they are going to support your idea. This doesn't mean they won't have tough questions and it doesn't guarantee that the outcome is a slam dunk. Creating organizational buy-in helps the process and ultimate outcome.

It can also help with the most significant challenge I mentioned at the beginning of this section—getting the person who can approve the pitch to attend. Often the more positive buy-in a pitch generates, the more enthusiasm there is to attend the formal pitch and give approval to move forward.

Before the pitch meeting

Once you've solicited buy-in for the idea or plan you're going to pitch, now it's time to prepare. The goal is to have your pitch approved—not to gauge interest. That happened in the buy-in meeting. So it's time to set expectations, refine the pitch, and gather any supporting information:

1. **Setting expectations**: Before the pitch meeting starts, you want to understand how the process works. Here are two questions to ask:

   ➢ **Who will be attending the meeting and what role do they play in the organization?** This will tell you the individuals involved in the process. Hopefully, it will also tell you who is making the decision and who is influencing the decision. Whether you're an employee pitching to the management team or an external consultant pitching to a prospective client, this is necessary information.

   ➢ **What is the typical process?** You will want to know when to expect an answer. Some organizations do not make decisions right away. Others do. You don't want to push for an answer during a first meeting if the company doesn't typically reach a decision right away. Knowing the company's process for decision making can help you craft the perfect pitch.

2. **Refining the pitch – be prepared**: When the goal of the meeting is to get approval for the idea or plan you're pitching, look like you deserve it. I've seen plenty of good pitches get turned down because the pitch was sloppily prepared. I know this sounds very elementary, but when a great idea is poorly presented, it puts a shadow of doubt on the idea.

   If you're planning to distribute materials, make sure to have copies for everyone. If you need equipment for the meeting—to do a demonstration or show visuals—make sure the equipment works. If you're an external consultant, have plenty of business cards to distribute. Always have a "Plan B" ready in case something doesn't work out—like a last minute conference room change or equipment that doesn't work properly.

3. **Gathering support information**: Personally, I've always enjoyed math and accounting, so I've never really shied away from formulas. However, in today's business world, simply knowing how to calculate a number isn't enough. While business metrics are important, you have to understand how they fit into the overall operation.

To get your pitch approved, you'll probably have to share some data to support your case. You'll want it to be the right data—the metrics that matter to the people you're pitching to. It might be obvious ones like EBITDA, market share, and profit margin, or it could be industry indicators. Anticipate questions and prepare your responses.

Tip

Business cards

I want to take a moment to emphasize the importance of carrying business cards. The business card is a marketing tool. Let me repeat that...it's a marketing tool. Where else can you have your name, title, contact info, and company logo all in a small rectangular piece of paper?

Even if your proposal is rejected, people will keep your business card. After all, it's easy to carry.

Forgetting to bring business cards to a meeting means you're giving people a reason to forget you. Not to mention that you can sometimes drop them in a fishbowl and win prizes.

Let me share a story that I think touches on all three of these points. Over the years, I've learned some very valuable lessons about how to pitch an idea to management.

My career has primarily been as a human resources generalist, but I did spend a couple of years totally focused on recruitment. I had always hated recruiting up to that point, and when my director gave me the role, I figured it was some sort of punishment. I was so wrong. I quickly realized that recruiting was about more than just interviewing people. There's a huge strategy component. And, as a recruiter, I needed to be keenly aware of what was happening in the business in order to be successful in my job.

I remember one day being in a meeting with a senior vice president of airline operations. We were discussing his future staffing needs, and I thought I was dazzling him with my recruitment statistics about time to fill and onboarding completion rate. But then he asked me a question: "What was yesterday's on-time performance?"

I didn't know the answer.

In the airline industry, on-time performance was (and probably still is) a key performance metric. Not to say human resources metrics such as turnover and cost per hire aren't necessary, but the person I was pitching to was focused on on-time performance.

He proceeded to tell me the number. Then he explained to me (in a very stern way, I might add) why I needed to know that number. Because the last thing I ever wanted was to be responsible for a flight not going out on time—because I hadn't found the right person at the right time to fill the job.

Several weeks later, I was in a team meeting with that same senior vice president. People were talking about staffing, training, and so on and it was obvious he was getting frustrated. He asked the group, "What was yesterday's on-time performance?" No one responded. He looked at me directly, and I answered the question. [Oh, I scored some major brownie points that day.]

Before you ever try to pitch a plan or idea, find out who the players are and what's important to them. Your pitch needs to speak to them and address their needs.

During a pitch meeting

A successful pitch meeting answers the question "What's in it for me?" (also known as the WIIFM). The goal of the meeting is still the same—to get approval for what you're pitching. But in order to do that, the conversation must move from what you want to what others will get.

Back in *Chapter 5, Training Meetings*, we talked about the principles behind adult learning, and a key component is telling participants what's in it for them. If you want people to buy into your idea, you have to tell them the reason on their terms. Customers will buy your product or service if it fixes one of their problems or makes their life easier. Perhaps Elmer Wheeler, the "World's Greatest Salesman", put it best with his often quoted "Don't sell the steak, sell the sizzle."

Today's audiences expect messaging to appeal to them. I'm all for creativity, but the best messaging is both authentic and geared to the audience. Listeners don't want to search for the uniqueness that applies to them. There's so much information available to us, especially on the Internet. It's hard to filter through all of it. More importantly, if I'm on the receiving end of your pitch, I shouldn't have to.

Make a note

The Internet, noise, and curation

The good news is that today's technology gives us the ability to find just about any kind of information we're looking for. The downside is there's so much, it's hard to separate the relevant information from the rest. The amount of information available to us is so tremendous, it's given a new meaning to the term "signal and noise". Signals represent relevant information and noise represents irrelevant info.

As business people, we need to be able to sift through the vast amounts of information available to us and find exactly what we're looking for at the right moment. There's so much available to us on the Internet; it can be a challenge to find good sources of information. And in our busy lives, we don't have unlimited time to find relevant information.

That's why we have to learn how to curate information. I like to think it's similar to being a museum art curator. Our skill is putting together works of art from multiple sources in various mediums to convey a story. Now translate that to the corporate world. As business curators, our role is to find data and information from global sources that will help us achieve our goals.

We should view curation not only from the standpoint of where can we go to find good information (that is who are good curators for us) but also in terms of the information we need to gather ourselves. Possibly something unique we can't find anywhere so we'll curate it ourselves. Or something that can be found in other places but we want to put our own point of view on it.

The only way we will become skilled curators is to start breaking down curation skills into manageable pieces and find out what works best for ourselves, our networks, and our companies.

During the pitch meeting, audiences expect the information to be curated for them. Only the relevant data should be presented. It might be tempting to present a lot of information to support your position. Choose quality over quantity.

Curating information for your pitch meeting will help you find and focus on the WIIFM. The information might help fix a problem or educate others on a subject they're interested in or maybe just makes people laugh or smile, but it connects them to the pitch in some way.

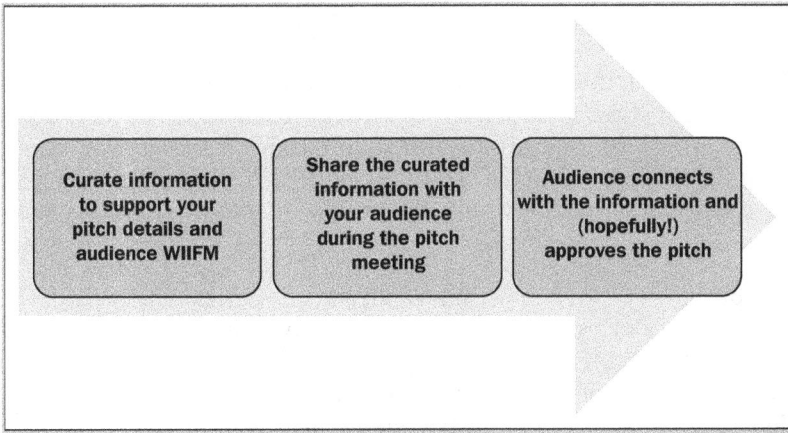

Where I've seen pitches not be a success is when audiences don't know the WIIFM. The person delivering the pitch doesn't understand why they have to tailor their messaging to their audience. They have the attitude that since they're pitching the idea or product means it must be valuable, and everyone should just approve it.

It doesn't work that way. We have to tell people what's in it for them. It's not realistic to think that everyone will figure it out on their own. Or that they'll even want to.

If you're saying to yourself, "I get it—communicate to others on their channel—but how?" Honestly, it's not hard.

Ask them.

If you're conducting training on time management, you can ask participants, "What would you do with an extra hour in your day?" After hearing responses, you can reply with, "Let me show you how."

Want someone to buy into your new meeting format? Next time you're having coffee together, say, "I have an idea that will reduce the time we spend in meetings. I'd love your feedback. Got a moment to discuss?" And if you ask people for their feedback, really be prepared to listen. Give them an opportunity to ask questions and offer suggestions. Feedback means feedback—not listen to my pitch, say nothing, and give me your support. You can use the non-verbal, following, and reflecting skills in *Chapter 7, Focus Groups*, as your guide.

A prospective customer tells you they are losing millions of dollars because the engineering department isn't diagnosing problems correctly. Your reply? "We've got a problem solving training session that can help with that."

The WIIFM isn't being selfish. It's a reasonable question. It's your business case. What will I get for listening, participating, buying, and so on? Value must be present. Customers and employees will not give their time and money to something with no value.

Take legitimate power seriously

Because a pitch has to do with approval, legitimate power plays a part in the process. In *Chapter 6, Employee Performance Meetings*, I defined legitimate power as *the power associated with a person's position or title*. It's possible that your pitch needs the approval of someone at a particular level or title within the organization. If you're giving the pitch, you will want to make sure that the person who is responsible for approving the idea attends the meeting.

When you're pitching an idea to a person with legitimate power, remember the rules for managing up. We all have a boss. Yes, all of us. Maybe they're called a supervisor or manager. Possibly your boss is a board of directors. Or maybe your "bosses" are customers and shareholders. But we all have a boss. Someone we're accountable to. And it's our responsibility to know our boss and the best way to manage them.

In the business world, we spend a lot of time talking about how managers need to manage and what great leaders should do. Sometimes we forget that the relationship goes both ways. Not only do managers and leaders need to know how to get the best performance out of their staff but employees need to know how to bring out the best in their manager.

When you're pitching an idea to your boss, you need to remember how your boss wants to receive communication. If you're trying to figure out how to manage your boss—ask them! Next time you have an idea: "When is a good time to discuss with you an idea I have?" After you present the idea: "Let me know if this is a good way to bring ideas to you in the future." Managers and leaders need to tell the people they work with how to get the most from the working relationship. Here are a few examples from my work history:

> ➤ One of my bosses was very difficult to schedule time with. She was busy all the time. The best time to speak with her was when she was driving home. If I tried to bring ideas to her in the middle of the day, she would be distracted, and I typically didn't get the attention I was looking for. So I started staying a few minutes later at the end of the day. I would ask her to call me on her long drive home. We got to talk. Really talk. And the time was valuable.

> ➤ Another boss was the opposite; he would come in very early in the morning. And he liked Starbucks. Every morning he would walk by managers' offices looking for someone to go with him to Starbucks. My colleagues wouldn't think of coming in early. Me? I got myself up at "zero dark thirty" for coffee. Why? Because I got quality time with my boss.

While those examples deal with quality time, I had another manager who preferred ideas in writing. If you were trying to pitch an idea, he wanted to see it in writing first. It helped me tremendously in terms of being succinct with my proposals and outlining the needs, costs, and benefits of my idea. After he had the chance to review and process it, we would discuss it in detail.

Obviously, there are times when the business forces us to work outside of our comfort zones. Emergencies occur. We have to compromise our style for the benefit of the team. But there is value in knowing how our boss likes to work. It helps to pitch our ideas in a way where they will be heard and considered.

Being able to manage your boss is a business necessity. It should not be considered or treated as manipulation. A good boss knows enough about themselves to share information about their working style.

Before wrapping up our conversation about legitimate power, I want to turn the table and talk about those times when you might not be delivering the pitch but instead you're approving them. People know when you have legitimate power and what you have the authority and responsibility to approve.

The way you handle being pitched to will speak volumes about your effectiveness as a manager:

> ➤ Ignoring pitches will come across as being closed-minded. As part of your position, people will want to pitch ideas to you. It comes with the job.

> ➤ Not approving pitches will be perceived as you're afraid of giving credit to others. Granted, the pitch has to be good. But if someone has a reputation for always saying no, people will begin to wonder whether they are valued.

> ➤ Always approving pitches might be a good thing. It's possible there are a lot of great pitches happening. But if every idea is approved, people might also assume a person is afraid to say no.

Lastly, when you have the ability to approve a pitch, it's important to know the difference between importance and popularity. You might be pitched an idea that's wildly popular but not in the best interest of the organization. There are two ways to answer those types of pitches:

> ➤ You can respond in a quiet or private way. Think of it as being a *whisperer*. It can be a very effective way to convey certain messages.

> ➤ Some information needs to be boldly, directly, and perhaps even loudly conveyed. I've seen on more than one occasion a small group win the debate or sell their idea because they were vocal and tenacious.

Individuals with the legitimate power to approve pitches/projects should take their responsibilities seriously. Never commit to something you don't have the authority to commit to. If you want or need a second opinion, ask for it. People will make judgments about your ability to make decisions based upon the way you handle these moments.

Whether you're delivering the pitch or responding to it, the most effective communications consider the content and the audience. Know what you need to say and how to say it, so the pitch meeting turns out the way you want it to.

Bringing technology into the meeting

Today's meetings are no longer confined to conference rooms. Video conferencing technology allows people to participate in meetings no matter where they are. It also means we have to be more aware of the reasons we're asking for a meeting in the first place.

People already complain that they have too many meetings on their calendar. When individuals are spread out all over the place, it could be said there's an advantage to in-person meetings. It makes the meeting organizer pause and ask, "Is this worth bringing everyone together?" After all, there's a cost to the meeting.

With video conferencing technology, meeting organizers have to be careful. It's still important to ask the question "Is this worthy of a meeting?" Just because no one has to travel to attend, doesn't mean a person's time isn't valuable.

As we've discussed earlier in this book, there are three reasons to conduct a meeting:

1. To convey information, as in the case of regularly scheduled status meetings, brainstorming, or networking.

2. To give or request feedback in training, employee performance, and focus groups.

3. To make a decision on a project, strategic plan, or idea pitch.

Another way to bring technology into meetings has to do with prereading or prework. According to the January 2014 Pew Internet Research on mobile technology:

➤ 90% of Americans have a cell phone

➤ 58% of Americans have a smartphone

➤ 32% of Americans own an e-reader

➤ 42% of Americans own a tablet computer

Honestly, I can't image these numbers going anywhere but up. This gives organizations some opportunities when it comes to distributing meeting materials. There are many file storage applications that allow the meeting organizer to download meeting materials in a folder for the group to review prior to the meeting. I've used them in several situations:

➤ Meeting organizers can place agendas, slide decks, articles, and so on in a folder for participants to review prior to the meeting.

➤ During the meeting, participants can access the documents using their devices.

➤ If someone requests a document that's not already in the folder, it can be added (instead of sent via e-mail).

➤ And the folder can stay in storage indefinitely. No more dealing with "I lost or can't find that e-mail, can you resend it?"

The Paperless Project is a grassroots coalition of companies focused on reducing paper usage through technology. On their website, they say the average organization spends 15% of their revenue creating, managing, and distributing documents. I wonder how many of these documents are specifically for meetings. Using a file storage application can reduce the amount of paper generated for meetings and potentially save the company money.

As we become more attached to our technology devices, meeting organizers should look for ways to bring technology into the meeting versus trying to find ways for participants to disconnect. If technology can help create a more effective meeting (both in terms of time and cost), maybe participants won't view them as such an intrusion.

After the pitch

After the pitch meeting concludes, it's all about follow-up.

When you pitch an idea or plan to someone else, you want to follow up and thank them for listening, even if you ultimately do not get approval. It's important to respect that someone took the time out of their schedule to listen to your pitch and consider it. You'll possibly want to pitch to them again sometime. Thank them. Even when a pitch meeting goes perfect, and you're 99.9% sure you're going to get approval, you still want to thank the person or group for their time.

Often during the pitch meeting, follow-up items will be generated from all parties. Here's an example of a pitch meeting I recently attended.

A company contacted me to do some work for them. The person who contacted me I've known for years, and she's very familiar with my work. She's in a decision-making capacity with the organization. We met and she shared with me the scope of work.

Great! Then she asks me to meet a few members of her team. No worries. I meet the team, and we talk about the project. As we're talking, a few more items get added to the project. This is a good thing—but it means she needs to send me some additional information.

I wanted to share this example for three reasons:

1. You never know where your next pitch meeting might come from.
2. Having to send follow-up documents isn't always a bad thing.
3. Follow-up is necessary.

Having a pitch turned down isn't about you

Well, it could be because the pitch was terrible. But since you know your stuff, have done your homework, and properly planned and prepared, chances are…it's not about you.

There are lots of reasons that pitches get turned down. Companies aren't ready to take a project on. Organizations don't have the budget or staff to make the idea work. People need more time to process and warm up to the idea.

My point is this—don't view a pitch being turned down as a personal attack on you or on the quality of your pitch. At the point you hear the pitch has been turned down, see whether there's an opportunity to get feedback about the pitch. Some people will tell you straight up why the pitch was turned down. Others might hedge a little. It doesn't hurt to ask, "Can you share with me why the idea or plan was turned down?" If you get an answer, great. If not, let it go and move on. There will be more opportunities for pitches.

Tip

On approval ratings

One of the best pieces of advice I've received in my professional career has to do with feedback after pitches. It also applies to presentations:

- We often have a tendency to focus on the negative. The pitch that wasn't approved. The presentation that didn't go well. When the reality is that plenty of things went great. The key is shifting our frame of reference.

- Next time you're faced with a pitch that didn't go as planned, think about this: if there were 100 people in the room and 10 of them didn't like your pitch, you have a 90% approval rating. Who wouldn't want that?!

Finally, once the pitch meeting is concluded, it could make sense to follow up with meeting participants on social media. Whether the pitch is approved or not approved, staying connected demonstrates that you think the relationship is important. It could also lead to new opportunities at a future date.

5 tips for better pitch meetings

Pitches come in all forms but do have some common elements. These business professionals share the secret to delivering a winning pitch.

Jeanne Achille is chief executive officer of The Devon Group, a public relations and integrated marketing communications firm. Here are the five pieces of advice she gives clients to maximize a pitch meeting:

➤ *Ensure the right editorial resources have been interviewed as sources and prepared to stand by for media interest.*

➤ *Include those resources (if possible) in the meeting; if that's not practical, ensure abstracts supported by research/trend data are on hand for discussion during the meeting.*

➤ *Research the editorial target before the meeting to ascertain tone, preferred content, and recent articles/interests to ensure fit.*

➤ *Publish an agenda prior to the meeting with details regarding objectives, timelines, and resources.*

➤ *Use the time during the meeting to gain consensus and determine how both parties will worth together in a sustainable manner.*

Rosemary O'Neill, president and cofounder of Social Strata, Inc., which provides online community technology, emphasizes the importance of listening:

"I've pitched and I've been pitched 'at' for more than 27 years of a career in marketing and communications. (No-one wants to be 'pitched at'.)

My primary tip for anyone who wants to be successful in pitch meetings is to listen first. In fact, don't even think of it as a pitch. Think of it as preliminary consulting. That mindset shift is the key to really learning what's going on with your prospective client's business.

If you go in with the idea that 'I'm going to sign a deal today, no matter what', then everything the potential client says will sound like, 'I need your service/product.'

Shift your brain into, 'I'm going to find out what the biggest challenge is for this person.' Everything changes, and all of a sudden, you're sitting on the same side of the table, helping to find a solution. And guess what? It might not be your service/product. If you discover that you're not a good fit, shake hands, refer them to the correct vendor/consultant, and know you've earned the undying respect of another fellow business person. That's the way to build an enduring business."

Ron Thomas, chief executive officer at Great Place to Work Gulf, based in Dubai, reminds us that all meetings have a cost:

"How much is it costing?

'We just spent over $5,000 for a half-hour meeting', one of the senior executives said. The meeting was to decide the scheduled lunch hour, and this was the second meeting. As I heard this, I could almost see an old-fashioned time clock at the conference room door that punched time in and time out. Taking that a step further, we could envision, at the end of the 'month', the exact cost for each one of these important meetings. It would be a sobering report if all of our meeting hours were calculated as such.

What if every meeting objective could be measured by the cost of the process? That number would be sobering, to say the least. Meetings are the bane of corporate existence. Whether it is a conference call or a physical meeting, these are part of our process of doing business, and for the most part, they are not going away. If it is a conference call, it is palatable (at least) because we can mute our lives away, continue our work, or scan the Internet. Yes, we have been there and done that.

Let's face it—most meetings are a drain and a waste of time. How many times have we sat there and realized that the meeting had turned into something else, and the discussion is like talking to an aged uncle where it starts in one direction and ends someplace else.

So how do we tame this beast? If you must have a meeting, please do the following:

➤ *If you are the meeting chairperson, don't be weak because you are the conductor. If it is bad it is because of YOU.*

➤ *Have a clear agenda. What, pray tell, are you trying to solve?*

➤ *At the end of the meeting, what decision should be made?*

➤ *Think—how much time do you really need to arrive at a decision?*

➤ *Always—always!—think about that meter that is running in the background.*

Remember: you do not want a consensus at the end of your meeting that everyone agrees that your meeting was a complete waste of time."

Susan Vitale, chief marketing officer at iCIMS, a leading provider of Software-as-a-Service (SaaS) talent acquisition software solutions, says bring the numbers:

The best advice for running any meeting is to always have a plan, leave time for questions, and stay on topic. When it comes to making a pitch, the same advice applies along with the following tips:

➤ *Use data to back up your point. Reinforce the validity of your message by relying on data to tell the story. Show industry trends, survey responses, any third-party validation that backs up your project. This way, it's not just your opinion they hear, but evidence that your idea is a solid one.*

➤ *Be concise in your pitching efforts. Keep your pitch direct and to the point, factoring in time for Q&A. Have answers prepared for the 5 W's: Who? What? Where? When? and Why? Additionally, prepare to be challenged. Take the time to think about how others might perceive your pitch and develop talking points ahead of time that address foreseeable roadblocks.*

Ray Wang is founder and principal analyst at Constellation Research, a company that provides research on business and disruptive technology:

The secret to a good pitch starts with psychology. You have to channel your audience and identify key drivers of self-interest. Understand the motivators before you make the pitch. Are they looking for career advancement? Are they just trying to keep their job? Are they aspirational or pragmatic? Are they looking for fame or fortune? The secret to the effective pitch is improving contextual relevancy. Without this, you are just noise.

Summary

Pitch meetings are a special kind of meeting. We have something invested in them. We want a certain outcome. However, there are common elements such as planning, preparation, and follow-up. Even when pitch meetings don't turn out the way we hoped, they still have the potential to be productive and worth the time.

Regardless of the idea you're pitching, one thing is certain—the work doesn't stop after the pitch. Now it's time to make that idea you've fought for a reality. In our next chapter, we'll discuss how to integrate those ideas the company has agreed to support into your strategic plan.

> 9

Strategic Planning

Whenever I think of strategic planning meetings, I'm reminded of a scene from Lewis Carroll's *Alice in Wonderland* between Alice and the Cheshire Cat.

> *Alice: "Would you tell me, please, which way I ought to go from here?"*
>
> *Cat: "That depends a good deal on where you want to get to."*
>
> *Alice: "I don't much care where –"*
>
> *Cat: "Then it doesn't matter which way you go."*

Strategic plans are our roadmap (aka strategy) for the company. Strategic planning is the process of creating that roadmap.

Strategic planning is different from operational planning, although they are related. Operational planning focuses on the daily activities of the organization. I tend to think of it as the tactical activities that happen each day with a focus on the internal organization. And obviously, proper execution of the company's organizational plan is critical to the success of the company's strategic plan.

However, strategic planning takes a wider scope. It's not just about what happens inside the company. Strategic planning looks at how the company fits into the community and the marketplace. It also looks beyond the immediate and short-term. Strategic planning considers the long-term goals of the business.

Strategic planning is often viewed as a complex process, but it really doesn't have to be. It has four essential steps:

1. Prior to the meeting, the **formulation** stage occurs. This is when information and data are gathered to help establish the organization's goals.

2. During the meeting, the **development** of action plans to attain organizational goals takes place.

3. After the meeting, **implementation** of the agreed upon action plans happens.

4. And lastly, there is constant **evaluation** of results to ensure success.

In this chapter, we'll cover each of these steps so you can conduct and participate in valuable and effective strategic planning meetings.

Creating a strategy and being strategic aren't the same thing

Before we can talk about strategic planning, it's important to discuss the difference between creating a strategy and being strategic. Just because someone can create a strategy doesn't mean they can think strategically.

According to the Cambridge dictionary, strategy is a detailed plan for achieving results. There are many different kinds of business strategies—marketing strategies, compensation strategies, recruitment strategies, social media strategies, even strategic plans. You get the point.

Thinking strategically means a person is capable of a thought process that allows them to facilitate a dialogue of critical thinking and innovation. This isn't to say that the two aren't interrelated. Creating strategy is important for business. But strategic thinking is a competency that needs to be developed.

If you are interested in exploring the connection between these two concepts, Jeanne Liedtka penned a fascinating article on the five elements of strategic thinking titled *Linking Strategic Thinking with Strategic Planning* (http://www.hrbartender.com/ images/thinking.pdf) that really deserves a read. As business professionals, I wonder how much time and emphasis we are placing on these elements:

> ➤ **Systems perspective** that is, having the ability to see the entire picture.

> ➤ **Intent-focused** which is being able to create a focus for employees to concentrate on the goal.

> ➤ **Intelligent opportunism** reminds us of the conversations happening about the opportunity economy and being open to new ideas that are good for business.

> ➤ **Thinking in time** refers to the view of referencing the past to create the future, and using the proper analogies to create linkages and anticipate trends.

> ➤ Lastly, being **hypothesis-driven**. Yes, the classic scientific theory rears its head. Being able to reason and test a hypothesis is the key to effective strategic thinking.

For business professionals, this means relying *less* on gut instinct and *more* on analytics. We need to shift our focus from a "been there, done that, so I know the answer" to a "been there, know what happened, now let's apply the learning to our current situation".

It's easy to see the value in strategic thinking. Being able to effectively apply our theoretical knowledge and in-the-trenches experience will serve us well.

The business case for strategic planning

Organizations can be torn about the idea of dedicating time to plan for the future. When business is going well and the company is making huge profits, it might be tempting to say, "Let's take advantage of these good times and make as much money as we can. We'll plan later." On the flip side, when the business isn't doing quite so well and money is tight, there's a tendency to say, "We can't afford to plan right now. We need to go out and make money."

Bottom line, businesses need to find time to plan during the good times and bad—and everything in-between. The future of their organization depends on it. Companies must understand their customer, their market, and their competition.

One component to strategic planning is identifying the mission, vision, and values of the organization. Even when a company has an established mission, vision, and values, this is a good time to review and confirm the purpose of the company.

Strategic planning meeting benefits

Strategic planning meetings can accomplish more than creating a roadmap for the organization. Some additional benefits include:

> ➤ Effective deployment of resources
> ➤ Increased productivity
> ➤ Strong team development
> ➤ Solving major problems

Here's an example from my past that includes all of these. I worked for a company that conducted strategic planning every year around budget time. They would invite about 50 managers to participate in the process. Before we went to the meeting, we would participate in a focus group (see *Chapter 7, Focus Groups*) to identify the top challenges facing the company.

After the top issues were identified, we were assigned teams. Our job title had absolutely no bearing on what team we were assigned. For example, the year that leadership development was identified as a top issue, I wasn't on that team. At the time, I was the human resources director and leadership development would have been my responsibility.

Teams would work together to do the following:

> ➤ Identify and research the problem
> ➤ Brainstorm options to solve the problem
> ➤ Agree upon a proposed solution

At the strategy session, the team would present their challenge and proposed solution to the entire group. The CEO and COO didn't dominate the conversation. They gave everyone the opportunity to participate. Sometimes the group approved the solution; sometimes not. Or they made some recommendations and then approved the action plan. The point is the group decided together.

So, in addition to the company creating a strategic roadmap for the future, the process helped to:

> ➤ Identify problems

> ➤ Create teams to work together

> ➤ Recommend solutions for those teams to solve problems

> ➤ Approve and allocate resources for the group to solve issues

> ➤ Work together as a team to increase the productivity of the company

The strategic planning meeting can bring many benefits to the company if the process is inclusive and transparent

Frequency of strategic planning meetings

Company culture and industry drive the decision regarding how often to conduct strategic planning meetings. Here are the three things to consider:

1. **Rapidly changing industries**: Some industries are moving so quickly that strategy should be reviewed more frequently. An example might be the technology industry.

2. **New products/services**: An organization introducing a new product or service might consider more regular strategic planning meetings. Another instance might be a company that is looking to grow via mergers and acquisitions.

3. **Budget planning**: Because strategic planning often raises questions about resource allocation, it's often combined with budget discussions.

There's no right or wrong when it comes to how often strategic planning meetings happen. The important thing is that they're productive.

Common strategic planning challenges

The goal of strategic planning is to prepare a roadmap for the organization. You need two things to put together a good roadmap—information and decisions.

Poor data collection is one of the most common challenges in the strategic planning process. Companies often fail to collect data at all, gather enough data, or pull together the right data. Environmental scanning is a process for collecting data and can help companies make sure they are well prepared. There are three types of information that should be collected for strategic planning:

> ➤ **Internal**: This is data about the company. Not just financials and marketing information, but also data about the workforce and existing resources.

> ➤ **External**: Data about workforce demographics trends can be extremely beneficial. Also, information about government influence in the industry can impact the meeting.

> ➤ **Market**: Information regarding economic conditions and business competition is key to making decisions about the future.

Not all of this information holds equal weight. It's possible that the business is facing a skills gap and workforce information might have greater importance. That will be one of the decisions the participants need to make during the meeting.

Provided the information brought to the strategic planning meeting is sound, the next challenge is making good decisions using the data. In *Chapter 1, Meeting Roles, Responsibilities, and Activities*, we talked about decision-making techniques. Companies sometimes abandon their regular (and good!) decision-making processes for something more complex because they feel the "strategic" in strategic planning means they should do something different. Strategic doesn't necessarily imply complicated. It's possible to keep the process simple and effective. Oftentimes, the more simplistic the process, the easier it is to communicate and execute. That's success.

Before the strategic planning meeting

Before the group starts on the prework that's required to conduct a strategic planning meeting, a few logistic items have to be finalized. The first is where to conduct the meeting.

Meeting location

While many of the meetings we've discussed so far will happen inside the normal office environment, a strategic planning meeting can be held onsite or offsite. Here are some of the advantages and disadvantages to each:

> ➤ Onsite meetings:

>> ➤ **Advantage**: Participants can address operational issues and questions when they arise. And it's cost effective because there are no offsite meeting expenses.

>> ➤ **Disadvantage**: Participants could be pulled away from the strategic conversation too many times and this might hurt the overall development of strategy.

> ➤ Offsite meetings:

>> ➤ **Advantage**: The meeting can be used to reward and recognize key staff members as well as the development of strategy. Participants can focus on the strategy portion of the meeting (versus the operation).

> ➤ **Disadvantage**: The additional cost to conduct meeting offsite. Participants might forget about operational responsibilities during the time away.

Whatever location you decide, be prepared to make accommodations in the meeting agenda to maximize the group's time. For example, schedule longer breaks so participants can take care of operational issues. Tell participants upfront that the schedule will give them time to address matters so when the strategy session is taking place, they can focus.

Session facilitator

Once the location has been decided, the next big decision deals with having a third-party facilitator. We've talked about outside facilitators before in *Chapter 5, Training Meetings*, and *Chapter 7, Focus Groups*. The pros and cons remain the same. A good rule of thumb is that the facilitator should not be someone who has a vested interest in the outcome. For example, having a department manager facilitate their own department planning meeting could influence the outcome. If employees made suggestions, the manager might want to comment or evaluate them.

The facilitator role is to help the conversation and not be a part of the discussion. If this can be done with internal personnel—terrific. If not, consider bringing in a skilled facilitator to lead the meeting and take notes.

Meeting participants

The last decision to make before starting actual meeting work is deciding the meeting participants. Some people will attend this meeting solely based upon their job title. Examples are the CEO, COO, President, and Controller. Others will be invited based upon their responsibilities such as the person in charge of company product lines or the person responsible for customer service. It's also possible that individuals could be invited because there's a strategy that might be associated with their area of responsibility. For example, let's assume the company is concerned about the quality of their applicants and succession plan. The vice president of talent acquisition and the vice president of organizational training might be invited to the strategy meeting for the first time.

These three decisions (setting the location, confirming the facilitator, and inviting the participants) set the stage for the first step in the strategic planning process, formulation.

Step 1 – Formulation

The purpose of the formulation stage is to confirm that everyone is on the same page when "forming" the strategy. If the organization hasn't created a mission, vision, and values (MVV for short), this is the time. If the company already has an MVV, they should take time to confirm that everyone knows the MVV and interprets it the same way.

Some organizations will refine or redefine their MVV every so many years because their industry is changing rapidly. Your organization should do what works best for your situation. But don't ignore this portion to save money or time. Creating a business strategy is incredibly important. The last thing you want to do is create a strategy with participants not aligned toward the company's mission, vision, and values.

Mission

Today's business world is moving very rapidly. I've seen plenty of companies start making money with a particular product or service that really never was a part of their strategy. A regular review to ensure that the mission statement aligns with the company *and* that everyone remembers the mission is important.

The mission statement tells people what the company is all about. They're used on various levels:

> ➤ A company level conveys what the business does

> ➤ At a department level, the mission statement shares the purpose of the team

> ➤ And at an individual level, it defines our reason for being at the company

So, mission statements are important. The actual mission statement itself defines the purpose of the business. What the company is trying to achieve and the reason they are trying to achieve it. Mission statements also share what products or services the business provides and why it's important.

Make a note

Examples of famous mission statements include:

■ Google's mission is "to organize the world's information and make it universally accessible and useful"

■ Part of Coca-Cola's mission statement includes "to refresh the world"

■ Retailer Wal-Mart's advertised mission statement and its advertising slogan are the same: "We save people money so they can live better"

I've always thought of mission statements resembling the classic elevator pitch. If someone asks you, "What does your company do?" then what is your 30-second answer? The reply is probably very close to your company's mission statement. At least it should be. It tells people what you sell and why you sell it.

Developing a mission statement

Because mission statements are all about the focus of the business, a key to developing a good mission statement is involvement. One of the biggest mistakes I see companies make is having a small group of people develop their mission statement. I've actually seen *individuals* decide the mission for an entire group.

If you're part of a team, then the team should create their mission statement. Otherwise, the mission statement doesn't truly represent the group. It only speaks for the individual or individuals involved in its creation.

One of the reasons it's tempting to create a mission statement alone or in a small group is because the process takes less time. And businesses want to avoid time-wasting meetings. (That's why this book exists.) But in order to get the best result, you have to invite the devil's advocates and the naysayers. And be prepared for their comments and debates. And, yes, that does take time.

Deep down inside, you know they should be there. If you exclude them, then you run the risk of them undermining your efforts. They will go around telling everyone how they weren't included. And, even if they are a PITA (translation: pain in the arse), you look worse because the process appears secretive and cliquish.

Once, I was challenged with the task of putting together a strategic plan for a nonprofit organization. In their 30-year existence, they never had one. I wanted to make the process as inclusive as possible but several people told me I was crazy to try to have 60 people work on a strategic plan. But we found a terrific partner to help lead us through the process.

Tip

Hire a professional

Even if you do strategic planning for a living like me, when I need to be part of the process instead of facilitate, I hire a professional. Trying to run the meeting and be a participant can be a recipe for disaster. You know that old saying about being your own lawyer…

One activity that really helped us solidify our mission was a three-question discussion about our organization. The facilitators put one condition on our responses—we had to answer everything in the affirmative—to keep our group focused on the positive. The three questions were:

1. What activities do we do now?
2. What things do we want to do in the future?
3. What steps do we need to accomplish in order to achieve the roadmap we created for ourselves?

It's a great exercise that really works. Besides being a positive way to talk about the organization, this type of process allows for a tremendous level of participation.

If your organization already has a mission statement, you can use this three-question activity as a way to confirm your current mission and to starting thinking about what the organization hopes to accomplish.

Vision

Sometimes the concept of strategic planning conjures up thoughts of long retreats at exotic resorts where you're locked in a conference room. The meeting ends with a pseudo-team building exercise and pep talk after which you receive a 2-inch thick binder with the notes from the meeting that ultimately ends up on a bookshelf collecting dust.

In today's fast-paced business world, that impression of strategic planning has to change. It's still important and essential to our business. But it needs to be streamlined while still effective.

Reviewing mission statements is one of the first steps in the strategic planning process. And, I don't see mission statements going away or losing value in the near future. Vision statements, on the other hand, are being reinvented to accommodate today's business climate.

Whenever I think of vision statements, it reminds me of a chapter in Scott Adams' book titled, *Principle*. He makes a joke about managers doing vision things when they should be doing mission things. The joke does have some bearing in the business world. Traditionally, organizations have always had vision statements—those declarations of what they want to be long-term. Their legacy, if you will. But with the mantra from Wall Street being, "you're only as good as your last quarter," are vision statements relevant anymore?

Even from a personal standpoint, we encourage people to develop personal vision statements, reflecting their contributions as an individual. When employees are just trying to make ends meet and willing to pick up a side hustle at a moment's notice, it calls into question how a personal vision statement supports a personal brand.

While I'm tossing out some musings about the future of vision statements, I'm not completely ready to eliminate the need for them. But I do think the vision statement needs to be more fluid than it has been in the past. Company vision statements used to be chiseled in stone and maybe today they should be written on paper...in pencil..., and have an eraser handy.

Vision statements take a long-term perspective. They tell people why the business exists. Whereas a mission statement that tells people what the company does, vision statements share the organization's legacy and what success looks like to them.

Make a note

Examples of famous vision statements include:

- Beauty retailer Avon's vision is "to be the company that best understands and satisfies the product, service, and self-fulfillment needs of women—globally"

- At one time, Microsoft's vision statement was "A personal computer in every home running Microsoft software"

- Nike's vision statement includes "help athletes of every level of ability reach their potential"

If a mission statement is your company elevator pitch, think of a vision statement answering the question, "What will your company be doing in five years?" How would you answer that in 30 seconds? And it really shouldn't be answered with "more of the same" or "I don't know."

I do wonder if we will see a trend where the new vision statement is less about what your business provides and more about who they service. Even if you have an alternative source of revenue, you can focus on the core customer which remains consistent. However, companies must have a clear understanding of their customer base.

I once facilitated a focus group where I asked the question, "Who are your customers?" and the answer was "Everybody." Hmmm…no. Everybody is not your customer. Sorry. At some point, we will all have to narrow our business strategy to be truly effective.

Values

We've talked about *vision* and *mission* statements, so it only seems fitting that we finish this strategy trifecta with some comments about organizational values. In my opinion, values are the most important of the three.

Values are the qualities that transform a company's mission and vision into reality. In essence, values outline *corporate culture* and play an important role in our everyday activities as managers.

> **Recruiting**: Values should be the qualities we look for during job interviews. People who demonstrate our organizational values should be the ones we hire. For example, if having a customer focus is one of your company values, then asking questions about delivering would be the key.

> **Training**: Every company should include their organizational values in *orientation*. In fact, they should be reinforced during every company-training program. Think about the impact of being able to link company values to leadership.

> **Performance**: Performance appraisal systems should include the company's organizational values. We should reward performance that supports organizational values.

Make a note

IBM values include:

- Dedication to every client's success
- Innovation that matters, for our company and for the world
- Trust and personal responsibility in all relationships

It seems so simple. Your organizational values help you achieve your success. Therefore, you hire for them, train to improve them, and recognize/reward based upon them. But in reality, we see plenty of cases where the values a business says are important aren't the ones that get emphasized or acknowledged. I wonder if that's because organizations are conflicted about which values to select.

For example, I know of companies that thrive on an entrepreneurial culture. They are competitive, profit/results-driven, and have a tremendous sense of urgency. But their values don't reflect any of these attributes. Why? Because those words may have some negative connotations.

Organizational values are unique to each company. They shouldn't just be politically correct marketing terms. Let me repeat that—your company values shouldn't just be politically correct marketing terms. Values should represent the culture of the business. It's okay to be competitive and profit-driven. In some industries, it's a necessity.

Make a note

The IBM "Values Jam"

In 2003, IBM undertook the first reexamination of its values in its 100-year history through an event they called the "Values Jam." It was an unprecedented 72-hour discussion on IBM's global intranet on the most important values to the company. Hundreds of thousands employees weighed in and worked together to define the essence of the company. The result? A set of core values, defined by IBMers for IBMers, that shape the way the company leads, makes decisions, and acts.

Values are the company standards of behavior, which includes ethics. A company's values should connect to the operation. The other connection that must exists is senior leadership must live the values of the organization. If the values aren't important in the C-Suite, they will not matter to anyone else.

Some organizations don't have formally defined values but they are easy to spot. Ask someone for the top five characteristics that align with the company. Give them a 1 minute to answer. Their response reflects the values of the company.

As you're starting the strategic planning process, think about your organizational values and whether they're representative of your organization. If they are, that's great. If they're not, could it be time for a change?

Communicating company mission, vision, and values

Once an organization has defined their mission, vision and values (again, let's call them the MVV for short), it's time to share them with the world. Internally, the MVV provides guidance for decisions and inspiration for employees. Externally, the MVV tells customers and shareholders the priorities of the company. Here are some of the ways I've seen organizations reinforce their MVV both internally and externally:

➤ **Business cards**: Many organizations, especially nonprofits, will publish their mission on their business cards for everyone to see. It's a great public relations and fundraising communication piece.

➤ **Letterhead, notepads, and so on**: Another piece related to the business card, including the mission and vision of the organization on common business items. If the mission is short, it can be easily incorporated into envelope design or included on invoices. It's a good way to keep the message out in the public eye.

➤ **Name tents**: Years ago, I served on a board whose meetings were open to the public. We had a name tent at each of our places so the public knew who we were. On the side facing us, was the mission of the organization. Obviously, we didn't need to see our own names so the organization created a reminder of the company mission. Every time the board took a vote, the mission was right in front of us.

➤ **Entrances**: Companies like to get employees involved in "blessing" or "buying-into" the company mission. They'll set up walls where employees can sign off on the mission. It's very symbolic and wonderful way to create a common goal. In my opinion, the mistake companies make is hiding it from public eye. One of my clients set up this "wall" in the foyer of their office. Every single person who came into the building saw it – employees, vendors, suppliers, applicants, etc.

➤ **ID badges**: If you work in a building with key cards or employee ID badges, make sure the organizational mission is visible on the badge. It keeps the message top of mind every time an employee has to show their badge or swipe it for access.

Companies have an MVV for a reason. It's to help guide decisions and the operation. However, it can be difficult to keep everyone focused on the mission. We're human, after all. Doing a recheck during strategic planning only makes sense. In addition, creating mechanisms for those employees who are not at the strategic planning meeting to stay connected is equally important.

Step 2 – Development

The logistics have been taken care of and the research has been completed. Now, it's time to conduct the actual meeting. A perfect way to start off a strategic planning meeting is with an icebreaker.

Make a note

What's an icebreaker?

An icebreaker is a game, exercise, or activity that welcomes the group. It comes from the nautical term, icebreaker, being a ship that is capable of navigating through tough patches of ice. The "icebreaker" allows participants to relax and become comfortable with each other.

There are lots of different kinds of icebreakers. In fact, there are whole books devoted to icebreaker activities. But let me share with you a classic icebreaker that works in almost any environment.

Make a note

Interviews

Ask participants to find someone in the room they don't work with on a daily basis and interview them. Include the common items such as name, title, and department but ask them to find out one additional thing. For example, "If you could have dinner with one person—living or not—who would it be and why?" It's a fun question and you'll get some great answers. You can also theme the final question to the meeting. Example: "Share one change you've made in your career that turned out well." The meeting starts off on a positive note and the facilitator can see each person's tolerance for change.

Once the icebreaker has been conducted, the group should be ready to start work. A traditional way to begin strategic planning is with an evaluation of the organization. This is called a **SWOT** analysis. SWOT is an acronym for strengths, weaknesses, opportunities, and threats.

Conducting a SWOT analysis

A SWOT analysis should include every aspect of the organization: finances, communication, marketing, operations, products/services, talent, and technology.

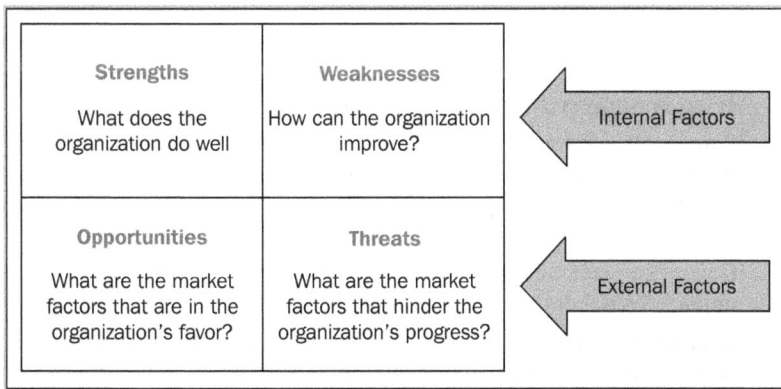

Strengths	Weaknesses	
What does the organization do well	How can the organization improve?	Internal Factors
Opportunities	Threats	
What are the market factors that are in the organization's favor?	What are the market factors that hinder the organization's progress?	External Factors

During each phase of the conversation, the participants can share their thoughts about the organization, operation, and overall business performance.

To identify the company's strengths, ask:

➤ What do we do well that our customers value?

➤ What do we do well that our stakeholders value?

➤ Are we in good shape financially?

To hone in on organizational weaknesses, find out:

➤ Where do we "drop the ball?"

➤ In what areas have we sensed dissatisfaction with our customers or stakeholders?

➤ Have we managed our finances well?

To determine potential opportunities, ask participants:

➤ What future opportunities do we anticipate in these areas:

   ➢ New customers?

   ➢ New or recurring sources of revenue?

   ➢ New products or services?

➤ What do we do that is unique in the marketplace and can be leveraged?

Lastly, to uncover threats to the business, ask:

➤ What challenges are we currently facing?

➤ What challenges do we anticipate over the next 3 years?

A SWOT analysis is an effective tool to help organizations get to the root of their challenges and opportunities. If there is a criticism of the SWOT analysis, it's that it can become a bit too focused on the negative. If you have a group that's facing tremendous challenges, you might find the group comes up with a long list of weaknesses and threats and a short list of strengths and opportunities. If that happens, one way to get the group out of the "glass half-empty" mode is to use a process called appreciative inquiry.

Make a note

What is Appreciative Inquiry?

Simply put, it's a process that advocates looking at situations from the positive perspective. Think of appreciative inquiry as two-steps. For the appreciative part, the group focuses on what's going well. That is, "This is what we're doing right." Instead of "This is what isn't working."

Groups can take the discussion one step further through the second step of inquiry, "What do we want the future to look like?"

Then connect the two. Point A is what we currently do well. Point B is where we want to be. Now let's figure out the steps to get from Point A to Point B.

If you like the idea of appreciative inquiry, you can bring this to your strategic planning meeting. Joris Luijke, author of the blog *Culture Hacking*, suggests that this approach of asking thoughtful positive questions can be a good way to keep meetings on track, encourage participation, and save time.

Documenting the conversation

In the last chapter on focus groups, we talked about the importance of documenting conversations. I don't want to rehash the same discussion but instead add a few tools that you can use specifically with strategic planning.

Mind map

A mind map is a visual outline of information. It's often created around a single word or concept. Sometimes it's referred to as a spider diagram. You can create mind maps by hand or use smart device apps that facilitate their creation. Below is an example of a conversation regarding creating better staff meetings using a mind map diagram:

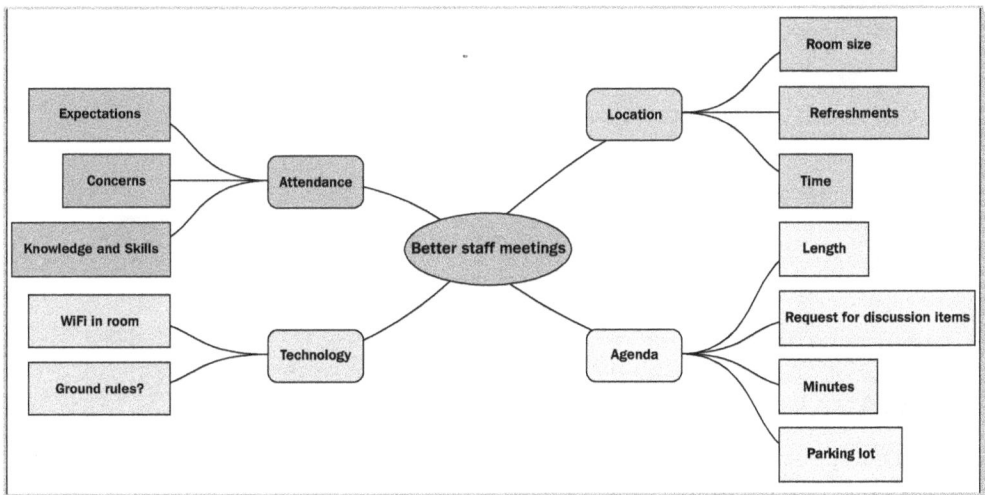

Fishbone diagram

Also called an Ishikawa diagram for its creator, a fishbone diagram shows cause and effect. The problem or challenge is the center line or spine of the diagram with the offshooting spikes (or bones) representing the other factors or categories of effect. Here's an example of a conversation that might happen regarding the challenge of poor employee morale and how it could be represented using a fishbone diagram.

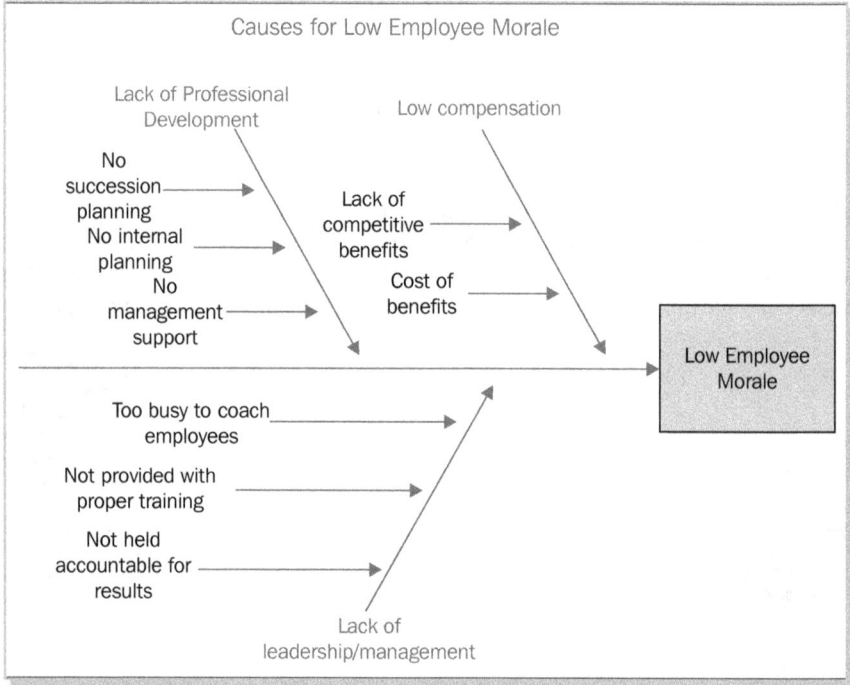

Causes for Low Employee Morale

5 whys

This is a questioning technique used to explore cause and impact. It's used to determine the root cause of an issue. Here's an example:

> **Problem***: Our latest product has an unusually high amount of customer returns.*
>
> **1st Why?** *Customers say a particular function stops working.*
>
> **2nd Why?** *We know the software has a bug.*
>
> **3rd Why?** *We haven't released the fix yet.*
>
> **4th Why?** *Our testing hasn't concluded that the bug definitely fixes the problem.*
>
> **5th Why?** *It's possible there's a flaw in the design and it's not a bug.*

These three techniques (mind maps, fishbone diagrams, and 5 whys) can add a valuable layer of detail to your strategic planning meeting documentation.

Step 3 – Implementation

When it comes to time, strategic planning is one very long meeting. So let's recap where we are so far...

> ➤ We've logistically planned the meeting, found the facilitator, and secured the location

> ➤ The participants have been invited and worked on their assignments

> ➤ The group has reviewed (or created) the mission, vision, and values

> ➤ The group has conducted a SWOT analysis of the organization

---

Tip

Have multiple meetings

If you decide to conduct your meetings on-site, one approach might be to break the strategic planning meeting into smaller parts. This gives participants time to process the information in between meetings. A common separation might be to conduct the MVV session as one meeting, then the SWOT analysis, and finally the strategy plans.

A lot of work has been done. But there's still a lot to do. Now it's time to develop the strategic plan itself. I know you might be saying to yourself, "Is all this prework really necessary?" And the answer is "yes". Emphatically, yes!

Creating the strategy for the organization is one of the most important meetings you'll have. Make it count by doing the necessary homework and prework.

As the group is putting together the organizational strategy, document your strategic plan using the SMART goals format we discussed in *Chapter 1, Meeting Roles, Responsibilities, and Activities*. It's perfect for remembering to ask all of the relevant questions, for example:

> ➤ What action do we want to take? (*Specific*)

> ➤ What is the desired outcome or result? (*Measurable*)

> ➤ Name the steps that need to be considered. Are there any potential barriers or obstacles we need to account for? (*Actionable*)

> ➤ Who will be responsible for each action step? Are there any other resources we need? (*Responsible*)

> ➤ When should each step be completed? (*Timebound*)

The goal here is to identify objectives that will be vital for your organization to achieve its mission and vision. The goals should build upon the company's strengths, resolve organizational weaknesses, leverage business opportunities, and avoid market threats. The action steps should offer short-term milestones for the company to benchmark their progress.

Tip

Short-term versus long-term thinking

One of the things that technology has changed is the definition of short-term and long-term.

I've been a part of strategic planning sessions that defined short-term as 3-5 years and long-term at 5-10. I remember facilitating a focus group and we talked about short-term being 1-3 years and long-term being 3-5. Today, I wonder if a year is really short-term given how fast the business world is moving!

Companies need to ask themselves, "What does time mean within our organization?" This is subjective and should be defined by the organization, its industry, and the competitive landscape.

Regardless of the actual time frame, I think we have a tendency to think of short-term activities with a different sense of priority than long-term. One we need to do right now and the other we can work on later. It might not seem like a big deal, but what if a business gets their priorities wrong? More importantly, can a business afford to get them wrong?

The final strategic plan should be a document that can be used for several purposes:

> **Organizational credibility**: Every organization, no matter how big or small, for-profit or nonprofit, wants to be taken seriously. They have a passion for their product or service. The strategic plan is their documented roadmap for success.

> **Resource allocation**: Every strategic plan will involve expenditures of some sort. The plan should clearly outline what those are so the proper resources are budgeted.

> **Employee communications**: While the final plan document might not be distributed company-wide, the key elements of the strategic plan should be known to everyone. This creates a sense of buy-in and tells employees how they impact the strategic goals of the company.

> **Stakeholder commitment**: If a company wants to be successful, they have to commit to change. The strategic plan provides documentation of the company's commitment to change.

A strategic plan is a living document, not a good looking binder full of paper that sits on a shelf in the office.

Power and its impact on strategic planning

Back in *Chapter 3, Brainstorming*, we talked about bestowed and earned power. Bestowed power being that influence we have because of our position or role within the organization. Earned power is related to the influence we have as an individual.

When it comes to strategic planning, bestowed and earned power play a significant role. Our job title or responsibilities (that is, bestowed power) might factor into whether we are invited to participate in the strategic planning session. Equally true could be that our lack of a particular title could exclude us from the meeting. Example being "vice president level and above attend the meeting." If I'm a senior director, I might not get an invitation.

This gets complicated if your organization likes to get creative with job titles. I've seen organizations promote someone to senior director (instead of vice president) even though they are doing the same work as a vice president. I'm not saying it's right. It just happens.

What can be helpful is to think of participation in terms of earned power. Regardless of their title, has a person earned the right to be there? Does their experience and knowledge bring value to the meeting? If a company is used to doing things based upon title, this can be a hard shift to make. One way to get everyone comfortable with the idea is to use the multiple-meeting suggestion I made a few pages ago. Break the meeting into smaller segments. It allows the traditionalists as well as the new participants a chance to get comfortable.

Bringing technology to strategic planning

One of the most important components to the strategic planning meeting is capturing all of the information being discussed. Participants will want a record of the SWOT discussion about the organization. They will want copies of the data and information shared during the environmental scan. Lastly, they will want the final strategy document and action plans. Most of this information will be supplied by the person responsible for facilitating the session. Likely, their role will include having someone on hand to be a note taker.

In addition to the notes from the meeting, participants might want to jot down their own notes. These notes could be things they want to share with their respective teams when they return to the office. It might also include specific action items they need to incorporate into their goals to support the overall strategic plan.

While some people still prefer paper and pencil, many individuals have moved to using electronic note taking applications. There are really too many different electronic note-taking applications to mention. What's important is to realize they exist so individuals can use their laptops, tablets, and phones to take notes.

It can be a little unnerving if you're not used to participants typing while discussion is happening. But we do have to move past those old perceptions and hold people accountable for the discussion and outcomes, not the way they choose to take notes.

On the plus side, electronic note-taking technologies also include bulletin boards and whiteboards so companies can capture drawings and sketches for distribution to the team. I remember the old days when someone would have to redraw a diagram so it could be copied and distributed. Thank goodness those days are behind us!

Step 4 – Evaluation

I think it's important at this point to offer a little reality check where strategic plans are concerned. There's a line taken from the movie *Field of Dreams*, "If you build it, they will come." The truth is…they won't. It takes more than just creating a strategic plan for people to use it. People have to understand **WIIFM (what's in it for me)** before they will embrace it.

Here's an example of how WIIFM can impact an organization: a company builds a robust repository of information for employees to use. It contains information such as the company phone directory, how to apply for a leave of absence, and the annual holiday schedule. It's great because all of the information is online and accessible anytime. But employees don't use it. Why? Well, there could be several reasons:

> ➤ No one knew it existed

> ➤ It's easier just to walk around the corner and ask someone

> ➤ The system has a lot of information but it's not updated regularly

> ➤ Information located in one section of the system doesn't match information found in another section

> ➤ And the list goes on

When we create things, even strategic plans, part of the process needs to be establishing a clear understanding of how it will be maintained. I've seen plenty of great things created that fall to the wayside because no one stopped to consider what happens once it's implemented.

Here's another common example I'm sure you've seen before. A group meets to discuss some sort of organizational challenge. Someone says, "We should do X." Everyone agrees. Then nothing happens. Why? Because the person who came up with the idea thinks they're done. They came up with the idea. The rest of the group wasn't specifically told they were supposed to implement the idea. So the idea never gets implemented.

Oh, and here's a final example. Let's say a group meets and decides they are going to create X, which is an information repository. And they do. The group designs and builds a terrific solution. Then they go back to their regular daily work. After several months, the group realizes no one is using the solution they created. Because the group thought communicating the new resource and maintaining it was someone else's job. They were just supposed to create it. And now the challenge is…all the information is outdated.

Once the strategic plan document has been created, it's should be referred to regularly. Your organizational structure could help decide how often the document is reviewed. For example, the senior leadership team might review the document quarterly. The board of directors might only review the document annually or semi-annually.

During the review sessions, a two-step evaluation process should take place:

1. Evaluate the process.
2. Evaluate the plan.

By evaluating the plan on two levels, the strategic plan stays current, results can be easily identified, and necessary adjustments can be incorporated.

During the plan evaluation, current information should be considered. This is a good time to confirm that the assumptions used to create the plan are still valid. Stakeholders should offer input regarding any new trends or recommendations that merit consideration. A few questions to ask during this review include:

> ➤ Are the company's strategic goals and objectives being achieved?

> ➤ Are goals being achieved on time?

> ➤ Does everyone have adequate resources?

> ➤ Are the goals still realistic?

During the process evaluation, the key stakeholders should confirm that everyone that should have provided feedback has been given the opportunity. Also, that roles and responsibilities are clearly understood. Some of the questions that can be asked during the evaluation are:

> ➤ Did everyone have the opportunity to provide input during the review?

> ➤ Can everyone explain the company's strategic goals?

> ➤ Does everyone have access to a copy of the strategic plan?

It's perfectly acceptable to refine action steps during a strategic plan review. In fact, it's even absolutely fine to deviate from the plan completely if circumstances warrant it. Think back a few years ago to the *great recession*. If we were a company planning to launch a luxury brand, it could have been disastrous for our business at a recessionary period. At the point we can see what's taking place, it only makes good business sense to postpone that launch.

After building a strategic plan, consider all the phases. Not just the planning and creation. But how to implement, communicate, maintain, and evaluate it. Otherwise, all of your hard work could be for nothing.

5 tips for better strategic planning

Clarity and accountability are key ingredients for a successful strategic planning session. Here are five tips from business pros on the best way to achieve it.

Jim Gallo, MS, SPHR, associate director at The Center for Organizational Effectiveness at Florida Tech, stresses simplicity.

> *"***Simple***: Rome was not built in a day! Therefore do not attempt building an entire organizational or departmental strategy in one day. Keep it simple and keep asking the pivotal question; "How is today's strategy meeting going to drive the company forward?" This should be at the top of every agenda, power point etc.*

Eliminate Distractions (time for a cruise): *Having a strategy meeting does not automatically mean a stuffy boardroom with big comfy chairs and a fancy power point. Sometimes we need to change it up a bit and find another location and or time away from the workplace. While taking an actual cruise may be a bit extreme for some, creating an environment in which participants will have difficulty contacting others and others contacting them can assist in reducing the distractions and keeping focus. If they can turn off their mobile devices for a cruise they can sure turn off for an important strategy meeting.*

Once it's done it's done, move on! (buzzer strategy): It is important for everyone to stay focused and on task. I'm sure most of us have experienced a strategy meeting that lasted much longer due to additional supporting opinions that add little to no value to the conversation. These wondering conversations lengthen strategy meetings unnecessarily and reduce focus. While we want to get all opinions out regarding the topic, we should try to eliminate those conversations that are restating the obvious or take the conversation off topic. But just how do you cut people off without possible hurting their feelings?

The answer is "team work". Have the meeting participants do it. One tip to keep conversations brief and to the point is the "buzzer strategy". This strategy involves a sound device (the larger and obnoxious the better) that is used to buzz people back to the conversation, close it out, table it or move on to the next. At the beginning of each meeting, designate an individual to be responsible for this esteemed buzzing honor. This honor should be rotated for each subsequent meeting. Another strategy is that once the buzzer is pressed it is given to another meeting participant. This gives everybody an opportunity to keep all conversations on track and brief and adds a little fun to the meeting. You may need to give a few buzzing examples.

Accountability: *Everyone leaves the room with a task related to the strategy, a timeline to complete the task and a scheduled follow-up meeting to present their task accomplishments. Once again this should not be a list of 15 to 20 tasks. Keep it simple and then hold everyone accountable. "*

Jennifer V. Miller, founder at People Equation Press, says preparation is essential.

"The most overlooked element in strategic planning is the setting of boundaries. Every person walking into a strategic planning meeting has a different definition in their minds of what "setting strategy" means. I've seen too many strategic planning meetings derail because half of the team was drilling into details that weren't yet relevant to the discussion, and the other half was rapidly becoming disengaged because they were tuned out of the process.

The meeting facilitator should meet in advance with the meeting sponsor (the person who's ultimately responsible for setting the strategy) and gain clarity on exactly how far to go in developing detailed plans. For example, is the aim of the meeting to set high-level expectations, with further work to be done at a later time? Or, will there be a detailed plan mapped out, with goals and milestones created? When the overall level of detail is predetermined, then the meeting facilitator can put measures into place to properly guide the discussion that will result in a productive planning session. "

Speaker, trainer, and human resources consultant Nancy Newell reminds us of the importance in creating clarity of and unity of action around the agreed upon vision.

"When groups are engaged in strategic planning, I have found that they successfully work through the process of recalibrating their mission and vision statement and reestablishing values statements with good brainstorming, inclusive communication strategies, and group management techniques. Groups can lose sight of the new direction pretty quickly once we move to the more tactical process of identifying objectives and resource allocation.

To keep groups focused on the new, and moving away from the old, we repeat the new mission and vision at every meeting, and have gone so far as to publish vision statements for the walls of the meeting rooms. One group even published the new vision statement at the top of every page on the notepads that were given to strategic planning participants for use in the meetings. This really helps keep the conversation focused, and is a quick touch point for everyone—"Does this activity that we're talking about really get us where we want to go?"

Mary A Stevens II is a ninja, leadership coach, and public speaker. As the owner of Boulder Quest Martial Arts, she's dedicated herself to helping people find, ignite, and carry their own light. Her tip is a new way to look at keeping the meeting focused and on track.

"Having an agenda is the best way to kill a meeting. An agenda gets you focused on the little details. Whether it's for sales, human resources, or a new project, meetings shouldn't be about what to do. The most successful meetings set a vision and everything in the meeting supports the vision. If you can create a strong image in the minds of your customers (or employees), then the "what" presents itself. Share from your purpose and you will inspire even the most mundane meetings to greater productivity and agreement."

Wm. Edward Vesely, executive vice president and chief marketing officer at SilkRoad, a leader in cloud-based, human resources technology solutions, shares strategies for planning in today's fast-paced business environment.

"The terms strategic planning, and process, conjure up a range of thought in today's fast-paced, competitive world. Combine them into a single phrase and there's ample opportunity to stray from the 'no nonsense' theme of this book.

The most effective strategic planning meetings involve a relatively small cross-section of smart and engaged people who have clear goals and great chemistry. That said, consider the following:

➤ ***Don't assume senior members are in alignment****: I've participated in important strategic planning meetings when a CxO didn't understand where we wanted to be in nine months. I also know the VP of Strategic Planning at a large, risk-averse multinational corporation who quips that her role involves preparing business plans for acquisition candidates, and then routing a given plan among the senior business leaders until someone rejects it.*

➤ ***Give everyone a voice****: Some of the best ideas have come from quieter, more cerebral team members. Facilitate the conversation, and be sure to call on people who can't get a word in edgewise or are too timid to contribute in the presence of more verbal or senior individuals.*

➤ ***Focus on an execution****: Sure, we need to improve processes in order to reach new levels of performance and scalability, but the most successful teams also eliminate bureaucracy where it stands. Deliver results, then learn and improve.*

Speaking of execution, I leverage an approach outlined by John P. Kotter of Harvard Business School in the article "What Leaders Really Do," to move teams through important growth stages, and drive change across a business:

➤ ***Create a sense of urgency****: Get the word out that "business as usual" is no longer acceptable for the ongoing viability of the company.*

➤ ***Create a solid execution team****: It's important to remember that it takes a village and you're often only as strong as your weakest member.*

➤ ***Create a shared vision****: The team needs to know where it's going and how much better life will be—for them and the business—when they arrive.*

➤ ***Communicate the vision****: Buy-in from key stakeholders across the business is vital. The CEO and heads of sales, marketing, engineering, and finance especially need to be on board.*

➤ ***Empower employees to act****: They need to be reminded they're not air traffic controllers—if they make a mistake, they're not likely to kill anyone. People need to take educated risks, and it's up to their leaders to encourage and support them.*

➤ ***Produce short-term results****: Launch a viral marketing campaign or other highly public effort, then publicize the success and give full credit to those who contribute and take the risks.*

➤ ***Build momentum****: From there, transform into a more optimized balance of methods and strategies that leverage the latest technologies, for instance.*

➤ ***Anchor behavior in organization culture****: Set the bar continually higher, empower people, recognize their accomplishments, and never tolerate the status quo.*

In the end, it's all about empowering and engaging people. Employee satisfaction should never be the goal, but instead successful leaders strive for a highly engaged workforce that can be ignited to create the results that are needed to truly make a difference."

Summary

Strategic planning meetings are some of the most important meetings that take place in the organization. It's possible we could say this meeting sets the stage for all the other meetings we're talking about. Ultimately, status meetings help us achieve our operational goals (which help us accomplish our strategic plan). Training meetings help us carry out our goals (which helps us achieve our strategic plan). And so forth.

In our next chapter, we're going to talk about project meetings. We're going to discuss how this meeting should be different from the regular status meeting and examine some project management tools to help the meeting be successful.

>10

Project Meetings

Projects are a regular part of business life. The organizations we are affiliated with, whether it's as a volunteer or employee, will always have some sort of project going on.

As business professionals, we need to know how to effectively manage and participate on a project team. Part of the team's effectiveness is how well the team conducts their meetings. There's a direct correlation between project meetings and the outcome of the project.

What is a project team?

Project teams are groups that come together to work on a specific, defined initiative. They usually have representation from many different facets of the organization. And once the project is completed, the project team is typically disbanded. An example might be a group of employees responsible for organizing a health and wellness fair.

Sometimes we use the term project team interchangeably with other groups such as task forces, work groups, and committees. While it's not a major faux pas to intermingle these terms, there are some subtle differences:

> **Committees**, like project teams, typically have representation from multiple areas in the organization. However, committees are often seen as having an ongoing purpose, charter, or set of governing rules. The safety committee is an example of a common workplace committee.

> **Task forces** are like project teams in that they are brought together to accomplish a specific task or initiative. The difference is usually in the initiative. Project teams tend to focus on short-term projects and task forces take on longer-term strategic projects. An example of a task force would be a group brought together to investigate workplace violence.

> **Work teams** or groups are responsible for a particular product or client group. They can be comprised of a single department or multiple departments within the organization. A work team would be responsible for implementing a procedure as a result of new safety legislation being passed.

Understanding the difference matters in the beginning when you're establishing the group. The team needs to have a clear understanding of their purpose, their authority and responsibility, and the duration of the assignment.

Roles within a project

The next key for project success is having the right people in the room. Most project teams have a project manager, sponsor, and cheerleaders.

Project manager

This individual has the responsibility of leading the team through the process of planning, implementing, and concluding the project. Good project managers wear many hats during the life of the project. If you're selecting someone to assume the role of project manager or considering taking on a project manager role yourself, here are some of the skills necessary for the job:

> **Team-builder**: Good project managers are able to bring together a diverse group of people to complete the project. This doesn't mean there won't be a conflict. Conflict is natural, sometimes necessary, and often a healthy part of team development.

> **Effective communicator**: Project managers are responsible for communicating both within the team and to external stakeholders about the project and status.

> **Collaborator**: Whenever you bring a group of people together, there will be differences of opinion. Project managers can help the group reach compromise and consensus.

> **Decision-maker**: If necessary, project managers must be able to make decisions on behalf of the project. As we discussed in *Chapter 1, Meeting Roles, Responsibilities, and Activities*, not every decision is a consensus decision. Project managers should be prepared to make decisions as appropriate.

> **Detail-oriented**: Successful implementation involves the perfect execution of details. Project managers need to understand the details surrounding the project. They do not have to actually do everything, but an understanding of the details allows them to support the team.

> **Organized**: One element of project success is time, which we will talk more about later. For now, it's important to note that project managers should be able to keep the project on task and on time.

> **Problem-solver**: Lastly, project managers must be able to work through challenges when they occur.

Many of these attributes should look familiar to you. They are the same qualities we talk about when discussing how to run a good meeting: organizing the agenda, communicating with meeting participants, working through problems, making decisions, and providing detailed minutes. Good project managers bring all of their skills to the meeting.

Project sponsor

Another key role in the project is the project sponsor. This person, usually in an influential position within the organization, helps the project team achieve their goal by securing resources and approvals for the project. They could be the person who helped get company support to start the project in the first place. Typically, a project sponsor doesn't attend all the meetings or have regular assignments. Instead, the project manager keeps the sponsor informed of the project status and the sponsor assists with issues when they occur.

One of the biggest roles a project sponsor has is being continuously supportive of the project. I'm reminded of a blog post I read years ago on the *ThoughtLeaders* blog (http://www.thoughtleadersllc.com/blog/) titled, *When the Boss Says Yes and Means No*. Project sponsors have to be clear in their support for the project and clear in how they communicate that support.

At some point, we've all heard the notion that if senior leadership doesn't support a projector initiative it's doomed to fail. But we need to define the word "support". Here are a couple examples of questionable support:

> ➤ Let's say the powers-that-be don't cancel the project. But they also don't attend the meetings, provide adequate resources, or promote the benefits of the result.

> ➤ Another possibility is leadership doesn't cancel a project but they also don't know how to support it. Maybe just giving the team the green light to do something (and see where it takes them) is support enough.

It might not seem like it at times but I have seen instances where the decision to *not* cancel a project is interpreted as providing support. The organization is willing to try something and possibly fail. In other situations, appropriate support might need to be much more, including leadership team presence and resources such as money, equipment, and staff.

Project sponsors have to set clear expectations where projects are concerned, including letting the team know the level of support the project will receive. This can avoid confusion and frustration from employees wondering why their project isn't getting the management support it needs.

Tip

Have multiple sponsors

More organizations are designating multiple sponsors to help their projects be successful. This gives the project a higher level of support. Project sponsors are chosen for their specific expertise and influence. When challenges occur that demand a sponsor use their influence, project sponsors are more comfortable because they know they're not using up all their internal influence.

Part of being a leader is organization. Support isn't a one-size-fits-all matter. Taking into consideration the task, its impact on the operation, and communicating clear expectations will make for a successful project.

Cheerleaders

We're not talking about the people at football games. Project cheerleaders are individuals who have a passion for the project and are willing to help "tell and sell" others. They may or may not be a part of the formal project team.

Years ago, I worked on a project team to introduce a new employee benefits program. As part of the program, we were making some changes to the company and employee contribution. The company paid 100 percent of the employee's medical coverage and, under the new program, was asking employees to pay $10. Senior leadership had already heard that employees were grumbling about the new program and felt their benefits were being taken away.

The project team decided to create a group of benefits ambassadors (read: cheerleaders). The ambassadors were people who wanted to know more about the benefits change, why it occurred, and so on. They attended informational meetings and became the internal experts about the new program. If employees had questions, they could go to human resources or an ambassador for answers.

After the rollout, many employees commented on how much they liked the ambassador program. When they had questions, they figured HR was going to "tow the company line" so going to an ambassador seemed like a good way to get the inside scoop. Then they realized the ambassadors supported the program too. Even the ambassadors that were a bit skeptical at first told others about the great features in the new benefit program and that $10 wasn't a large price to pay.

Regardless of the role a person plays on the project team—manager, sponsor, cheerleader, or team member—each person is responsible for clear communication.

The goal of a project meeting

Simply put, a project meeting takes place to make decisions about the project. It's different from the regularly scheduled status meeting we discussed in *Chapter 2, Regularly Scheduled Status Updates*, for three reasons:

1. Project meetings have one focus—the project. Status meetings can involve multiple subjects, including projects.

2. Project meetings are about accomplishing the project. As such, they involve making decisions to move the project forward. Status meetings are about sharing valuable information. Both are important but not the same.

3. Project meetings should only have a life within the context of the project. Once the project is over, the project meetings should end.

The first key to a successful project meeting is having a well-defined scope. In defining the project scope, Wikipedia draws an interesting distinction between two variables in a project: the work and the outcomes. They define the work tasks as the project scope and the deliverables or outcomes as the product scope. This makes total sense. The project scope is what the team hopes to accomplish and how they hope to get there.

Depending upon the project and organizational culture, scope documents can get into more detail. The project scope might include a brief background or history leading up to the project. It might outline the resources available to accomplish the project, as well as the individuals involved on the project team.

If you've never drafted a project scope before, there are many resources available. A couple of my favorite project management blogs are *The Project Management Hut* (http:// www.pmhut.com) and *Herding Cats* (herdingcats.typepad.com/my_ weblog/) Also, Microsoft Office provides project scope templates.

Project scope documents are often used to solicit senior leadership support. In order for that to happen, the project scope should be directly tied to business goals. The closer the link between the project/initiative and organizational goals, the better the chances that senior leadership will have a high level of support and engagement for the project.

You might be asking—shouldn't every project have a direct impact on business goals? The reality is, many projects don't. Things like painting the building or upgrading furniture are projects that don't always have a direct business impact, but they are necessary for other reasons. That's why the project scope is so important. It documents what the project entails, why it should be supported, the resources necessary, and the final outcomes (that is, goals and ROI). It tells participants what the meeting is all about.

Common project meeting challenges

The single biggest challenge for project teams is scope creep. This is defined as uncontrollable changes or additions to the project's scope. Usually, this happens because the project wasn't clearly defined, or the group wasn't clearly communicating, or a bit of both.

Scope creep can have a detrimental effect on team interaction and project outcomes. Here is an example of what scope creep might look like in a project:

> ➤ A company decides to build a mobile app so customers can purchase their products via their smart devices. The company isn't sure about all the specifics, but they hire a mobile app developer to help them design the app.

> ➤ The developer conducts their assessment of what the company needs and begins work on the project. As they are working, the company starts sending over requests for new features they would like to see in the app.

> ➤ At the end of the project, the developer delivers the app. The company isn't thrilled because the app doesn't work exactly as they discussed. The developer explains that all the additional features impacted the final product. And the final cost was more than double the original budget.

To avoid scope creep, both parties must communicate clearly:

> ➤ There's nothing wrong with adding features. However, as the company starts adding features, they need to make sure to ask about the budget and how the new feature would work within the approved design.

> ➤ Even though the developer was willing to add new features to make the company happy, they need to be sensitive to the company's budget and delivering a good product. Reminding the company about functionality can be seen as a positive step in making sure the outcome is what the company wanted.

During meetings this means using the active listening skills we discussed in *Chapter 7, Focus Groups*. Using our mobile app example, here are a few things the meeting participants should do:

> ➤ Watch for non-verbal cues that might indicate that participants are not listening intently. The last thing anyone wants is for participants to be looking at their smartphone and miss the introduction of new features.

> ➤ Ask open-ended questions. One person says during the meeting, "Can you add these new features?" The reply is "yes". That's a closed question. What doesn't get asked is how much additional money will it cost or how long will it delay the timetable.

> ➤ Paraphrase requests for changes in scope. When changes are requested, clarify the change by paraphrasing. Look for confirmation that the change is understood, and document the change so there is no confusion.

The second biggest challenge in projects is balance. When a project team is working, they are trying to create the best quality, on time, and within budget. I like to think of it as good, fast, and cheap.

A number of years ago, an astute friend of mine was talking about his industry—technology. He mentioned that, most of the time, tech projects could be delivered good, fast, or cheap—pick two. In other words, you can't get all three. Over the years, I've seen the same concept applied to just about any industry.

Most of the time, our customers want a product or service to be reasonably good, delivered in a timely manner and at a cost-effective price. This is what we call value. And, if we're able to consistently deliver our product or service in this manner to a wide enough customer base, chances are good that we'll be successful.

Now let's say our customer has a unique circumstance—they want the product or service much faster than customary. We can tell Mr. or Ms. Customer that it's possible, but will cost extra because of the added expenses in accelerating production. So they'll get it fast and good, but not cheap.

If they're unwilling to pay extra, we have a choice—decline the sale or tell the customer the deliverable won't be up to usual standards because we have to rush it. The customer will get fast and cheap at the expense of good.

You can probably see how this plays out in other circumstances. Say a customer wants good and cheap. Sure, you can do that, but it will take longer because you'll fit the project in around more profitable pieces of business. Think of the companies you deal with—I'm guessing they work with you in much the same way.

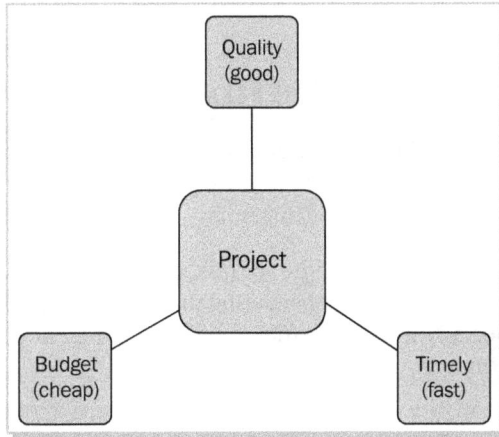

```
                    ┌─────────────┐
                    │  Quality    │
                    │  (good)     │
                    └─────────────┘
                           │
                    ┌─────────────┐
                    │             │
                    │   Project   │
                    │             │
                    └─────────────┘
                   ╱             ╲
        ┌─────────────┐      ┌─────────────┐
        │  Budget     │      │  Timely     │
        │  (cheap)    │      │  (fast)     │
        └─────────────┘      └─────────────┘
```

If you're able to accept the "good– fast – cheap" model as a somewhat universal truth, let's bring it down to the project meeting:

➤ If a project team wants the deliverable to be of the highest quality but isn't willing to put additional resources behind the project, there's a chance the project will take longer than expected. (Good and cheap, but not fast.)

➤ The project team wants a high quality outcome, and they want it quickly, then they need to be prepared to budget for additional resources to make it happen. (Good and fast, but not cheap.)

➤ Lastly, the project team wants results quickly and inexpensively. Chances are it will not have the same level of quality. (Cheap and fast, but not necessarily good.)

We all want the veritable trifecta of projects—teams that will deliver quality work, in a timely manner using a reasonable amount of resources. When they do that, the project delivers value to the company.

During project meetings, the project team must constantly ask themselves if they are achieving their goals. Are we producing the best quality? Is the project within budget? Are we producing results on time? I've worked on project teams where we wrapped up the meeting asking these three questions. And if we didn't feel we were, then we took time to identify where the project was lacking and how to get it back on track.

Having a project go off track isn't a failure. It happens to the best project teams. That doesn't mean it shouldn't be addressed. The only way to overcome these challenges is with clear expectations about the scope of the project and clear communication to everyone involved.

Before a project meeting

For the first project team meeting, consider making it special. The group may or may not have worked together before. This is an opportunity to build a sense of teamwork. A few items to consider for your project kickoff meeting:

> ➤ Incorporate some element of fun. We talked about icebreakers in Chapter 8, *Pitch Meetings*. This is another type of meeting that can be well served starting with an icebreaker, especially if team members are from different departments and don't work together on a regular basis.

> ➤ Consider a personality profile. To help the team learn about each other, the project manager might want to have team members do a personality profile or communications profile. This allows team members to learn about each other and the best ways to manage conflict and problem solving within the group.

> ➤ Establish a communications protocol. Whether it's a printed list of names, e-mails, and phone numbers or internal collaboration software, the team needs to know right away how to communicate with each other.

> ➤ Give participants an opportunity to discuss the opportunities and risks attached to the project.

Digital Marketing Director Erin Everhart uses an activity called the sailboat exercise to identify risk and opportunities during her initial client meetings. This is something you can adapt for any project.

Here's how the activity works:

Action Point

Activity: Sailboat exercise

Draw a sailboat.

Wind in your sails: Have participants identify the positive attributes of the project. These could be the skills of the team or resources available.

Anchors: Discuss the things that can hold the team back. It might be a change in team members, losing resources, or a change in company policy.

Icebergs: Recognize what can derail the project. An example could be losing sponsor support.

The sailboat can help the team visualize the project and be a constant reminder to stay on task.

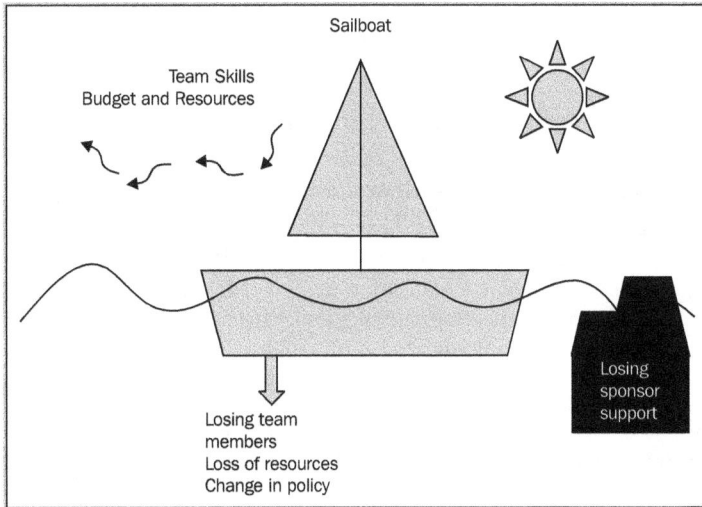

Sailboat

Team Skills
Budget and Resources

Losing team members
Loss of resources
Change in policy

Losing sponsor support

After the initial or kickoff meeting, planning for subsequent meetings remains equally important. Project teams can still include icebreakers or reconnect activities in the agenda. They do serve a different purpose. Instead of using the activity to get to know each other, the goal might be to catch up since the last meeting. This is especially helpful with groups that are working on a project but do not regularly meet in person.

I used to assist in the planning of an annual human resources conference. There were about 20 people on the project team. The group did most of their work in smaller groups of 4-5 people via e-mail and phone calls but the whole group got together quarterly to discuss overall progress. I remember one project manager having reconnect activities at the start of each meeting to create a sense of camaraderie. It was essential that the whole group worked well together onsite, so the reconnect activities help to achieve that goal.

In addition to icebreaker activities, every project meeting will still require an agenda with discussion and decision items.

Tip

Note decisions on the meeting agenda

When I was a volunteer leader, I found it helpful to put a note next to agenda items the board would need to vote on. That way, board members came to the meeting prepared to make a decision about something.

I've carried that practice over to my consulting practice. When I plan meetings where a decision must be made, I note those items on the agenda. It keeps the meeting moving, and participants come prepared to discuss and decide on key items.

We talked about how the goal of the project in general is to keep the project focused. To some extent, that's still the goal when it comes to actually running a project meeting.

During a project meeting

At this point in the book, we've talked about several essential components of meetings: agendas, parking lots, facilitation, meeting notes, and so on. Because a key component in managing a project is time, I want to focus on managing your time during the meeting. It's easy to forget the cost of conducting a meeting.

The cost of a meeting

We've probably all heard the old cliché "time is money". It's very true, and meetings are a perfect example.

Let's say you're a part of a project team that has seven other members (eight total). For the purposes of simple math, each person makes $50,000/annually. This doesn't include the cost of benefits. The total compensation for the entire team is $400,000 ($50,000 x 8).

The project plan is for one year. Let's also assume each person works 2,000 hours per year (that's 40 hours per week for 50 weeks). I know it might seem unrealistic, but it's a place to start. That puts each person's compensation at $25/hour ($50,000/2000). Here's the price for their meetings:

> ➤ **Weekly**: The group decides to meet weekly, so they stay on top of their deadlines and details. Each person would attend 50 one-hour meetings. That's $1,250 per person. The annual total is $10,000 for all 8 project team members.

> ➤ **Monthly**: The group decides that a weekly meeting is too much, so they are going to meet monthly but allocate a half-day. That way they can have deeper discussions. Each person would attend 12 four-hour meetings. The cost is $1,200 per person which comes to an annual total of $9,600 for the entire team.

> ➤ **Quarterly**: The group wants to do most of the work virtually and get together quarterly for status updates and major decision-making. But since there will only be four, they agree to full-day meetings. Each team member will attend four eight-hour meetings. The cost per person is $800 and for the whole team is $6,400.

Keep in mind that while there are some savings in terms of people's time between the weekly, monthly, and quarterly meetings, there could also be an additional expense in terms of logistics such as location, refreshments, and so on. The point is, meetings cost money.

From a project perspective, groups need to decide the right meeting schedule to accomplish their goals. Meeting weekly could be exactly what the team needs to succeed. Or maybe quarterly is perfect.

Project teams should meet when it makes sense for the project. Otherwise, they are wasting time and money.

Now that we've established that time is money, let's take that concept to the timeline of the project.

The cost of finishing the project on time

There are many reasons that projects are not completed on time, but one of them is that the project timeline wasn't well managed. Have you seen any of these before?

> ➤ The project manager doesn't control meetings so what should have taken one meeting ends up taking two. Or possibly three.

> ➤ The project team cannot make a decision, which delays the next step in the project.

> ➤ The group doesn't meet enough (that is, they hate meetings!) so a key piece of information isn't shared with the team in a timely fashion.

The project is important. The meetings about the project are important. They keep the project focused and on-time. Project timelines can be managed many ways. I'm a fan of these two methods.

SMART milestones

It's simple and effective. The group develops a list of milestones that should be accomplished by certain dates. This is perfect for the SMART (Specific, Measurable, Actionable, Responsible, Timely) format we discussed in *Chapter 1, Meeting Roles, Responsibilities, and Activities*.

> ➤ Specific can refer to the specific milestones in the project.

> ➤ Measurable can be the noticeable or measurable indication that the milestone has been achieved.

> ➤ Actionable would be the steps to accomplish that milestone.

> ➤ Responsible are the people or persons accountable for the action steps.

> ➤ Timely references the timeline to complete the milestone.

By now, you realize what a fan I am of SMART planning, and this is the reason. The SMART approach is very flexible and easy to remember.

Gantt chart

If your project requires more detail, another option is a Gantt chart. A **Gantt chart** is a popular way of reflecting activities in a project. It's commonly used in formal project management. Typically, it has a list of all the tasks or activities that need to be completed in a column. Then across the other axis of the chart is a timeline.

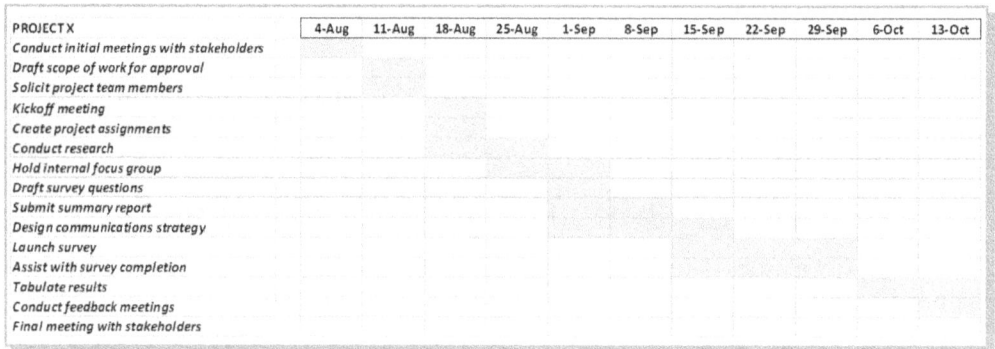

PROJECT X	4-Aug	11-Aug	18-Aug	25-Aug	1-Sep	8-Sep	15-Sep	22-Sep	29-Sep	6-Oct	13-Oct
Conduct initial meetings with stakeholders											
Draft scope of work for approval											
Solicit project team members											
Kickoff meeting											
Create project assignments											
Conduct research											
Hold internal focus group											
Draft survey questions											
Submit summary report											
Design communications strategy											
Launch survey											
Assist with survey completion											
Tabulate results											
Conduct feedback meetings											
Final meeting with stakeholders											

A Gantt chart explains:

> ➤ The activities or tasks that need to be completed for the project

> ➤ When each activity starts and ends (there could be multiple activities happening at the same time)

Gantt charts can take a lot of time to create and maintain. Luckily, technology has made working with Gantt charts much easier. You can find templates and software fairly easily. Lynda.com, the online learning company, offers educational videos on project management, including using project management tools. And remember you can always search YouTube for additional assistance in using and maintaining Gantt charts.

Remembering the three-legged stool of project management success (quality, budget, and time) makes me realize how critical managing time during meetings can be. If the project timing goes off track, there's a huge potential for the budget to increase in an effort to get things back on time, and that ultimately impacts the success of the project.

Using expert power on your project team

One of the people who will be on your project team is the subject matter expert (SME). This individual has specific expertise that you need for the project to be a success. When you're an expert at something, you have expert power.

Let me add some clarification. In my opinion, everyone is an expert at something. We are all subject matter experts. A challenge happens when:

1. A person claims to be an expert in something they know little or nothing about. For instance, I should never claim to be an expert in computer programming. While I am capable of turning my computer on and occasionally downloading software, I don't know how to write code.

2. Others rely upon a person like they are an expert when they're not. While I know the principles of compensation, there are other people who have more extensive experience. They are the ones who should be relied on as the SME.

Often we are conditioned to think that if we say we're an expert, that's being conceited or arrogant. We're only allowed to accept the expert label if someone else gives it to us and then we're supposed to hem and haw about it, "Oh me?! Gosh no, I'm no expert." until someone firmly tells us to stop it. The truth is we need to get comfortable with being an expert, especially when we are on a project team because we are an expert.

This also means we need to know what we are an expert at. It's about being self-aware and knowing what you do well. We should be able to articulate those things we do well, along with what we did to get there. Here's an example of what someone should be able to say:

> *I'm an expert at designing training programs. I learned the principles of training design taking coursework at ABC University. I was able to take what I learned in class and immediately apply it in a company project to revamp our existing onboarding program. My work with the onboarding program led me to be selected as the project lead to design the company's leadership development program. I'm particularly proud of this program because it was recognized by the local professional training association as one of the best leadership initiatives in the state.*

You get the picture. Regardless of your role in the project, you need to be able to comfortably say things like this. In today's workplaces, where everyone is a SME about something, companies should consciously take steps to manage their all-SME workforce.

In order for project teams to be successful, employees must become comfortable with the idea of being an expert so they will share their expertise with others. This is a central part of the knowledge transfer process, whether that sharing takes place informally or during meetings, mentoring, coaching, or training.

Additionally, managers need to embrace the idea of managing a workforce of experts. They need to become comfortable working with someone who has more expertise in a subject than they do. Otherwise, employees will not feel comfortable sharing their expertise in meetings.

Everyone is an expert. We must work with people who share the same expertise as us and with others who don't. I can't help but think that if we allowed people to embrace their expert status (versus labeling it a narcissistic behavior), then maybe we wouldn't have to worry about people claiming to be experts in topics they're not. Ultimately, it's all about leveraging your strengths and using your expert power.

Seating arrangements

Speaking of power, the other power aspect to consider is the room setup. Back in *Chapter 5, Training Meetings*, we talked about room setup for training meetings. But room setup for status meetings, project meetings, or other types of meetings can be an important dynamic.

Remember King Arthur and the Knights of the Round Table? The idea of a round table provides everyone with equal authority. Yes, there will be people who have more power in a particular way—legitimate power to make a decision or subject matter expert power. But the round table offers a way for everyone to feel welcome at the same level.

If you don't use a round table, there are clearly chairs of power at the meeting.

The head of the table is usually called the *power position*. Many leaders will intentionally not sit at the head of the table as a way to encourage balanced discussion. On the other hand, if you have a meeting where you're trying to make a point, sitting at the head of the table can send a message that you have legitimate power as the project manager.

The position opposite the head of the table can be viewed as the "opposition" simply because it's opposite the project leader's position.

The positions on either side of the project leader are favored positions because it's thought these individuals have the project leader's ear. Conversely, the positions on each side of the opposition can be thought to support the opposition. Lastly, the people in the middle? Well, sometimes they can be considered out of sight and out of the conversation. On the upside, if you have to attend a meeting and just want to blend in—this might be a perfect place to sit.

Understanding the power dynamic is an important part of meetings. It won't ever go away so using it to your advantage is key.

After a project meeting

In 1965, Bruce Tuckman published his research on group dynamics and team development. The four phases of team development are Forming, Storming, Norming, and Performing. Here's a brief description of what happens during each phase:

➤ **Forming** is the phase where the team gets to know each other and the group learns about the task they've been brought together to accomplish.

➤ **Storming** is a period of conflict every team goes through. It's a healthy and necessary part of team development. The group learns how to deal with internal conflict and differences of opinion. It is possible that a group cannot effectively move past this stage.

➤ **Norming** is when the team comes together to work on the assigned task. At this point, the group is considered a functional group.

➤ **Performing** takes the group beyond a normal functioning team. In this stage, the group is considered high performing. They have a common goal that guides their activity. The group members have been trained and demonstrate leadership ability.

Years later, in 1977, Tuckman added a fifth phase to his work—adjourning. During this phase, the group accomplishes their task and separate as a team.

Once the project team has completed their work, the group should be given an opportunity to properly celebrate and separate. Often this is done with a final team meeting that's called a team celebration or wrap-up meeting. I've also heard them called debriefs or post-mortems.

The purpose of the meeting is two-fold:

1. Give the team an opportunity to celebrate. They've worked hard. The team has accomplished their goal. Chances are there have been some tough moments and challenges. This is a moment to recognize the success of the team.

2. Record lessons learned for the next project. Throughout the course of the project, there have been many times when someone says, "We need to remember that for next time." This is an opportunity to note those tips somewhere for future use.

Tip

Remember the feedback model

In *Chapter 5, Training Meetings*, I shared with you a feedback model. You can use those same questions and same format during a project meeting wrap-up session:

■ As a project team, what did we do well? Encourage the group to focus on their successes.

■ As a team, what could we have done differently? While there will be things to remember, often many mistakes were only seen by the team.

■ Give the group a chance to respond before the project manager.

Completing a project is quite an achievement. It takes effort, skills, excellent communication, and flawless execution. Giving the project team time to debrief and celebrate is only fitting. The best way to wrap up a project is with a dedicated meeting.

Today's project management technology

We've already talked about one way that technology can help with project meetings—project management software. Another way is using social collaboration software.

Social collaboration platforms allow multiple people to interact and share information. It's a bit different to social networking in that social networks focus on the individual and their interactions. Social collaboration tools are designed for the needs of the group.

Ideally, social collaboration software moves project team communications to a central location. No more project emails back and forth. Team members can access a repository of project files. When one person updates a file, everyone has access to it at the same time. It's incredibly efficient.

There are free social collaboration platforms that students and volunteer groups can utilize as well as enterprise solutions for large organizations.

5 tips for better project meetings

When we think of project management, we tend to think of structure and focus. Here are some tips and resources from business professionals to help your next project meeting run smoothly.

Katie Hurst, marketing manager at OpenSesame, a leading eLearning provider, shares the concept of *Gamestorming*.

> *"The problem with 99 percent of meetings today is that no one takes the time to plan. "But Katie!" you say, "No one has time to PLAN a meeting! They are just a necessary evil." My response to this argument is a simple cost/benefit analysis. If all it took was 5-10 minutes of planning to create a meeting that resulted in healthy discussion, great ideas, clear action items AND ended on time—wouldn't you take the time?*

> *My go-to tool to help with planning is "Gamestorming" by David Gray (http:// www.gamestorming.com/). I first saw David speak at South by Southwest, where he managed to get a room of 600+ folks working together using the techniques in his book. The goal of Gamestorming is to break folks out of the meeting rut and encourage creative problem-solving through drawings, sticky notes and moving around the room. The activities focus on everything from product development and goal-setting, to change management. Activities can be furthered narrowed down by number of participants and time. Many of the activities can be accomplished in the traditional meeting window of 30-60 minutes, with minimal planning.*

> *Gamestorming has completely transformed the way I view meetings—and I never have trouble getting coworkers to attend!"*

Carmen Miller, vice president of client services at McKinley Insurance Services in Fort Lauderdale, shares her secrets for keeping a project focused:

> *"Anytime I'm working on a project, I make sure meetings are productive and stay on track. Here's just a few things I do:*
>
> *Have a facilitator. One person can take the lead, set the agenda, and be accountable for goals and accomplishments.*
>
> ➤ *Review: At the start of each meeting, take time to remind everyone of the Big Picture and what needs to be accomplished in this meeting.*
>
> ➤ *Stay focused: Give everyone an opportunity to provide input but keep on subject and be timely.*
>
> ➤ *Take notes: Have someone designated take notes on the decisions made, action items, and who is responsible for each. Also make note of items that are completed so they can be taken off future agendas. Distribute them promptly after the meeting.*
>
> ➤ *Debrief: After the project is over, conduct a debrief meeting to discuss what worked, what didn't work, and how to be effective in the next project."*

Becky Robinson, founder and CEO of Weaving Influence, emphasizes the importance of planning:

> *"To have an efficient meeting, send out an agenda in advance and ask meeting participants to e-mail any additions or changes. If your meeting is not going to be in person, arrange all technology in advance—I find that the most efficient virtual meetings happen when teams can look at each other (my team and I use GoToMeeting). Send any instructions for using technology in advance so your meeting is not delayed by people downloading software. Identify someone in advance who can take and distribute notes. Be clear about any expected time constraints for the meeting and, if possible, designate someone to be the time keeper, moving the meeting forward according to the agenda.*
>
> *Start every meeting with introductions and some way for everyone to state their intention for the meeting. What do they want to accomplish during the meeting? How do they hope to contribute?"*

Shari Roth, Managing Partner of CAPITAL iDEA, a consulting company that works with organizations to help them bridge the gap between talent and results, says there are two key components to running a successful project meeting:

> *"When given the responsibility to head a project there are two very critical things that can make or break your success. The first is having the right people on the project and the second is being able to lead successful project meetings. There are few simple fundamentals that when ignored, projects can get derailed.*
>
> *The success of a project has as much to do with how it is launched as how it's run through the duration of the project. Make sure the right people are on the project. That means they have the needed skills, time available, proper attitude and align with the goal of the project.*

When it comes to leading the meeting, planning is key. The agenda for the meeting should be sent to participants in advance of the meeting. The greater the amount of preparation needed for the meeting, the earlier the agenda should be sent. Once in the meeting, stay on topic. Take issues up offline if something comes up that needs to be addressed, but wasn't on the agenda.

When you send out the agenda, it's critical that the people that need to provide updates and make decisions are in attendance. If a key person cannot attend, make sure someone is sent in their place that can speak intelligently about the project. Don't allow bodies to show up to be a place holder or just to take notes because it will cause your meeting to be ineffective.

Make sure to start the meeting on time. Don't wait for everyone to arrive. And don't back track. Be consistent. If necessary talk one on one to attendees that continue to show up late. Also respect the team's time and end on time. There may be times when discussion is needed that causes the meeting to run over. It is important to check in with your attendees to see if they can stay a bit longer. If not, schedule another time to deal with that one issue.

Before attendees leave the meeting, everyone must be clear on the actions to be taken, and the due dates. Nothing should be left up in the air. The action items should be distributed after the meeting and request everyone to be in communication. As a leader of the project it is your role to talk to anyone that drops the ball more than one time. If necessary, that person may need to be replaced, or often their manager needs to understand how the project is being impacted. Too often managers are overloading their employees and don't keep in mind the work required on the project."

Bob Sparanese, a marketing consultant specializing in the technology industry, recommends making people feel a little uncomfortable so they can do their best work:

*I've always found that people get too comfortable in meetings. I always thought that a tech company called Cabletron got it right many years ago – they didn't install chairs in their conference rooms, just high-top tables. You can read about it here—*http://www.fundinguniverse.com/company-histories/cabletron-systems-inc-history/.

People who had worked there said the meetings went really fast and to the point. People would get tired of standing and no one would even think of grandstanding. I've always wanted to remove tables from a room and try this approach to see if we could review project timelines, have owners report on their progress and see if it works.

That being said, here are a few ground rules for conducting a productive meeting:

➤ *Only those whose input are pertinent to the goal of the meeting should be invited. All attendees should understand their role as it pertains to the goal of the meeting.*

➤ *Expectations for the outcome of the meeting should be set by outlining the goal of the meeting, listing objectives to meet the goal and sending an agenda with action items to the invitees with action items to be discussed included.*

➤ *The agenda must be direct and discussion controlled by the facilitator. Limit and control domination of discussion by any one person. Get everyone's input if possible. Avoid digression to other topics not relevant to the goal of the meeting. One diplomatic way to do that is to say, "that's a great point but I believe we're off topic so let's get back on track by focusing on the task at hand".*

➤ *It is essential to start and end on time.*

➤ *Conclude by identifying action item strategies agreed on by the attendees.*

Summary

In *Chapter 8, Pitch Meetings*, we pitched an idea and got support for the idea. In *Chapter 9, Strategic Planning*, our idea was included in the strategy of the organization. Now, we're managing the project.

In order for a project to be successful, it must have well-conducted project meetings. Those meetings need to support the scope of the project. They should be facilitated well, so the team stays focused on the goal. But the meetings should also focus on project deliverables, making sure the outcomes are of high quality, are on time, and are within budget. Using tools such as Gantt charts and SMART milestones will help manage the project.

However, once the meeting has ended, the work isn't over. In fact, an important part of the work takes place outside of meetings. In our final chapter, we'll talk about the things that must be done to make sure all of the hard work that happens during the meeting doesn't go to waste.

>11

The Work Doesn't End
When the Meeting is Over

Throughout this book, we've talked about planning and executing the best meetings possible. Now that the meeting is over, we cannot let all of our hard work go to waste.

At the end of any meeting, participants should be on the same page regarding the following three things:

1. The actions that need to take place outside of the meeting.
2. The individuals responsible for those actions.
3. The timeframe for accomplishing the agreed upon actions.

This means the work doesn't end when the meeting is over. In fact, some might argue that the real work has only just begun. The meeting leader must make sure this work happens, on time, by the individuals assigned to the task.

Before launching into after-meeting assignments, it's not unusual to discover that the meeting discussion is still taking place. In many office or organizational environments, this is referred to as the meeting after the meeting.

The meeting after the meeting

Yes, it's true. The meeting after the meeting does exist. It's not an urban legend.

In fact, the meeting after the meeting (or let's call it the MATM for short) can actually be more important than the original meeting. Many people think it's really a big gripe session about the meeting. But a true MATM is very important—it often provides insight into the people and discussions that you usually can't get during the meeting itself.

As a business professional, you want to be included in the MATM. Here are six dynamics to watch for:

1. **The purpose**: Typically, the MATM is part venting and part strategy. Usually, participants are frustrated about something that happened during the meeting (the venting part) and the conversation turns toward brainstorming ways to fix the situation (the strategy part).

   A MATM of only griping? Well, that's just a gripe session. Not to say a gripe session isn't noteworthy, but it's beyond the scope of this book. Often gripe sessions are about not communicating something well or not getting proper buy-in. We covered getting buy-in in *Chapter 10, Project Meetings*, with pitch meetings.

   A meeting where you discuss strategies to fix something, that is, make a decision: that's the reason for a "real" meeting.

2. **The attendees**: From an office politics perspective, the individuals who attend a MATM are influencers where this particular matter is concerned. The influencers can change from issue to issue. In each chapter, we've talked about power during meetings and who has power based upon the meeting. In most cases, the influencers are those with the most power.

   Something to note: try to notice who initiates the MATM. Figure out if they are the person who ultimately is accountable for this issue (and it appears they're soliciting feedback) OR are they trying to influence the person who is ultimately accountable?

3. **The timing**: Sometimes the MATM is spontaneous and other times, it's planned. If the influencers happen to be at the same place together, the original meeting might just turn into a conversation. "Hey, what did you think of yesterday's meeting?" And the conversation starts.

   The other way is that someone might plan to get a group together quietly. For example, you invite a couple of people to lunch. Either before or during lunch you say, "Hey, I've been thinking about last week's meeting and wanted to get your thoughts."

4. **The location**: Often, but not always, the MATM takes a more casual tone. It might be a mid-morning coffee run, lunch, or drinks after work. I've seen a lot of people miss the opportunity to participate in a MATM because it looked like a social event and their opinion is "work is work, and I don't want to socialize with my co-workers".

   This can be unfortunate because if you don't recognize the signs, then you can't participate. On the other side, I've seen organizers of the MATM intentionally choose a venue knowing certain people wouldn't attend. For example, Carol doesn't ever join us for happy hour, so let's meet then.

   This is a tough decision. I can't tell you the right answer. What I can recommend is don't be naïve and believe business only happens in office buildings and boardrooms. It happens everywhere—on golf courses, social networking platforms, at coffee shops, and during happy hour.

5. **The discussion**: I mentioned earlier that the MATM can often be a gripe session. If you're at a MATM, listen carefully to the complaints. Try to understand the frustrations and also why that frustration may or may not have been addressed during the meeting.

   The other conversation that happens during a MATM is strategy, for example, what people plan and agree to do next, as a result of the MATM. This can offer valuable insight into what happens behind the scenes in the organization. It can also tell you a lot about the individuals involved and their comfort zones, spheres of influence, and workplace power.

6. **The commitment**: There's an over-quoted line from the 1999 movie starring Brad Pitt and Edward Norton called "Fight Club":

   "The first rule of Fight Club is: You do not talk about Fight Club."

   The same rule applies here. What people share in the MATM must be respected. The reason MATMs are important and can work well for organizations is because people let their guard down. They talk about what challenges them and they might share something they plan to do. Unless your role in the organization is to go forewarn someone, then you have to respect the tradition of this meeting.

Instead of trying to eradicate the MATM, find a way to play a positive role in them. As a human resources professional, I found that when I was being invited to the MATM, it was to help the group in a specific way:

➤ **To clarify something**: Someone at the meeting didn't understand something that happened. Instead of asking during the meeting, they might choose to wait until after and ask some questions. They might also choose to ask someone other than the meeting leader.

   This can occur a lot with new supervisors and managers, especially when they haven't had prior exposure to these types of meetings. They need to learn from someone they can trust. This is the part of business that never shows up in the employee handbook or in a training program. Years ago, I had a boss tell me, "Over the years, with each job, I learned a little bit about human resources and a whole lot about office politics." That line stuck with me. It's my job as a manager to share the realities of the workplace with others.

➤ **To be a sounding board**: Participants want to say something, but they don't know how their comments will be received. They are looking for someone to offer a different perspective. Not approval or support, only a point of view.

   This relates to my comment about sharing the realities of work. Books, articles, and media will tell you it's important to be open, honest, and share with your boss. This is totally true and I completely agree with it. This doesn't mean you should be unprepared. Having a sounding board gets you prepared. If you choose the right person, they can help you to potentially see a different point of view.

Bottom line: your reputation and relationships matter. They will help you get a seat at the MATM.

Gossip after the meeting

While you want to be a part of the meeting after the meeting, it's not always advisable to attend the "gossip after the meeting". There is a difference.

Gossip is usually associated with talk about another person or people, often with details that aren't true or are negative in some way. I'd like to think we can all agree backstabbing and undermining behavior are totally inappropriate and unacceptable and should not be encouraged in any way.

Gossip is also considered the informal channels of company communication. It might also be called the rumor mill, grapevine, and so on, and it can be valuable every once in a while.

Thinking we can eliminate the grapevine of conversation is naïve. I'd suggest that, instead of spending energy to eradicate gossip, learn how to leverage it. That's right. Use it to your advantage. Again, I'm not talking about spreading nasty comments here. If people make mean-spirited remarks about their co-workers, then you deal with it by holding the employee accountable and coaching.

As an example, let's say you have a message you want the masses to start hearing… but you're not in an official position to write a memo or have a meeting. Letting the rumor mill get the word out can be a good thing. The rumor mill can start getting people comfortable with the idea. Then when you do make that official announcement, people say, "I had a hunch it was coming."

If people just want to grouse, that's not really productive. However, if there's an opportunity to unofficially make a remark, then it could be worthwhile to declare the grapevine your friend and use it to your advantage.

Recovering from a bad meeting

Sometimes bad meetings just happen. The reasons are varied. Some situations we must take responsibility for and others are out of our control. One thing is true however…you can recover from a bad meeting. In this section, I want to share some of the common reasons participants complain about meetings and how you can recover afterward.

The meeting leader is unprepared

This is probably first on the list. When the meeting organizer is unprepared, it shows in everything. From big things such as not distributing an agenda to small details such as refreshments, the meeting leader sets the tone of the meeting and needs to properly prepare.

So why does it happen? Well, here are the three excuses I've heard the most.

> *"It's a regular meeting, so everyone knows what to do."*

Regular meetings need as much structure as impromptu ones. One could argue regular meetings need more preparation. Nonregular meetings have the benefit of appearing important because well...because they're not regularly scheduled. The weekly meeting can easily fall into the trap of being labeled worthless, dull, or boring if there isn't a concerted effort to keep the meeting relevant. A meeting where everyone is just going through the motions will quickly get the label of being irrelevant.

> *"I want to let the creative juices flow, so I'm not going to stifle the group with an agenda."*

Creativity and anarchy are two very different things. It is possible to allow creativity while still using an agenda. The purpose of a meeting agenda is to plan the time and topics, not to dictate the outcome of the discussion. Let me suggest that sometimes putting just a few parameters around the conversation can actually increase creativity, not stifle it. When the scope of discussion is too big or too broad, participants might not know where to start. The meeting agenda provides the starting point.

> *"It's an emergency, so I didn't have time to prepare."*

If you have enough time to figure out that you need a meeting, then chances are you have enough time to prepare. Preparations do not have to take days or hours. Depending upon the agenda, preparation could take minutes. For instance, the weather service has declared a storm warning. The company needs to put their emergency plan in place. The leader of the emergency response committee calls a meeting. The agenda for this meeting would not be long:

➤ Request for participants to review the emergency manual (prior to the meeting)

➤ Current status regarding the weather

➤ Next steps for each department to prepare

➤ Agreed upon next meeting date

The purpose of this meeting is to communicate information. The purpose of subsequent meetings could be different. In this situation, the meeting leader wants to inform and heighten awareness.

The solution for unprepared meeting leaders? Prepare next time. Participants will be forgiving if someone is unprepared for one meeting. It's when the meeting leader is unprepared on a regular basis that participants realize the meeting isn't going to change.

Being unprepared has an impact on the credibility of the meeting leader. It's so much easier to prepare than deviate from the agenda than the other way around. It's very difficult to create and communicate a meeting agenda on the fly.

Meeting participants are unprepared

This ties into the meeting leader being unprepared. One of the things that the meeting leader needs to do is tell participants what they need to read, review, bring, and so on to the meeting. This helps participants come to the meeting prepared. It also helps keep the meeting on track, especially where time is concerned.

A personal peeve of mine is when the meeting leader sends out information for review prior to the meeting and participants do not take the time to do their own preparation. We get to the meeting and, when that item comes up on the agenda, a participant will say, "Oh sorry, I didn't have time to read it prior to the meeting." Now what ensues is those people who did prepare sit around twiddling their thumbs (or checking their e-mail) while the people who didn't prepare get up to speed.

I don't know of a polite way to say this, but coming to a meeting unprepared is disrespectful. It's a waste of time for everyone in the room. It says you don't care enough about the people at the meeting and their time.

There are two solutions for when meeting participants come to the meeting unprepared. First, it's important to know if the meeting leader made a request of the participants. If so, there's no excuse—participants should have completed the task. If the meeting organizer didn't send a request, then unfortunately, it's the meeting leader's responsibility.

If you find that the meeting leader isn't sending out homework requests prior to the meeting (and they should), see if you can find a way to suggest it. This can be done privately prior to the meeting. For example, when the meeting agenda is distributed, just ask—"Is there anything you'd like for us to read prior to the meeting?" Hopefully the meeting leader will get the hint and distribute materials. If they do, be sure to mention during the meeting how helpful it was to get the reading materials prior. Other participants might share their appreciation as well and the meeting leader is likely to continue the practice.

On the other hand, if the meeting leader doesn't take the hint, seek out an opportunity to share feedback on an individual level. You can mention, "It would be helpful to me to read these materials prior to the meeting. I would feel better prepared and able to participate at a higher level."

Now if the meeting leader is sending out materials and participants are reading them, then the meeting leader must hold participants accountable. And holding them accountable isn't making them read the material during the meeting. That's just punishing the people who did what they were supposed to do.

After the meeting, the leader should have a private conversation with the participant using the steps we discussed in *Chapter 6, Employee Performance Conversations,* on employee performance conversations. The purpose of the conversation isn't to discipline the employee. It's to change their behavior. And you can use the same steps (with minor modifications) for conversations with volunteers and vendors.

The wrong people attending the meeting

A key reason that individuals might come to a meeting unprepared is because they probably shouldn't be at the meeting in the first place. When people are invested in the meeting, they have a tendency to plan and prepare. It's when people who aren't invested or not invested at the same level attend, that levels of preparation vary. Here are a few examples:

You feel compelled to invite your boss. Yes, your boss is invested in the project. They want you to succeed. Their next bonus, pay increase, or promotion might be resting on it. The question is, do they need to attend every meeting? Maybe but maybe not. Invite the boss to the meetings they really need to attend. Tell them the reason they need to be there and the role you need for them to play during the meeting. The other meetings? Tell them you'll keep them informed.

You don't want to hurt any feelings. A co-worker is very interested in the meeting. Maybe they want exposure to the people at the meeting. Possibly the project is fascinating and they want the inside scoop. Or they could just be downright nosy. The point is they're a friend and you don't want to say "no". Allowing a person to attend when it makes no business sense isn't a reflection on them; it's a reflection on you as the meeting leader. If you can't control the attendee list, what else can't you control? Offer to buy your colleague a cup of coffee and keep them in the loop outside of the meeting.

Inviting everyone means you're transparent and inclusive. I'm a total believer in the value of transparency and inclusion. But this is one of those times when more doesn't immediately translate into better. There are other ways to be transparent and inclusive. You can share meeting minutes with everyone or hold occasional town hall meetings with project updates.

The solution is to invite the right people to meetings. The people who need to be there. Remember the attendee list could change with the meeting agenda. It's possible to solicit feedback and buy-in outside of a meeting. People can participate in the process without attending the meeting.

Participants take over the meeting

There's a fine balance that must be struck between allowing conversation and allowing a takeover. In my experience, I've found that when the wrong people attend, coupled with them being unprepared, it's easy for a person or small group of people to hijack the meeting. Before you know it, someone else is in charge.

This usually happens because the person who probably shouldn't have been at the meeting has a different agenda from the meeting leader. Think about it. If the person attending the meeting was there to support the meeting leader, they wouldn't take over the meeting. The best solution for keeping people from hijacking your meeting is not to have them there in the first place.

But let's say you have no choice. Your boss says, "I'm going to stop by your meeting next week." What can you say - no?! In those situations, make sure that each participant understands their roles and responsibilities. In *Chapter 1, Meeting Roles, Responsibilities, and Activities*, we talked about task and process responsibilities. These can be used to help keep structure.

The other step that meeting leaders should do is introduce the new face at the meeting and the reason they're present. For instance, if the boss comes to the meeting, you can say, "Before we get started, let me introduce Kate to everyone. Some of you might already know her. She wanted to stop by and see how the project is progressing." The reason you want to do this is two-fold.

Everyone knows who the person is and why they're there, putting the group at ease. Even if everyone in the room knows the person. It's a sign of respect to introduce them and the reason they've shown up.

More importantly, if by chance the person decides to step out of the role that was explained at the beginning of the meeting, everyone then knows they are trying to hijack the meeting. This usually doesn't bode well for the meeting hijacker. Often participants will empathize with the meeting leader and the meeting hijacker doesn't get what they were looking for.

Additionally, once a person gets the reputation for taking over meetings, they get invited to fewer meetings. This can have a snowball effect and ultimately lead to the person becoming ineffective. Fewer meetings means being left out of the loop or not getting critical information. Fewer meetings means fewer people ask for feedback.

Once the group realizes that the meeting has been taken over, often participants will simply shut down. They know no more work will get accomplished during the meeting.

Meeting leaders take note. If one of your meetings is taken over and the meeting participants are gracious and suffer through the rest of the meeting, it's your responsibility to thank them. Whether that's to talk with each person individually or as a group at the next meeting, the group will only allow that to happen a few times.

Meetings that go off track

It's possible that a meeting hijacker will also take the meeting off track. But not always— the hijacker could keep the meeting on topic and just want to control the outcome. The meeting hijacker only attends to make sure a specific decision is made (or not made).

However, it's also possible the actual meeting participants can take the meeting off track without that external party. One way this can happen is when meeting participants start making all sorts of recommendations or new idea pitches. Remember the strategies we've discussed so far for keeping the meeting on agenda:

➤ Plan a reasonable agenda to accomplish during the meeting (*Chapter 2, Regularly Scheduled Status Updates*)

➤ Invite the right people (*Chapter 8, Pitch Meetings*)

➤ Assign a gatekeeper who will speak up when the meeting is starting to go off-topic (*Chapter 1, Meeting Roles, Responsibilities, and Activities*)

➤ Create a parking lot for off-topic items (*Chapter 2, Regularly Scheduled Status Updates*)

A common way that any type of meeting can go off track is when a participant tends to ramble. Some people might call it grandstanding or monopolizing the meeting. Bottom line, it can be frustrating. Amy Gallo, writing for Harvard Business Review, offered a suggestion for dealing with people who tend to dominate the conversation. She recommended the meeting leader meet with those individuals who tend to ramble prior to the meeting. Get to know them and find out their point of view. Then, during the meeting, summarize their perspective—with permission of course. Yes, this does put additional responsibility on the meeting leader, but it alleviates the frustration and keeps the meeting on target.

Another strategy that works, especially with training meetings, is to budget time for the group to occasionally go off track. When I design training, I am intentionally generous with time. This allows participants to ask questions and have a discussion. If we go off track for a couple minutes, it doesn't impact training. I've always found participants are fine with a few distractions as long as they aren't going to pay for it by running late.

Meetings that run too long (or too short)

Speaking of time, nothing upsets meeting participants more than running over the scheduled meeting time. People budget time on their calendars for meetings. Those meetings are supposed to be productive. Meeting leaders need to be good at budgeting time. Think about how long each agenda item will take. It's fine to adjust meeting times based on the agenda:

> *"This week's meeting agenda has a couple of topics that could involve some longer than typical discussion. I'd like for all of us to budget an extra 30 minutes for this meeting. That way we can all participate in the discussion and not feel rushed."*

> *"Because of the holiday, next week's meeting agenda is shaping up to be lighter than usual. I'm thinking we will only need 30 minutes, instead of the usual hour. Feel free to adjust your schedules accordingly."*

Ideally, meetings should end on time. It's fine to end the meeting early, but it's not okay to end the meeting late. There's one exception to ending the meeting early. That's when you end the meeting ridiculously early. You might be thinking, isn't ending a meeting early always a good thing? Not when you've been asked to attend an off-site meeting and cannot get home.

True story. I was invited to attend an all-day meeting in another state. So I had to buy a plane ticket, arrange for hotel, and so on. Instead of taking all day, the meeting took a couple hours. So when the meeting was over, I tried to get an earlier flight home. No options available. For a 2-hour meeting, I could have called in. It would have been cheaper and I would have been more productive.

While we're talking about time, another consideration is when the meeting is being held. I know it's virtually impossible to find a time that works perfectly with everyone's schedule, but there is value in determining the best time for a meeting.

For example, I've worked many places that never held meetings on Mondays or Fridays. Employees were always using those days to take a long weekend, so to avoid an employee missing a meeting, we didn't hold meetings on those days. Interestingly, as a consultant, Mondays and Fridays are now great for me to have networking meetings because it's not a day clients usually ask to meet. It totally depends on the culture and the nature of the meeting.

Often right before a holiday isn't a good time for meetings, unless of course, there's some sort of emergency that needs to be handled. On the other hand, some industries, like hospitality, work every holiday so it's not an issue for them.

The point I'm trying to make is that you shouldn't schedule meetings when people might be distracted. For example, during the World Cup soccer playoffs, I must say I was amazed when someone asked me to schedule a meeting during that time. You know the game where U.S. goalie Tim Howard had 16 saves and broke all kinds of world records. I was like, "okay—let's meet". Then they no-showed for the meeting. You know why? Yes, you guessed it: because they were caught up in the soccer game.

The solution is to find meeting times that work for everyone. Times when everyone can focus. If a holiday or special event comes along, just reschedule.

> *"Hi everyone! I noticed that the U.S. versus Belgium soccer game is Tuesday during our normal meeting time. I know not everyone is a soccer fan but in fairness to those who are, let's reschedule the meeting for Wednesday. It's a one-time thing and I appreciate everyone's flexibility."*

Meeting leaders, as well as meeting participants, should take responsibility for their preparation and participation. Meetings are not the sole responsibility of the leader.

Monitoring progress after the meeting

In *Chapter 1, Meeting Roles, Responsibilities, and Activities*, I shared with you SMART (specific, measurable, actionable, responsible, and time-bound) as a way to document and monitor progress toward goals. Using SMART is a great method to stay in touch with people outside of meetings to make sure goals are being worked on. Each person knows what is taking place, who is responsible, and when it is scheduled for completion.

Meeting leaders can use the SMART plan to check in with individuals and see if they need any resources or support. If someone has a question about priorities, they can contact the meeting leader for clarification.

If you are a meeting leader, it's important to know if someone is falling behind schedule or unsure of what to do. If you're a team member, it's important to tell the team leader what's going on so you can get support. This should be done outside of the meeting. No one wants to say they're behind schedule or that they made a mistake during a meeting. It will appear as if they are being singled-out and this is embarrassing for everyone.

Having a way to touch base with individuals outside the meeting structure creates a monitoring situation. It could be as simple as walking by a person's desk and asking, "Are we still on track to finish phase one by the end of the week? Please let me know if you need my help." The goal isn't to create another meeting. It's to make sure the action items from the meeting stay top of mind.

Because that's what meetings are all about—getting things done.

Summary

The work that happens inside the meetings is dependent on what happens outside of the meetings, and vice versa. A great meeting can create enthusiasm and excitement that fuels teams to do their best work. A bad meeting can deflate a group and slow the progress of a project. Individuals and organizations should put equal emphasis on the meeting and the work. And if a meeting doesn't go as planned, take steps to make it better next time.

People also have to realize that informal gatherings will take place outside of the scheduled meeting structure. These so-called meetings can provide a forum for individuals to vent, share, and formulate ideas. If they remain productive, the "meeting before the meeting" or "meeting after the meeting" can make the formally scheduled meeting even more valuable. (Yes, feel free to read that sentence twice. I had to when I wrote it!)

At the beginning of this book, I mentioned the natural tendency for people to eliminate meetings. Honestly, that's not the answer. There will be times when you need to disseminate information, offer feedback, or make a decision and the best way to do it is … you guessed it, via a meeting.

The solution to eliminating ineffective and frustrating meetings is to run a better meeting, not eliminate them.

I hope this book has offered you insights on how to plan, prepare, and lead a productive meeting. If you know someone is struggling as a meeting organizer, I hope you'll share some of the stories and tips in this book. And when you're asked to be a part of a meeting, you'll pull this book off your bookshelf (or open it on your phone/tablet) and use it for what's it's meant to be—a resource.

Organizations will always have meetings. The people who attend meetings have the opportunity to demonstrate their skills and leadership. Instead of viewing meetings as drudgery, maybe it's time to see them as an opportunity to showcase your skills.

References and Resources

This appendix contains all the references and resources that have been used in various chapters of this book.

Preface

- *How 3 Billion Meetings Per Year Waste Time, Money and Productivity in the Enterprise* by Mark Horton, Socialcast by VMware, August 10, 2010
- *Let's Stop…Scheduling 60 Minute Meetings* by William Tincup, Human Capitalist blog, October 3, 2013

Chapter 1, Meeting Roles, Responsibilities, and Activities

- *Decisions, Decisions, Decisions* by Jay Hall, Psychology Today, November 1971
- *The Managerial Grid III* by Robert R. Blake and Jane S. Mouton, Gulf Publishing Company, 1985
- *Process consultation: Its role in organizational development* by E.H. Schein, FT Press, 1969
- *Functional Roles of Group members* by Kenneth Benne and Paul Sheats, Bill Staples, ICA Associates Inc., 1948
- *Solutions: A Guide to Better Problem Solving* by Steven Phillips and William Bergquist, University Associates Inc., 1987
- *Why Do Your meetings Go Nowhere?* by Tina Samuels, Liz Strauss Successful and Outstanding Blog, October 9, 2013

Chapter 2, Regularly Scheduled Status Updates

> *No Meeting Wednesday: A Way Toward Focused Flow* by Dustin Moskovitz and Jason Womack, TheBuildNetwork, September 9, 2013

> *The 22 Minute Meeting* by Scott Berkun, ScottBerkun.com, 2010

> *Make Yourself 'Interruptible' for Better Meetings* by Mihir Patkar, Lifehacker, October 20, 2013

> *5 Ways to Get More From Your Meetings* by Alexa Von Tobel, Inc., November 22, 2013

Chapter 3, Brainstorming

> *Brainstorming is Dead* by the Build Network Staff, Inc.com, July 31, 2013

> *Brainstorming vs. Braincalming* from The Heart of Innovation blog, October 29, 2013

> *A Better Way to Group Brainstorm* by Mikael Cho, Lifehacker, October 14, 2013

> *Try Sitting Somewhere New at Work for a Brainstorming Boost* by Mihir Patkar, Lifehacker, October 20, 2013

> *Why Leaders Shouldn't Lead Brainstorming Sessions* from The Heart of Innovation blog, November 3, 2013

> *Lay's Joins Growing Trend of Brands Crowdsourcing through Facebook* by Justin Lafferty, Crowdsourcing.org, July 20, 2012

> *Tips and Tricks for Effective Meetings* by Renie McClay, November 2011

Chapter 4, Networking Meetings

> *Meeting Madness! The 4 Biggest Time Wasting Meetings You'll Find* by Andy Porter, Fistful of Talent, October 21, 2013

> *Should Mobile Devices Be Allowed in Meetings?* by Gary Vilchick and Karen Leland, The Build Network, September 12, 2012

> *Four Tips for Saying No With No Regrets* by Lynne Curry, Ph.D., SPHR, Results Based HR Strategy blog

> *Take Your Search for a Job Offline* by Dennis Nishi, The Wall Street Journal, March 24, 2013

> *Benefit from networking* by The Marketing Donut: Resources for Business

> *The Advantages of Networking* by the American Optometric Association

Chapter 5, Training Meetings

> *Tips for PowerPoint: Go Easy on the Text – Please, Spare Us* by Jared Sandberg, The Wall Street Journal, November 14, 2006

> *#ASTD2011: 7 tips to enhance your next presentation* by Sharlyn Lauby, SmartBlog on Leadership, June 21, 2011

> *Statistics on Visual Learners* by Kydiam S., StudyMode, November 2012

> *What's the Difference Between Training, Facilitating, and Presenting*, Langevin Learning Services blog, July 19, 2012

Chapter 6, Employee Performance Conversations

> *Four Ways to Increase the Power and Quality of Virtual One-on-One Meetings* by Carmela Southers, Blanchard Leaderchat, January 23, 2014

> *Meeting Madness! The 4 Biggest Time Wasting Meetings You'll Find* by Andy Porter, Fistful of Talent, October 21, 2013

Chapter 7, Focus Groups

> *Focus Groups for Beginners* by Jacqueline M. Barnett, Texas Center for the Advancement of Literacy & Learning, 2002

> *Advantages & Disadvantages of a Focus Group* by Alexis Writing, Houston Chronicle

> *When to Use a Focus Group and When Not to* by Diane Loviglio, Mozilla UX, August 21, 2012

> *Survey or Focus Group: Which to Use When* by Susan Eliot, The Listening Resource, December 14, 2010

> *Focus Groups Tip Sheet* published by the University of California at Berkeley, September 2006

> *Qualitatively Speaking: The focus group vs. in-depth interview debate* by Carey V. Azzara, Quirk's Marketing Research Media, June 2010

> *When and Why to Choose Focus Groups vs. One-on-One Interviews* by Roger A. Straus, The Research Playbook, January 21, 2010

> *Designing and Conducting Focus Group Interviews* by Richard A. Krueger, University of Minnesota, October 2002

> *Focus Groups: A Tool for Evaluating Visitor Services*, Park Studies Unit, University of Idaho

> *How to Run Useful, Inexpensive Focus Groups*, The Fieldstone Alliance Nonprofit Guide to Conducting Successful Focus Groups

➤ *People Skills* by Robert Bolton, Touchstone Books: New York, 1986

➤ *Focus Group Facilitation Guidelines* by Jill Dixon, University of Wisconsin, May 2005

➤ *Toolkit for Conducting Focus Groups*, Rowan University

Chapter 8, Pitch Meetings

➤ *Made to Stick* by Chip Heath and Dan Heath, Random House, 2007

➤ *The Ins & Outs of Video Conferencing*, Blue Jeans Network eBook

➤ *Mobile Technology Fact Sheet*, Pew Research, January 2014

➤ *Facts about Paper: The Impact of Consumption*, The Paperless Project (www.thepaperlessproject.com)

Chapter 9, Strategic Planning

➤ *How Nike Comes Up With Great Ideas* by Urko Wood, Strategy Innovations, Inc., March 29, 2013

➤ *What is a Vision Statement?* by Elaine J. Hom, BusinessNewsDaily, October 23, 2013

➤ *Can Asking More Questions Create Great Meetings?* by Joris Luijke, The Build Network, April 16, 2013

Chapter 10, Project Meetings

➤ *5 Ways to Make Your Client Kickoff Meeting a Success* by Erin Everhart, SearchEngineLand, October 22, 2013

➤ *7 Must-Have Project Management Skills for IT Pros* by Jennifer Lonoff Schiff, CIO, January 15, 2013

➤ *Module 5: Employee and Labor Relations*, SHRM Learning System, 2014

➤ *What is a Gantt chart?*, Gantt.com

Chapter 11, The Work Doesn't End When the Meeting is Over

➤ *Ask These Three Questions at the End of Every Meeting* by Mihir Patkar, Lifehacker.com, December 25, 2013

➤ *The Seven Imperatives to Keeping Meetings on Track* by Amy Gallo, Harvard Business Review, December 20, 2013

➤ *The End of the Meeting Blues* by Mitch Ditkoff, Idea Champions blog, January 23, 2014